Theomatics

Theomatics

GOD'S BEST KEPT SECRET REVEALED

Jerry Lucas
Del Washburn

STEIN AND DAY/*Publishers*/New York

DEDICATION

With the exception of the Lord Jesus, there is no single individual worthy of the dedication of this book. The message of *Theomatics* is for all Christians.

For this reason, we shall dedicate this book to those of God's children who have put their trust in Jesus, by faith, and have accepted Him as their personal Lord and Savior.

Therefore, we proudly dedicate this book to the

Body of Christ

Contents

ACKNOWLEDGMENTS

Special recognition is given to the following persons: My parents, Ira and Tracy Washburn, who allowed me to live at home, while I did all of my research. Their constant prayers and belief in my call of God will never be forgotten. Frank DeSpain, God's servant, through whom the whole subject was introduced to my attention. His influence on my life has been a constant source of inspiration and always will be. Dr. Albert Nobell, who pointed my research in the right direction. Rich and Valerie Cox, who introduced me to Jerry Lucas and have been a constant source of inspiration throughout this entire project. Arjan Bhatia of Boeing Aircraft Co., Seattle, Washington, and Dr. Laverne Stanton of California State University, my two statisticians, who did a masterful job in the area of statistics and probability.

DEL WASHBURN

Foreword

Many of you may remember me as a three-time All-American basketball player; twice, I was college player-of-the-year. I am also an Olympic gold-medal winner and was awarded the *Sports Illustrated* magazine's Sportsman-of-the-Year award. In college I was a Phi Beta Kappa graduate and upon graduation played professional basketball for eleven years, seven of which I was all pro. Before my recent retirement, I played on a world championship team with the New York Knickerbockers.

All during my life I was considered the "All-American boy." I had all that the world could possibly offer—fame, honors, awards, prestige, influence, and money. Many people would come up to me and say something like this: Jerry, you sure are lucky. I wish that I had what you have and could do the things you do. However, at that time in my life, there was something I could not tell those people. Deep down inside I was really miserable. I was lost. I had no peace or contentment in my life and didn't know what to do about it. I was ashamed to tell anyone, because I was supposed to have everything.

One day before we were married my fiancée Sharalee suggested that I read the Bible. I had never read the Bible before, but I began. As I continued to read I began to believe. I believed that there was God, that Jesus was the Son of God, and that He could change my life. And praise God He has—miraculously. I am now a new person. I am not in the spotlight as I used to be, but I have much, much more. I have peace of mind, and I am content for the first time in my life. The love of Jesus has made a new creature out of me. I'm not the same any more and never will be again. What has happened to me and so many millions of others can only happen when the living God becomes real in your life.

The Bible became the most important thing in my life. Since I have accepted Jesus into my heart and into my life, I have been using my God-given talents in the area of memory training to teach people how to remember the Bible and founded Memory Ministries. It was during one of Memory Ministries' seminars in Portland, Oregon, that I met a young seminar student by the name of Del Washburn. After becoming acquainted with Del, I saw some of the research he was doing. The voluminous work and its implications were impressive. I had known that many men had worked with numbers and mathematics in the Bible, but this appeared to be something totally new and different. Apparently, Del had found a key that would unlock a whole new dimension in the Word of God.

After a closer examination of Del's research papers, I invited him to move down to Los Angeles, so we could work on the project together. After several months of continued research we submitted our findings to a team of statisticians. Their convincing conclusions will be found in the last chapter of this book.

We could find no existing word to describe this mathematical continuity in the Bible, so we had to come up with a new word: Theomatics. It cannot be found in any dictionary. It is actually a combination of two words. The Greek word for God is *Theo*, and when combined with the suffix for the word *mathematics*, we then have the word *theomatics*. It means "the numbers or the mathematics of God."

Another reason a new word was needed was to avoid confusion between this work and any other work related to numbers. The material you will find in this book is as new as the word *theomatics* but also as old as the Bible itself. It has been there for thousands of years, but its secret has just been discovered.

The Bible was written over a period of 1,600 years by over forty different men. Yet, there is a mathematical consistency flowing through the whole Bible that defies explanation. People who have denied, joked at, and laughed about the Bible may think of it differently after coming to grips with the facts contained in this book.

As you read this book, you will have to form an opinion, and I believe that it will be the same as mine, which is: God did indeed write the Bible, as the Holy Spirit inspired men to write. I believe that this book scientifically proves that a mind far beyond human capabilities and understanding planned, constructed, and formed every word in the Bible as it was written in its original languages.

This book was written to reveal these findings to Christians, as well as a nonbelieving world. Its purpose is to glorify the Lord Jesus Christ. No matter what your theological, doctrinal, or denominational background might be, this book should increase and multiply your faith. I personally believe by faith alone that—although He used human instruments to do it—the author of the Bible was God Himself. These findings add scientific evidence to what I accept by faith.

How many times have you heard people say things about the Bible like the following: I am skeptical about the Bible. The Bible was written by men just like you and me. It is nothing more than just an old newspaper. Why should I accept the Bible as the final authority? I know that people make statements like these, because I used to, myself. But that was before I began to read the Bible.

My role in *Theomatics* has been one of direction, suggestion, guidance, and prayer. Del deserves the majority of the credit for this work. He found the key, did the research and the writing. Only time will tell how the Lord will direct Del's future activity with theomatics. I will always be available to assist him in any way I can as a brother in Christ.

My hope and prayer is that nobody will make anything more or less of theomatics than what it is. There may be nonbelievers and believers alike who scoff at it. And there may be those who will seek to ride further on their own doctrinal horses by using this information.

In spite of all this, one thing is sure: Theomatics exists! Del didn't put it there, and I didn't put it there. No human being put it there. Not even those who physically wrote the Bible. God put it there!

The fact that it is there cannot be denied—scientifically or otherwise. The only thing a person can say is, "I just don't believe it, simply because I choose not to believe it."

May God richly bless you as you read this book.

In the Memory of Jesus,

JERRY LUCAS

A disciple who abides in His Word.

Foreword

Born of missionary parents in Colombia, South America, I was, from birth, surrounded by influences conducive to the growth of godly aspirations. I knew that the Lord had a purpose in my being alive, and that someday I would be able to serve Him and my fellow Christian brethren.

Yet strangely enough during my early twenties I fought God's call with all my heart. After many failures, I realized that like Jonah I could no longer run from God, nor counter His will. "Many are the plans in the mind of a man, but it is the purpose of the Lord that will be established" (Proverbs 19:21). Inevitably, God so won my heart and soul by the work of His spirit that I turned my life over to Him completely—and without reservation. It was not long before the Lord began to make known to me a truth of great significance.

One day while visiting a dear friend I was introduced to some old manuscripts from the 1800's. I read these and everything else I could get my hands on concerning numbers and mathematics in the Bible. Finally, after much research, I realized that the depths of this study were not yet complete. During my discouraged moments, a still small voice kept telling me that there was a key, not yet found up to this time in history, which would begin to unlock the mathematical structure of God's Word. One day while looking over a particular work, I came across two theomatic features that started the ball rolling in the right direction.

At first, I was only aware that the design which was opening itself up appeared to be entirely new. As these two initial features were being developed, I began to see another great truth—that they were uniting various Scriptures in such a way as to bring forth a distinct clarification of truth. As time went on, the theomatical structure of God's Word continued to unfold itself before me. I was completely overwhelmed by the awe-inspiring magnitude of the design that God had placed in His Word.

But why? Could it be that God was now revealing the indelible stamp of the divine authorship of His Word in such a manner that man could now take that which is holy and spiritual and subject it to the crucible of mathematical science, only to find that the authorship of His Word is solely divine—untouched by man?

It was only a short time ago, in January of 1975, that I began my adventure. At that time, I had no idea how far the road would lead. But then, all of sudden, things started happening. The simple curiosity with which I had begun my research quickly changed into something far more meaningful and significant. Here, before my very eyes, lay the mathematical design of God's Word. What was I supposed to do? I felt so helpless. The significance of this discovery was astounding, but how was I going to tell people about it? I had never been to Bible school or seminary. I had never received any formal theological training. In fact, my qualifications were almost zero. Still, I knew that the Lord had called me for the express purpose of making known to His people the truth of theomatics. But why had God chosen me?

Then I was reminded of a verse in 1 Corinthians: "But God hath chosen the foolish things of the world to confound the wise; and God hath chosen the weak things of the world to confound the things which are mighty; and base things of the world, and things which are despised, hath God chosen, and things which are not, to bring to naught things that are: That no flesh should glory in His presence" (1 Corinthians 1:27–29).

And then something else emerged. In going through the Bible, I discovered that as a rule, whenever God chose somebody for a particular task, He always chose the individual with the fewest qualifications, the most unlikely candidate. Moses is a perfect example of this. He had a speech impediment and little confidence in himself. Yet God chose him to lead the children of Israel out of Egypt.

When Goliath stood before the armies of Israel and defied the living God, whom did the Lord send forth to go out and fight the giant? Did He choose one of Saul's soldiers? Instead, He choose a shepherd boy by the name of David.

When Christ chose twelve men to be His first disciples, whom did He choose? Somebody from the Sanhedrin? No! Instead, He chose a bunch of illiterate fishermen.

Of all the candidates least likely to be the recipient of God's mercy, it was Saul of Tarsus. He was persecuting the Christians, yet God chose him, who became Paul, to be the prime instrument in the writing of the New Testament.

As my research progressed, I had no idea how the Lord would have me present this truth to the Christian world. I showed my findings to very few people and continuously prayed that God would open the right door. By a miracle of circumstances, the Lord brought me into contact with Jerry Lucas. I had followed his career in basketball and had also read *The Memory Book,* which he co-authored. It had been on the *New York Times* best-seller list for fifty weeks. Needless to say, I was elated to find out that Jerry had accepted the Lord into his life and was now teaching Bible memory. While attending one of his seminars in Portland, Oregon, I met him, and upon looking over some of my research papers, he flew back up to see me.

One thing Jerry and I would like to express about this book is the following: The facts contained herein will only serve to establish and confirm the beliefs of all true Christians and those who believe the Bible to be the inerrant Word of God—as it was written in its original text. Theomatics is a truth all Christians should rejoice over, and it may be one of the means that God will use in the last day, to help us more clearly understand the true meaning of Scripture. Since the mathematical structure of the Bible clearly establishes a common denominator of Scripture, related by meaning, the means is thus provided for God's people to become more united in their views.

Let me hasten to say, however, that even though theomatics may be used by God to help us more clearly understand the Bible, perhaps no one is more convinced than I that God has reserved the interpretation of His Word to the work and enlightenment of the Holy Spirit. Let each reader then be convinced, as the spirit of God bears witness to his heart, concerning the findings presented in this book.

Our only hope and prayer is that what is contained herein will bless the reader's heart and show all those willing to see that God is indeed sovereign and that everything happening in the world today is in God's plan of the ages—including the discovery of theomatics. The Christian has nothing to fear, but rather can take refuge in the fact that God is still on the throne and has placed in the hands of His people this truth, which may better prepare them for what is coming to pass on the face of the earth.

May God richly bless you as you read this book.

In the Memory of Jesus,

DEL WASHBURN

Another disciple who abides in His Word.

INTRODUCTION:
What Is Theomatics?

Theomatics scientifically proves that God wrote the Bible. If you do not believe this, and if your mind is closed, then this book is not for you.

Furthermore, this book sheds new light on Bible prophecy and end-time events. If you are not interested in what is going to happen in the future, then this book is not for you either.

The facts to be presented herein are the culmination of over 3,000 hours of research; however, this work is in no way exhaustive or complete. It is only the beginning. It could best be described as a "John-the-baptist book," or a forerunner of that which is to come.

At this time we are gearing up for a massive research effort, particularly in the Old Testament. For this reason, the facts contained in this book will deal for the most part with the New Testament. In the future we will publish research showing the mathematical design, or continuity, that is present in both the Old and New Testaments.

While this work was being prepared, we realized that its purpose would have to be twofold. First of all, it must be written for the general public, and it must be easy for anyone to understand. We believe that we have achieved this goal.

We also realized that, at the same time, evidence and statistical data would have to be provided that would satisfy those who are more scholarly. For this reason, almost all the technical aspects of theomatics have been placed in the last chapter dealing with the science of statistics and probability. There, conclusive proof is given that the facts contained in this book are scientifically correct.

1

God's Best Kept Secret
Revealed

Guess what the Lord has done? God has written His entire Word mathematically! Within the Bible there is a mathematical design, which reveals God's divine origin of authorship in such a way that the faith of Christians can be built up and strengthened in a brand-new way. This mathematical design we call "theomatics," and it means the "mathematics, or numbers, of God."

Before we examine this marvelous truth, however, let us ask ourselves a question. Who is regulating the affairs on this earth today— God or the devil? That God reigns supreme in heaven is generally conceded. That He does so over this world is almost universally denied. More and more are men, in their intellectual reasonings, relegating God to the background. Take the material world as an example. Not only is it denied that God created all things by personal and direct action, but few believe that He has any immediate concern in regulating the creative works of His own hands. Everything is supposed to be ordered according to the abstract and impersonal laws of nature. Thus, God the creator is banished from His own creation. We need not be surprised that men, in their totally depraved state of mind, exclude Him from everyday human affairs.

But, again, who is regulating the affairs on this earth today—God or the devil? Attempt to take a serious and comprehensive view of the world. What a scene of confusion and total chaos! Sin is rampant, crime has reached epidemic proportions, lawlessness abounds, and everywhere evil men and seducers are growing worse and worse. Moral conditions have fallen to rock bottom, and family life in many quarters is a thing of the past.

Let us take a more specific view of the political scene and world conditions in general. Thrones are creaking and tottering, governments are falling, and new, less stable ones rising to replace those that have fallen. Communist aggression threatens the Free World on every continent, and instead of the world being safe for democracy, we find that democracy is very unsafe in this world. Men's hearts are "failing them for fear, and for looking after those things which are coming on the earth."

Let us turn aside for a moment now, and focus our attention on the religious world. After almost twenty centuries of gospel preaching, Christ is still "despised and rejected of men." Worse still, the Christ of Scripture is proclaimed and magnified by very few. Recently a religious leader of great influence made the declaration that he believed the men who wrote the Bible were God's penmen, but they were not His pen. Such a statement would make the average Christian question this man's faith, for we who have been "born of the spirit" know that the entire Word of God was given to us directly by God, and that it was His very pen which wrote it.

But, again, we must ask ourselves the question: Do not all these things seem to indicate that the devil may have taken the upper hand, and that we Christians have failed in our efforts to effectively preach the gospel? And what of God? Does He not see and hear? Is He impotent or indifferent? Many are declaring that Christianity is a failure, and as a result not a few of the Lord's own people are perplexed, and their faith is being severely tried. People everywhere are asking the question: How can I know for sure that the Bible is the inspired Word of God?

But there is another side to the story, and this one must be emphasized or else God will be robbed of His glory. Even though all appears to be in a state of confusion, there is a powerful move of the Holy Spirit taking place in the church today. God is gathering His people into the one fold of the One Shepherd. Everywhere a person looks, he can see the tremendous hunger and thirst among Christians for more knowledge of the Word. God's people are gathering everywhere: in homes, churches, rallies. And then there is the tremendous growth in the publication of Christian books and literature. Sales are at an all-time high, and the presses are unable to print Bibles fast enough. Many church leaders have referred to this fresh moving of the Holy Spirit as "a new awakening." There is a feeling of expectancy among Christians everywhere that the end is upon us, and that God is preparing His people for the closing days of history. For this reason, could it be that now is the time God has chosen to make known to His people the truth of theomatics? Could it be that God is now revealing scientific evidence that He alone is the author of His Word?

In reply to this, you may ask, How can this be so? Are not Christians supposed to walk by faith? The answer to this question is yes, for "without faith it is impossible to please Him." Even though the truth of theomatics is scientific in nature, its purpose is not to replace faith, but rather to build up the faith of the saints. To the lost and dying world, theomatics will have no meaning, but to those who are saved and know Jesus, it will only serve to strengthen their faith, because it will be a confirmation of that which they already know to be truth.

Bible Prophecy—1976

Two hundred years have passed from the time this nation was founded to the writing of this book. But what a change has taken place! In only a few short years this country has developed from a few English colonies to the greatest nation on earth. As the Christian looks about, he cannot help but realize that the words spoken in Daniel 12:4 are rapidly being fulfilled: "But as for you Daniel, conceal these words and seal up the book until the end time: many shall run to and fro, and knowledge shall be increased."

From the earliest times, one area of Scripture more than any other has attracted the attention and fancy of Bible scholars and all people in general. Bible prophecy is receiving more attention today than ever before. The main reason for this increase in popularity is the keen sense of expectancy among Christians that the age is drawing to a close. World conditions change almost daily, and the situation in the Middle East has caused many to stop and take a second look at world events in light of the Scriptures.

If one were to turn on his radio, he would hear a multitude of preachers expounding everything from current events to the second coming of Christ. If he were to walk into a Christian book store, he would find the shelves loaded with books on every area of prophetic studies, particularly the book of Revelation. Man has always been eager to know what lies in the future, and Christians are no exception. The fact that such a huge percentage of the Bible is prophetic in nature has only served to whet the appetite of the believer to try and unlock the the prophetic meanings of Scripture and find out what is going to happen next.

In the midst of all the excitement surrounding prophetic subjects, however, there has been a certain aura of uncertainty. Bible scholars have differed widely as to the interpretation of certain prophetic events, and as a result, speculation has prevailed. For this reason, many have given up entirely on trying to understand Revelation, and come to the conclusion that God gave us prophecy so that we could confirm the events after they happened. To a degree, this is true; however, we must also realize that the purpose of prophecy is to forewarn and foretell events before they occur, so that we will know what is going to happen ahead of time and, thus, be prepared. So why, then, all the confusion?

God's Secrets Are Hidden Until the Proper Time

In Revelation 13:18 we find the following words: "Here is wisdom. The one therefore having wisdom, let him calculate the number of the beast: for it is the number of man, and it is 666."[1] This passage of Scripture has taxed the ingenuity of the world's greatest theologians from the earliest times. What could this number possibly mean? There is tremendous significance to the number 666, which will be discussed later on, in Chapter 7, but for now the interesting part of this verse is the clause, "the one therefore having wisdom, let him calculate. . . ." These words tell us that there is a time coming when this will be understood, because the book of Revelation was written to and for the end-time saints of God.

The word for *calculate* in Greek is ψηφιζω, pronounced *psefizo.* In Greek, it is defined as "to count with pebbles, to compute, calculate, reckon." In Revelation 13:18, the word means to explain by the process of computing. The same word is found in Luke 14:28: "For which one of you, when he wants to build a tower, does not first sit down and calculate the cost, to see if he has enough to complete it." In Webster's dictionary, the word *calculate* is defined as "to determine by arithmetic, compute, reckon, to ascertain by reasoning."

[1] This English translation of Revelation 13:18 is based on the earliest known copy of the book of Revelation (Chester Beatty Papyrus).

In Daniel 12:9 it says, "Go your way Daniel, for these words are concealed and sealed up until the time of the end." These words along with Revelation 13:18 tell us that certain things are sealed up, concealed, kept secret, until God wishes to have them revealed. Let us examine this statement for a moment.

From the time of Adam, one finds that all of God's revelation throughout history has been progressive. The patriarchs during Abraham's time had a very limited knowledge of God's plan of salvation, as compared with the early Christians. Throughout God's dealing with the Jews, knowledge increased as God gave further revelation through the prophets.

When Jesus came, the age of grace began. It was at this time that the full revelation of the gospel became known. In Colossians 1:26 Paul refers to "the mystery which has been hidden from past ages and generations, but has now been revealed to His saints." Paul constantly referred to the mystery of the gospel which had been hidden in the past, but now revealed. Did the Old Testament saints have knowledge of all this? They did only in form, but not in fullness. Even the New Testament saints were somewhat limited as to the full knowledge of God's plan of redemption. In the early church, the apostles were continuously teaching from the Old Testament. Today, in the twentieth century, we have a much fuller revelation with the sixty-six books of the Bible.

Now, not only does this principle of progressive revelation hold true of the spiritual world, but of the natural as well. Why was it that Columbus did not discover America before 1492? Why was it that electricity was not discovered before the nineteenth century? Why has it been that so many of the great scientific discoveries were not made until the turn of this century? The reason is very simple. God withholds certain things from man until the proper time. It must be noted as a point of interest that when inventions such as the radio and airplane were being made, men all over the world were receiving the same inspiration at the same time. It is God who gives this inspiration, and it is also God who withholds it.

A perfect example of how God brings forth a further understanding of hidden truth is found in a comparison made to the human body. For thousands of years, mankind could only marvel at the wonder of creation found in the human body. He could see that all of the body's systems functioned in a systematic manner, which defied explanation.

Man could see, hear, taste, smell, touch. His body could digest food, which gave him nourishment. When he was tired, he could recuperate and feel rested through sleep. If he was sick or injured, the body would heal itself automatically. If he wanted to reach down and pick something up, he could do so. If he wanted to run, he could do that also. But even though man could see that all of these body systems functioned and operated in a systematic order, he knew very little about the hidden structure inside of the body which made it all possible.

Then along came medical science. Here it was that man began to unlock the mysteries of how the human body functioned. He discovered that within the body there were systems built in that could fight disease. He also found out about the blood and nervous systems, and how the musculature worked. He then looked into the eye and discovered how the eye could take in light and transmit an image to the brain. All of these discoveries led to further investigation, and as a result doctors began to discover new forms of medicine and surgical techniques. Revolutionary findings were being made almost on a daily basis. To try and compare today's knowledge of the human body with that of even a hundred years ago would be an insurmountable task.

But here is the important part of this truth. For thousands of years, all that man could see of the body was simply the outer shell. He could see and appreciate that it all operated in a systematic manner, but he knew little about what lay beneath that shell. As time passed, he began to discover that underneath all of this there existed a design—a design which made possible the outward and visible functions of the body. Even though this hidden design had been there for thousands of years, man did not realize it until just recently. Could it be, then, that this is the case with the Word of God?

For almost 2,000 years now, Christians' hearts have been blessed and filled with joy from the written words contained in the Bible. At times the Scriptures have brought peace and assurance when nothing else could. In time of trial or illness, comfort and reassurance have been found. The loss of a loved one has been easier to bear. Broken homes have been reunited. But most important, countless souls have come to know Jesus. The Bible has done more good for mankind than all other works of literature throughout history combined. More things have been written and said concerning the book of books than any other book in history. The very nation in which we live was founded on the principles and laws set forth in the Bible. Because of America's freedom of worship, she has enjoyed the greatest prosperity of any nation on earth. All of the blessings, the comforts, and the spiritual prosperity which we have enjoyed down through the years have come about solely through the written Word of God.

The only Word of God that we have ever known has been the written Word of God, words like those you are now reading. All of our comprehension concerning God's revelation through His Word has been limited solely to what we have seen on the surface, with our physical eyes.

Could it be, then, that underneath this written Word there exists a design—a design which has not been known up to now, because it is hidden beneath the very surface of the original Bible text, a design which ties together the hidden meanings of Scripture? Could it be that what we have seen up till now has only been the outer shell? Let's find out.

God's Works Are Perfect in Number

The Bible tells us that everything God does is perfect in number (Job 28:25, Psalms 147:4, Isaiah 40:26, Luke 12:7). We find that this is true when we look at nature and the expanse of the heavens and the magnitude of the universe. As one gazes up at the stars, he cannot help but agree with the words of the psalmist when he says: "What is man that thou art mindful of him, or the son of man that thou dost care for him?" The dimension of the universe with its billions of galaxies is something that our finite minds cannot even begin to comprehend, let alone appreciate.

Not only does God's design exist in the universe; it can also be carried right down through nature to the intricate design of the atom. And here is the most exciting thing: All creation, no matter how large or small the scale, can always be reduced to numbers. If we look at the world of light and sound, we find that each light and sound wave consists of so many vibrations per second. The same principle also holds true with music, because each musical note has its own particular number of vibrations per second. The design of numbers also exists in the plant and animal kingdoms. Each part of a biological structure is composed of so many cells arranged in a geometric pattern. Furthermore, these millions of tiny cells are thus arranged by number to compose the complete structure. All of God's creative works, no matter how large or small, can always be reduced to numbers.

At this point we would like to pose to the reader a profound question. The Bible plainly teaches that God created all things. "For in Him all things were created, both in heaven and on earth, visible and invisible" (Colossians 1:16). Throughout Scripture, God is constantly portrayed as the very creator of the heavens, or the universe. If one were to gaze through the telescope on Mt. Palomar and view the billions of galaxies and island universes, he could not help but realize that the design present in all of this is beyond the wildest comprehension of man. On the other hand, if a person were to gaze through the electron microscope and view the molecular structure that comprises all of the chemical elements, he would see the same design present as found in the universe. Now here is the question: The Bible is the very Word of God, the One through whom heaven and earth were created. If the Lord God is the one who designed and created the universe and all of the atomic elements, then why would not His book contain the same vast and intricate mathematical design?

Furthermore, Jesus said that "heaven and earth will pass away; but My words shall not pass away." This then tells us that the Word of God is more enduring, priceless, and valuable than all created matter. On this basis alone, we can readily assume that the Bible should contain a mathematical design as vast as all creation.

In 2 Timothy 3:16, it states that "all Scripture is inspired by God." The word *inspired* in Greek means literally "God breathed." In the Old Testament, in Exodus 32:16 it says that "the tablets were God's work, and the writing was God's writing engraved on the tablets." Since it was the very hand of God that wrote the Bible, we are now going to discover something absolutely remarkable.

The Old and New Testaments as we know them were originally given to us as written language or words. These words are composed of letters. Now what the Lord has done is to assign each letter and in turn each word of the Bible with a number, or *theomatic*, value. This means that all of the meanings in the Bible can be reduced to numbers —the same as everything else in creation. Sound fantastic? It is, and that's what theomatics is all about. Everything in the Bible was composed and written mathematically. Related meanings in Scripture all tie together by theomatic design.

2

The Theomatic Structure
Defined

In the last chapter we sought to lay a foundation of spiritual values for the subject in which we are about to engage ourselves. In this chapter we will become directly involved with theomatics, and from here on all of our attention will be focused on the actual design in the Word of God.

The truth of theomatics is not difficult to understand. God did not put a design in His Word that would be confusing to His people and as a result impossible to comprehend. In fact, the exact opposite is true. There are five basic concepts that must be learned, and then the rest is easy. After you have learned these concepts, you will be ready to embark on one of the most exciting adventures of your Christian life.

Concept 1: The Theomatic Number Codes

In the English language we always express numbers by the Arabic digits 1, 2, 3, 4, 5, 6, 7, 8, 9, and 0. The early Greeks, however, had no way of expressing numbers in their language system, so they used the letters of their alphabet as numbers. For example, number 1 would be the letter α, number 2 would be letter β, number 3 letter γ, and so on. If a person wanted to express the number 14, he would take the letter for the number 10 (ι) and number 4 (δ), and place them side by side: $\iota\delta = 14$. The number 237 would be expressed by the letters for 200 (σ), 30 (λ), and 7 (ζ): $\sigma\lambda\zeta = 237$. The Romans also incorporated this idea of using letters for numbers and, as is well known, used the letters I, V, X, L, C, D, and M to express numbers.

Now in order to confirm the Greek number code as we have given it, a person needs to look no further than Webster's dictionary. The complete number code is found in the section entitled "Special Signs and Symbols," which lists all of the Greek letters with their appropriate values.

The Hebrew number code, following a similar concept, has been in use since the time before Christ. In fact, if you were to look in a present-day Hebrew Bible, you would find the chapter and verse numbers given with the letters of the Hebrew alphabet.

Shown below are the Hebrew and Greek alphabets. The Bible was, of course, originally written in these two languages, the Old Testament in Hebrew, and the New Testament in Greek. Following each letter of the alphabets there is a number. This number is the equivalent *number*, or *theomatic*, value of that particular letter. The Hebrew alphabet contains twenty-two letters, and the Greek has twenty-six. See chart on the next page for the number codes.

What an amazing thing! Has God's best-kept secret been in Webster's dictionary all of these years? God's secrets are sometimes hidden this way. Once they are found, it is hard to believe that we never saw them before, but until then there is not even the slightest chance that someone is going to uncover them before God's appointed time.

As it has been shown, each and every single letter of the Hebrew and Greek alphabets has a number, or theomatic, value assigned to it. Now this is not only true of the individual letters, but it is also applicable to each and every single word in the Bible. To illustrate, we will take the word for *Jesus* in Greek, which is Iησους. By following the chart for the Greek number code and adding together the numbers for all the letters in this word, we would obtain the following total:

$$(\text{I} = 10) + (\eta = 8) + (\sigma = 200) + (\text{o} = 70) + (\upsilon = 400) + (\varsigma = 200) = 888$$

So by adding together the numbers $10 + 8 + 200 + 70 + 400 + 200$ we have a sum total of 888. Therefore the number, or theomatic, value of the name *Jesus* is 888. But this value is not only possible for the name of Jesus. It also applies to every single Hebrew and Greek word in the Bible, which has its own number, or theomatic, value.

Not only do words have number values, but also complete thoughts and sentences as well. To illustrate this, let's take the first verse of the Bible: "In the beginning God created the heaven and the earth."

HEBREW ALPHABET		GREEK ALPHABET	
א	1	α	1
ב	2	β	2
ג	3	γ	3
ד	4	δ	4
ה	5	ε	5
ו	6 ←	→ ς'	6[2]
ז	7	ζ	7
ח	8	η	8
ט	9	θ	9
י	10	ι	10
כ-ך	20[1]	κ	20
ל	30	λ	30
מ-ם	40[1]	μ	40
נ-ן	50[1]	ν	50
ס	60	ξ	60
ע	70	ο	70
פ-ף	80[1]	π	80
צ-ץ	90[1]	ϙ	90[2]
ק	100	ρ	100
ר	200	σ–ς	200[1]
ש	300	τ	300
ת	400	υ	400
		φ	500
		χ	600
		ψ	700
		ω	800

[1]These double letters are the same. The second letter is used in place of the first letter when it occurs as the last letter in a word. There is no difference in number value between the two.

[2]Those who are familiar with New Testament Greek may be surprised to see the addition of the letters *vau* (number value = 6) and *koppa* (number value = 90). The letter *vau*, sometimes represented by the symbol for the letter *sigma*, appears in only one passage of Scripture (Revelation 13:18). At one time in the history of the Greek language both of these letters existed, but later on they became extinct.

296   407   395   401   86   203   913 $= 2{,}701$

As the reader can see, the number that is the theomatic value for each word is directly above it. What we can do now is take all of these numbers and add them together, and we would have 296 + 407 + 395 + 401 + 86 + 203 + 913, for a total of 2,701. Thus, the theomatic value of the first verse in the Bible is 2,701. So each and every word of the Bible has a theomatic value, and also each and every sentence or complete thought as well.

When Del began his research, he did something which, to our knowledge, no one had ever done before. In order for him to effectively pursue the study of theomatics, a research tool was needed, one that would save hours of labor and at the same time open up the complete theomatic design in the Word of God. This tool was a *theomatic Greek-English New Testament*. Since no such tool existed at the time, it was necessary for Del to develop his own. He obtained a copy of a Greek-English New Testament and began to work.

Shown on the next page is a copy of one of the pages from the theomatic Greek-English New Testament. As the reader can see, underneath each Greek word there is the English equivalent of that word. Above each Greek word is the appropriate theomatic value of that word, written in Del's own handwriting. In the left-hand margin is the English from the King James Version of the New Testament.

Those readers who have seen a copy of a Greek New Testament are well aware that above almost every Greek word, there are a multitude of accents and breathing marks. Del first of all had to white out each and every one of these in order to make room for the number values of the words. After doing this, he then underlined each word for emphasis.

This research tool contains over 1,000 pages just like the one above and took well over eight months to complete. The entire work was done by hand, and then all of the theomatic values were later checked to insure the utmost accuracy. This tool later saved hundreds of hours on the calculator, because each letter did not then have to be added. Furthermore, Del could see the number, or theomatic, value of each word, which let him immediately know the significance of that particular word. Without this tool, Del's research would have been next to impossible.

366   **JOHN 3**

but he that came down from heaven, *even* the Son of man which is in heaven.

14 And as Moses lifted up the serpent in the wilderness, even so must the Son of man be lifted up:

15 That whosoever believeth in him should not perish, but have eternal life.

16 For God so loved the world, that he gave his only begotten Son, that whosoever believeth in him should not perish, but have everlasting life.

17 For God sent not his Son into the world to condemn the world; but that the world through him might be saved.

18 He that believeth on him is not condemned: but he that believeth not is condemned already, because he hath not believed in the name of the only begotten Son of God.

19 And this is the condemnation, that light is come into the world, and men loved darkness rather than light, because their deeds were evil.

20 For every one that doeth evil hateth the light, neither cometh to the light, lest his deeds should be reproved.

21 But he that doeth truth cometh to the light, that his deeds may be made manifest, that they

---

70 25 770 1091 525 70 680
Ο   εκ του ουρανου καταβας, ο υιος
the [one] out of – heaven having come down, the Son

770 1510 31 1030 1648 2155
του ανθρωπου. 14 Και καθως Μωυσης υψωσεν
of man.   And as   Moses   lifted up

420 630 55 308 953 1770 1978
τον οφιν εν τη ερημω, ουτως υψωθηναι
the serpent in the desert, so to be lifted up

819 420 530 770 1510 1281 70
δει τον υιον του ανθρωπου, 15 ινα πας ο
it behoves the Son – of man, that everyone

1845 55 1501 613 865 991
πιστευων εν αυτω εχη ζωην αιωνιον,
believing in him may have life eternal.

1770 104 355 70 284 420
16 ουτως γαρ ηγαπησεν ο θεος τον
For thus   [2]loved – [1]God the

450 1305 420 530 420 296
κοσμον, ωστε τον υιον τον μονογενη
world, so as the Son the only begotten

884 61 281 70 1845 215 821
εδωκεν, ινα πας ο πιστευων εις αυτον
he gave, that everyone believing in him

48 500 613 865 991
μη αποληται αλλ' εχη ζωην αιωνιον.
may not perish but may have life eternal.

470 104 686 70 284 420 530
17 ου γαρ απεστειλεν ο θεος τον υιον
For [2]not   [2]sent – [1]God the Son

215 420 450 61 188 420 450
εις τον κοσμον ινα κρινη τον κοσμον,
into the world that he might judge the world,

61 61 1017 70 14 1171
αλλ' ινα σωθη ο κοσμος δι αυτου.
but that [2]might be saved [1]the [2]world through him.

70 1845 215 821 470 496
18 Ο πιστευων εις αυτον ου κρινεται·
The [one] believing in him is not judged;

70 48 1845 466 380
ο μη πιστευων ηδη κεκριται, οτι
the [one] not believing already has been judged, because

48 1155 215 370 231 770 958
μη πεπιστευκεν εις το ονομα του μονογενους
he has not believed in the name of the only begotten

880 770 484 709 565 8
υιου του θεου. 19 αυτη δε εστιν η
Son – of God. And this is the

540 380 370 1500 537 215 420
κρισις, οτι το φως εληλυθεν εις τον
judgment, that the light has come into the

450 31 351 80 1120 221
κοσμον και ηγαπησαν οι ανθρωποι μαλλον
world and [2]loved [1]men rather

370 860 8 370 1500 58 104 1551
το σκοτος η το φως· ην γαρ αυτων
[2]the [4]darkness [3]than the light; for was(were) of them

309 301 109 281 104 70 932
πονηρα τα εργα. 20 πας γαρ ο φαυλα
evil the works. For everyone evil things

1431 265 370 1500 31 490 1021
πρασσων μισει το φως και ουκ ερχεται
doing hates the light and does not come

450 370 1500 61 48 301 109
προς το φως, ινα μη ελεγχθη τα εργα
to the light, lest is(are) reproved the works

1171 70 1010 358 114 1021
αυτου· 21 ο δε ποιων την αληθειαν ερχεται
of him; but the [one] doing the truth comes

450 370 1500 61 1473 1171 301
προς το φως, ινα φανερωθη αυτου τα
to the light, that may be manifested of him the

Before we present Concept 2, let's do some quick reviewing. In Concept 1 we saw how each letter in the Hebrew and Greek alphabets has a number, or theomatic, value assigned to it. Furthermore, by adding all the number values for the letters in a word, we find that each word has a number value. And last, by adding all of the number values for the words in a phrase, we find that each phrase also has its own number, or theomatic, value.

Concept 2: Multiples

Even though this concept is relatively easy to understand, we will give it a somewhat detailed explanation in order that the reader may understand its true importance. The concept is: *Everything in theomatics operates by multiples.* Let us explain.

Here is the number 300. If we divide the number 300 by 3, we would find that $100 \times 3 = 300$. In other words, 300 is a multiple of 100, because it can be divided evenly by 100. The same thing holds true for the number 700. It is a multiple of 100, because it too can be divided by 100. $100 \times 7 = 700$. Likewise, the numbers 500, 1,200, 200, 1,000, and 1,700 are all multiples of 100, because they can all be divided by 100.

Our next example is a little more complicated. Here are five numbers: 481, 1,073, 185, 3,219, and 1,110. At first glance these numbers do not appear to have anything in common with each other, do they? But they all have one remarkable similarity: They are all multiples of the number 37, because they can be divided evenly by 37.

$$
\begin{array}{rcl}
481 & \text{is} & 37 \times 13 \\
1,073 & \text{is} & 37 \times 29 \\
185 & \text{is} & 37 \times 5 \\
3,219 & \text{is} & 37 \times 87 \\
1,110 & \text{is} & 37 \times 30 \\
\end{array}
$$

At this point there is only one important thing that you will have to remember. Later on, when we present the theomatic designs, it will be shown that each major Bible truth has a key number assigned to it by God. For example, if you examine the many different references to Jesus, you find they are all multiples of the same number. And the many different references to Satan are all multiples of another number.

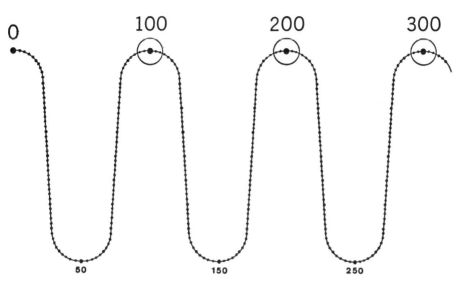

Concept 3: Clusters

The last concept we looked at showed how everything in theomatics operates by multiples of certain key numbers. Concept 3 is the *clustering of numbers around these multiples*. The easiest way to illustrate this is by drawing a line graph showing all of the numbers from 1 to 300. (This line graph could have been drawn as one straight line, but it was curved in order to save space on the page.) Each dot represents a number. At the top of the graph are the numbers 100, 200, and 300. These, of course, are all multiples of 100. Surrounding these multiples of 100 there is a circle. *This circle forms a cluster of the multiple of 100.* To further illustrate, let's draw a detail of this circle, or cluster.

As the reader can see, the large dot in the center of the circle represents the number 100. On each side of the large dot, there are two smaller dots. These represent the numbers 98, 99, 101, and 102. All five of these numbers (98, 99, 100, 101, and 102) form a cluster of the multiple of 100.

These circles, or clusters, are rather like shooting a basketball through a basketball hoop. If we were to take the many different

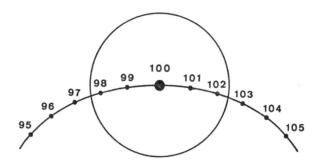

references to Jesus, Satan, and so on, their number values would all fall into the appropriate circles, or clusters. Here is an example. Let's say that we had a phrase in Greek with a theomatic value of 799. This feature would fall within the cluster of the multiples of 100, because 800 is a multiple of 100, and the numbers 798, 799, 800, 801, and 802 form the cluster. Another example would be the number 2,602. A phrase with a theomatic value of 2,602 would also fall within the cluster, because 2,598, 2,599, 2,600, 2,601, and 2,602 form the cluster. Everything in theomatics operates on the principle of clusters.

The dictionary definition of the word *cluster* is "a number of things of the same sort gathered or bunched together." One example in creation brings this truth out perfectly. In the universe, galaxies are all structured around clusters of stars. Toward the center of a galaxy, there exists the largest concentration of stars. But as one moves further out from the center, the stars become fewer and fewer. Theomatics operates on the same principle. The greatest percentage of the features to be presented in this book are exact multiples of the key numbers. A smaller number of the features are within minus 1 or plus 1 of the multiples, and fewer still are within minus 2 or plus 2. The numbers are all clustering around the direct multiples, and this is the same principle by which God has designed the galaxies.

Concept 4: Grammar of the Hebrew and Greek Languages

So far we have covered three of the four concepts: (1) *the theomatic number codes;* (2) *multiples;* and (3) *clusters.* Concept 4 is going to be a little different. Here we will discuss in very general terms some fundamentals of Hebrew and Greek grammar. You will find this concept extremely interesting, and perhaps you'll learn some things you never knew before.

Throughout the past centuries, man has tried in vain to answer many of the questions pertaining to the grammar of the Hebrew and Greek languages. In fact, if you were to walk into a Christian book store and look for a text on New Testament Greek grammar, you would probably find the words "in light of historical research" following the title. The reason for this is that what the scholars are trying to do is find manuscripts contemporary with the time of the Bible events, and compare them with the Greek of the New Testament.

Because of the mystery surrounding the Greek of the New Testament, many people throughout the centuries referred to it as being a "language of the Holy Spirit" (which it no doubt is). However, later investigations revealed that the Greek of the New Testament was the common marketplace Greek of the people of Jesus' day. This is why it is presently known as *koine Greek,* which means "common Greek."

In Concept 4, we will not attempt to give the reader a long discourse on the grammatical structure of Hebrew and Greek, but there are a few essentials which should be understood before we proceed. The first of these are the *cases,* and the second is the *article.* Our discussion will be from the standpoint of Greek, but the Hebrew language is very similar in these grammatical respects.

THE CASES

In the English language, how many ways are there to spell the word God? The answer is simple. There is only one way. The word *God* is spelled *G-o-d.* But this is not true in the Greek language. In fact, for just about every single noun in Greek, there are at least four possible spellings.[3] These spellings are called *cases,* and they each fulfill a basic grammatical purpose that we will not go into here. Each word has a basic root, or stem, and the ending of the word, or suffix, is the variable. To illustrate, we will list the four different spellings in Greek for the word *God.* (The Greek is in parentheses, followed by the English pronunciation.)

[3]These spellings are referred to by Greek grammarians as declensional forms, or case endings (nominative, genitive, dative, and accusative). Some grammarians also include the vocative as a fifth case.

(Θεος) Theos   (Θεου) Theu   (Θεον) Theon   (Θεω) Theo

As the reader can see, the basic word remains the same, and the only thing that changes is the ending. This is true with practically every single Greek word. If one were to spell *God* in the plural as *Gods*, the plural form also has four different spellings. *With this concept, God has provided Himself with a language that is extremely flexible.* In a few moments we will show why.

THE ARTICLE

The article of Hebrew and Greek is indeed one of the most fascinating things in all human language. To those readers who are familiar with grammar, the words *a, an,* and *the* are known as *articles.* The two articles *a* and *an* are *indefinite* articles, while *the* is *definite.* In the English language we have both definite and indefinite articles; however, in Greek there are no indefinite articles. *All of the articles in Greek are definite.*

It would take several pages to explain more fully the function of the Greek article, but that will not be necessary. There is only one thing you have to remember, and it is the following: There are no "rules" for the use of the article in Greek.[4] The Greek article has absolutely no meaning whatsoever (beyond the translated meaning of "the"). Because it is the definite article, it can add emphasis and act as a pointer, but it has no significance otherwise.

A perfect example of this would be the following. The word for *man* in Greek is ανθρωπος. With the article, the word *man* would mean simply *the man,* ο ανθρωπος. As you can see, there is no real difference between the two. The only difference between *man* and *the man* is that *the* adds emphasis to the word *man.* Otherwise, it has no real meaning. And here is the interesting fact. Without the article the word *man* in Greek could still be translated as *the* man. It is not necessary for the article to be present in Greek for a word to be definite. In fact, the article in Greek has no bearing at all on translation.

If all of this is a little confusing to you (and sounds like Greek), don't worry about it. The only important thing you should remember is that the article in Greek has no special significance whatsoever. In

[4]H. E. Dana and Julius R. Mantey, *A Manual Grammar of the Greek New Testament* (Toronto: Macmillan, 1955), p. 141.

fact, if you were to take a verse from the Bible and remove the articles, it would not change the translated meaning at all. Let us explain.

Here is a sentence in English: I was driving down the street in the car while I was listening to the radio. As you can see, this sentence contains three the's. The word *the*, of course, corresponds to the definite article in Greek. Let us again quote this phrase and this time remove all the articles: I was driving down street in car while I was listening to radio.

We have said exactly the same thing, even after removing the articles. This phrase has the same meaning when the articles are present and when they are deleted.

In John 11:4, Jesus is referred to as being "the Son of God." The Greek words for "the Son of God" with the articles are ο υιος του Θεου. But in Mark 15:39 Jesus again is referred to as "the Son of God." In this verse, the words "the Son of God" appear without the articles (υιος Θεου); but the translation still remains the same. So, therefore, a Greek phrase has the same meaning—with or without the article—and the same is true of Hebrew.

Now, as has been shown, practically every Greek word has at least four possible spellings. These spellings also have four different articles to match. In English there is only one way to spell the article *the*, but in Greek there are a multitude of possible spellings for the articles. To illustrate this, let us now look at the four spellings of God, along with their appropriate articles:

$$o \ \Theta\epsilon o\varsigma \qquad \tau o\upsilon \ \Theta\epsilon o\upsilon \qquad \tau\omega \ \Theta\epsilon\omega \qquad \tau o\upsilon \ \Theta\epsilon o\upsilon$$

As you have been reading these words concerning the Greek article, one question may have been going through your mind: If the Greek article has no meaning, then why did God place it in the Bible? He put it there because of theomatics! The reason the Hebrew and Greek languages are structured the way they are is that they are theomatic languages. Each of the various articles, along with the multitude of possible spellings for the words, all have different number, or theomatic, values.

What God simply does is to use the right combination of words (with their various spellings), along with the different articles, to construct a sentence, phrase, or thought that adds up to the proper theomatic value He has chosen.

This would be totally impossible with any other kind of language, such as English, and once this discovery becomes widely understood, it should excite Bible scholars in a way they have never known before. Theomatics throws definite light on why the Hebrew and Greek languages are structured the way they are.

Now at this point, it is quite obvious that in order for God to place the mathematics in His Word, He also had to be a grammarian and design the languages He was to use. Every single Hebrew and Greek word in the Bible was designed mathematically by God to fit together with the other words and thus form the complete theomatic structure of the Bible.

What an amazing thing! God took the languages of the ancient Hebrews and the common Greek people of Jesus' day, and thus constructed His entire Word with an intricate mathematical design. Everything had to fit together perfectly.

All of the computers in the world working together could not even begin to construct the design you are about to see demonstrated in this book. And even if the computers could do it, they would have to simultaneously bring out all of the spiritual truth and meaning of the Bible. Then, to top it all off, the languages would have to make sense grammatically. Only God could accomplish a feat like this. Praise His name!

Concept 5: Rules and Guidelines for Theomatics Research

As we illustrated in Concept 4, there are many spellings for words in Hebrew or Greek. This means that if a person wanted to, he could play "match-up" and invent almost any theomatic feature he desired. By playing match-up we mean that a person could take Greek words or phrases with related meanings from different parts of the Bible and start adding their number values together, playing with totals to see what kind of theomatic features he could come up with.

But if one were to go to the actual text of the Hebrew or Greek and find features without changing, matching, or adding the different words and phrases together, then his selection would be limited to the actual words God placed in the text of the Bible. This brings us to a certain guideline which must be followed at all times. We will call it the Golden Rule of Theomatics.

Every single word or phrase that is used for a theomatic feature must come right out of the text, in exactly the same manner as God put it there. No words may be changed or added at any time for any reason. All words to be used for a theomatic feature must come from the same spiritual context contained within that particular line, sentence, or verse.

The only allowable variable in theomatics is sometimes to eliminate the article altogether. In an earlier example, we showed how "Son of God" was spelled in one verse with the article and in another without the article. Either one of these examples would be a valid theomatic feature. Another example would be found in Ephesians 2:2, where Satan is referred to as "the prince of the power of the air." These words are preceded by an article in Greek. Therefore, this phrase could be shown with or without the article. Either way, the meaning remains the same: "the prince of the power of the air."

This is one of the reasons why God put the article in the text. Understanding the use of the Greek article is the key that unlocks the complete theomatic design in the Word of God. When the article is present, or when it is deleted, the meaning remains exactly the same, but the theomatic value changes. The Greek article is the one thing that makes it possible for all of the theomatic designs in the Bible to flow together.

In the Golden Rule of Theomatics, all words must be taken from the same spiritual context. This does not mean, however, that the words from the Greek text must always appear side by side, or bumper to bumper. Here are several examples of what we mean: In Mark 2:28 we find the following words: "Therefore the Son of Man is Lord also of the Sabbath."

ωστε   κυριος εστιν ο υιος του ανθρωπου και του σαββατου
Therefore Lord   is the son — of man   also of the Sabbath

As you can see from this example, the Greek words are arranged in a completely different order from the English translation. This verse means that the Son of Man is the Lord of the Sabbath, but in Greek the two words *Lord* and *Sabbath* do not appear side by side. They are separated by seven other Greek words. But because this verse concerns the "Lord of the Sabbath," it would be valid to take the two Greek words for "Lord" and "Sabbath," and place them side by side (κυριος σαββατου). The result would be "Lord of the Sabbath," and that's exactly what this verse is talking about.

Another example is found in The Acts 4:30, which says: "that signs and wonders may be done by the name of the holy child of thee Jesus."

ονοματος	του αγιου	παιδος	σου	Ιησου
name	of holy	child	of thee	Jesus

When the Greek word "of thee" (σου) is removed from the middle of these words, we have the perfect phrase "name of the holy child Jesus" instead of "name of the holy child of thee Jesus." Since these words carry perfect meaning, it would be valid to present a theomatic feature in this manner. This principle will be further supported later in this book.

WHICH TRANSLATION?

Have you ever wondered why there are so many English translations of the Bible on the market? The reason for this is the way the Greek language is structured grammatically. The ideas can be expressed in so many different ways when a verse is translated into English. There are so many meanings and shades of meanings possible. All the translators are saying basically the same thing, only with a different choice of words.

Because of all the variations throughout the translations, we would like to point out something to the reader that cannot be overemphasized. Beginning in the next chapter, we will start presenting the actual theomatic designs. This book contains well over 1,000 features, or quotations. During the process of compiling these features, we realized that we were faced with a problem. Which version or translation of the Bible were we going to use? Some people prefer the King James translation. Others favor the Revised Standard Version. Still others prefer the American Standard Version. So which translation were we supposed to use?

After researching this for some time, we came to the firm conclusion that there was no way we could stick to any one major translation. Why? Because the Greek language is so utterly different from English. The major complication lay in the fact that many times the words from the Greek text are arranged in a completely different order from that found in the English. Therefore, for this book we compared several of the major translations, and by comparing their wording with the Greek we came up with what we thought to be the most accurate translation. If sometimes our translation sounds a little different or unusual, the reason for this is that we are trying to keep as close as possible to the original Greek arrangement of the wording.

If the reader were to compare the features in this book with his favorite translation, he would immediately find that more than ninety-five percent of the features agree nicely with his version. However, there are a few (very few) which will not make sense when compared with any translation. If the reader should question this, we would suggest one of two alternatives: (1) Take this book to your pastor or someone else who knows Greek, and have him confirm it for you. (2) Purchase a Greek-English New Testament.[5] This will enable you to follow along comparing the Greek words with the English words.

In conclusion, let the reader understand that theomatics is not a truth to be understood in English. It is meant to be understood in Hebrew or Greek. In presenting the features we are simply saying: Here are the Greek words. These words add up to a certain number value. We have done our best to translate them as accurately as possible. If you think there is a better translation, then please feel at liberty to take the same Greek words, and put your own translation to them.

Theomatics: On What Basis?

As you have been reading the words contained in this chapter, one question may have been going through your mind: On what is all of this based? Where do you get the proof that God had anything to do with the assignment of number values to the Hebrew and Greek alphabets? Where is the verse in the Bible that tells us there exists any such thing as theomatics? These questions are vital and demand an answer. It is to these that we address the last portion of this chapter.

In order to establish the basis for the assignment of number, or theomatic, values to the letters of the Greek alphabet, we are going to use the two greatest authorities in the world: Webster's dictionary and the Word of God.

Let's face it. There are no two other authorities in existence as

[5]We recommend Marshall, Rev. Alfred, *The Interlinear Greek-English New Testament* (Grand Rapids: Zondervan, 1958), Nestle text.

reliable or trustworthy as these. Earlier in this chapter we mentioned how the theomatic values can be found in Webster's dictionary. This means that these numbers are not something we arbitrarily chose ourselves, but they are established and commonly known and accepted. In other words, it's standardized. (Even though the Hebrew alphabet does not appear in Webster's dictionary, the number values for the Hebrew letters are just as commonly known and accepted.)

And here's something else. If the reader will turn to the first portion of this chapter and look at the Hebrew and Greek number codes, he will see something remarkable. The list of number values is not haphazard but follows an even progression throughout. The first nine letters in the alphabet are numbered 1, 2, 3, 4, 5, 6, 7, 8, and 9. But notice what happens next. The letters which immediately follow also progress from 1 to 9. The only difference here is that a zero follows each digit: 10, 20, 30, 40, 50, 60, 70, 80, and 90. And the last of the letters from the Hebrew and Greek alphabets have values of 100, 200, 300, 400, and so on.

This numbering sequence in the list of theomatic values is proof of the fact that this arrangement was put together with orderly thought and design. In other words, the numbers are not all mixed up, but systematically arranged in an even sequence. Everything that God does is perfect in number.

Still, this does not prove that God had anything to do with it. Or does it? It is at this time we present something that very, very few people know exists. Guess what the Lord has done? God has put the entire basis for the theomatic values of the letters—right in His Word! The entire thing can be found in the earliest known manuscripts for the book of Revelation. These manuscripts are known as the "papyri." Let's talk about them for a minute.

When the books of the New Testament were written, in the first century after Christ, there existed no such thing as paper. Instead, a form of paper made from a sedge plant, papyrus, was used. This plant grew abundantly in the Nile River delta and reached a height of fifteen feet or more. The papyrus could be used to make rafts or canoes when bound in bundles, but the stem from this plant also gave man his first cheap and practical writing material. The papyrus was cut into thin slices and the pieces placed crisscross on a board and beaten together and pressed until the natural glue from the plant bound the pieces into a strong, thin form of paper.

All of the earliest manuscripts of the New Testament were originally written on this form of material. Some of the documents from this period remain to this very day, and they are considered to be the most treasured and priceless artifacts in existence, for they are the earliest known copies of the New Testament.

One such manuscript exists in Dublin, Ireland, in a collection of manuscripts owned by a man named Chester Beatty. It is unquestionably and by far the earliest known copy of the book of Revelation.[6] The date of this papyrus has been placed in the third century, or somewhere between 200 and 300 A.D.

The most amazing thing about this particular manuscript is the fact that it gives all the numbers in the book of Revelation with number, or theomatic, values. That's right. Every single number in the book of Revelation is shown with the letters of the Greek alphabet; for example, the number 7 is referred to many times in Revelation. In the papyri this number would be expressed with the letter ζ, which has a value of 7. The number 12 would be expressed by the two letters $\iota\beta$, and so on.

Revelation 13:18 is, of course, the verse which describes the number of the beast—666. If you look at the picture of the papyrus, you will notice on the left side the number 666 with a little arrow pointing to the right. Follow the arrow for about an inch and a half, and you will see the following symbol with a line over it: $\overline{\chi\xi\varsigma}$. This is the number 666, given with theomatic values. The first letter χ has a value of 600, the second letter ξ has a value of 60, and the last letter ς has a value of 6. When you add up all three of these numbers you have 666.

Therefore, in Revelation 13:18, the verse states that the one having wisdom is to calculate the number of the beast; and it gives the number 666 with theomatic values. Nothing could be plainer than this.

Verse 1 of chapter 14, which immediately follows, describes how the lamb stood on Mt. Zion, and with Him there were 144 thousands. If you look at the picture of the papyrus again, you will see beneath the 666 the number 144 with an arrow pointing to its right. Follow this arrow for about an inch and a half, and you will see the symbol $\overline{\rho\mu\delta}$. This is the number 144 given with theomatic values. The first letter ρ has a value of 100. The second letter μ has a value of 40. And the third letter δ has a value of 4. Together these numbers equal 144. Immediately following the number values is the Greek word for *thou-*

[6]Frederic G. Kenyon, *The Chester Beatty Biblical Papyri* (Emery Walker Ltd.: London, 1936), p. 1—Foreword. The catalogue identification number of the Chester Beatty papyrus is P⁴⁷.

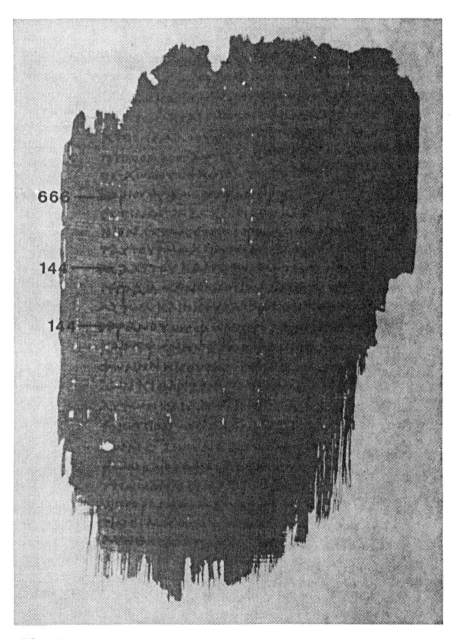

This photograph from one of the pages of the Chester Beatty manuscript shows the last few verses in chapter 13 along with the first portion of chapter 14.

sands. Also, the number 144 appears again toward the bottom of the page in verse 4.

As the reader can now see, the concept of assigning number values to the letters of the alphabet is a well-documented and established practice in languages that have no numerals. The values of the letters are standardized and can be found in Webster's dictionary. And to top the whole thing off, God has put His stamp of approval on the entire concept by giving the numbers in the book of Revelation with theomatic values.

At this point, let the reader understand one thing. Beginning in the next chapter, we will start presenting the theomatic designs that God has placed in His Word. Here it will be demonstrated and proven that God designed His entire Word mathematically, which will be confirmed in the last chapter dealing with the science of statistics and probability. We are basing the evidence and proof for the existence of theomatics not on the fact that the earliest manuscripts contain number or theomatic values, but rather on the fact that it can be demonstrated that it is there, that theomatics exists! That God has given us textual evidence, as we find in the papyrus, is icing on the cake.

The Chester Beatty papyrus is only one example. Many other manuscripts of Revelation, particularly the earliest, contain number, or theomatic, values. This fact can be easily confirmed by a little research on the part of the reader.

FORMAT AND LAYOUT OF THE FEATURES

You have just graduated. Now that you are familiar with the concepts presented in this chapter, you are ready for a full presentation of theomatics. There are, however, a few basic things that should be explained to the reader concerning the format of the features. All features will be shown in the following way:

1. *Son of Man* 37×80
   Mt 13:37 υιος του ανθρωπου

2. *Ruler of this world* 666×7
   Jn 16:11 αρχων του κοσμου τουτου'

In the above examples, there are two numbers following each English translation: 37×80 for "Son of Man" and 666×7 for "Ruler of this world." The first number is the key number, or *multiple*, for that particular topic. Take feature 1 as an example. The number, or theomatic, value of "Son of Man" is 2,960, or 37 × 80, the key number, or multiple, in this case being 37.

Feature 2 is a little different. Here the total number, or theomatic value, of "Ruler of this world" is 4,661, a cluster by 1 of 4,662, which is 666 × 7. At the end of the Greek phrase there is a little mark '. All clusters will be expressed by either ' (if within plus or minus 1 of the key multiple) or " (if within plus or minus 2).

3
Jesus

If a poll were taken to determine who was the most famous person in history, one name would stand above all the others. Furthermore, the impact of this man's life on all mankind would be of a magnitude too enormous to measure. The word *history* means "his story," and Christ's birth into this world marked the turn of all recorded history from B.C. to A.D.

To the Christian, however, the name of Jesus has far more meaning than just that of a historical character who lived 2,000 years ago. Not only does all secular history revolve around Him, but, to us who have put our faith in Him, He is the very cause of our existence—and our reason for living. The Bible is a book made up of sixty-six different books, and from the first word to the last, there is one central theme —the person and work of Jesus Christ, Son of God and Son of Man. He is portrayed in the Word of God as the one through whom the heavens and earth were created (Colossians 1:16), very God Himself, Who took on the form of a servant and came to this earth to redeem us through His blood sacrifice on Calvary. All rulership, power, and authority in the universe have been placed in His hands (Matthew 28:18), and it will only be a short time before we see Him face to face and share all eternity with Him as His beloved bride.

No study in Scripture is more revealing and rewarding than the one having to do with the names, titles, and attributes of Jesus Christ. When we began our research, we had no idea that the names of Jesus were so many and so vast. There is hardly a page in the Bible that does not mention or refer to Him in some way. Theomatics ties together each of the magnificent names of Jesus in such a way that your heart will be blessed and filled with joy as never before. After reading this chapter, you will gain a new understanding of Christ's glorious person, character, attributes, offices, and qualities.

Every name of Jesus has been placed in the Bible by the Holy Spirit of God to help us more clearly understand and intimately know Him. God's spirit has been eloquent in revelation about the person of the mighty Jesus. Every one of His names is vital, powerful, revealing, and all important to us.

Ιησους: 888

The name for Jesus in Greek is Ιησους, and it has a theomatic value of 888. This number is extremely significant throughout the theomatic design of the Bible, and later in this chapter we will discuss its significance in full. At this point, however, there is only one important fact that you the reader must remember, and that is the following: The many different references to Christ in the Bible are all structured around the number 888.

Here is how it works. If we were to take the number 888 and cut it in half, what is the result? The answer is 444. In other words, 444 × 2 = 888. But let us break down the number 888 even further, and cut the number 444 in half. We would now have the number 222. And if we were to cut the number 222 in half again, we would then have the number 111.

What we are going to do now is show the reader a complete design where all of the features work out to multiples of 111. This design covers the complete topic related to the birth and coming of Christ and the child Jesus.

THE BIRTH AND COMING OF CHRIST

The account concerning the birth and coming of Christ is found primarily in the two gospels of Matthew and Luke. Let us begin by examining Matthew's account.

In verse 20 of Matthew, chapter 1, the angel is found speaking to Joseph. Here are his words: "Joseph, son of David, do not be afraid to take Mary as your wife; for the one, her begotten of the spirit, is holy." From this Greek phrase come the following Greek words with their proper translation.

Her begotten of the spirit is holy   111 × 28
Mt 1:20 αυτη γεννηθεν εκ πνευματος εστιν αγιου΄

Now the most distinct portion from this feature is the simple words "her begotten." These words have a theomatic value of 111 × 8, or 888, the same as that of Jesus. Many of the features that we will be showing throughout this chapter are not only multiples of 111, but also of 888. If the theomatic value of a feature falls within this category, then the number 888 will be placed in parentheses, following the multiples of 111. The only important fact you should remember is that everything is working out to multiples of 111.

Her begotten   111 × 8 (888)
Mt 1:20 αυτη γεννηθεν΄

The next verse in Matthew begins with these simple words:

And she will bear a son   111 × 11
Mt 1:21 τεξεται δε υιον΄

This next quotation is probably the most famous statement in the Bible concerning the virgin birth:

Behold, a virgin shall conceive and bear a son   111 × 27
Mt 1:23 ιδου η παρθενος εν γαστρι εξει και τεξεται υιον΄

And when this verse is completed, the second half would read:

And they will call the name of Him Emmanuel, which is   111 × 53
being interpreted—with us God
Mt 1:23 και   καλεσουσιν   ονομα   αυτου   Εμμανουηλ   ο   εστιν
μεθερμηνευομενον μεθ ημων Θεος΄΄

Let us now put the two halves of this verse together, and see what happens:

Behold, a virgin shall conceive and bear a son,   111 × 80 (888)
and they will call the name of Him Emmanuel,
which is being interpreted—with us God
Mt 1:23 ιδου η παρθενος εν γαστρι εξει και τεξεται υιον και καλεσουσιν
ονομα αυτου Εμμανουηλ ο εστιν μεθερμηνευομενον μεθ ημων
Θεος΄

Finally, in Matthew 1:25, it states that, "He [Joseph] took his wife, and knew her not until she bore a son and called the name of Him Jesus."

She bore a son and called the name of Him Jesus   111 × 34
Mt 1:25 ετεκεν υιον και εκαλεσεν το ονομα αυτου Ιησουν"

Luke's account concerning the birth of Christ is quite extensive. In verse 31 of chapter 1, the angel is found speaking to Mary:

You will conceive in your womb, and bear a son,   111 × 51
and you shall call the name of Him Jesus
Lk 1:31 συλλημψη εν γαστρι και τεξη υιον και καλεσεις ονομα αυτου
        Ιησουν

The next feature is phenomenal:

The power of the most high will overshadow you,   111 × 64 (888)
and for that reason the holy offspring will be
called the Son of God
Lk 1:35 δυναμις υψιστου επισκιασει σοι διο και το γεννωμενον αγιον
        κληθησεται υιος Θεου'

One of the more significant references to Christ's birth occurs in verse 21 of chapter 2, where Jesus is actually named by the angel:

His name was called Jesus, the name given by   111 × 75
the angel before He was conceived in the womb
Lk 2:21 εκληθη ονομα αυτου Ιησους το κληθεν υπο του αγγελου προ του
        συλλημφθηναι αυτον εν τη κοιλια

One of the most impressive aspects of the theomatic design which God has placed in His Word is the fact that complete phrases break down to smaller portions that also work out to the same design. The following three features from the above will illustrate perfectly what we mean:

His name was called Jesus, the name given   111 × 32 (888)
by the angel
Lk 2:21 εκληθη ονομα αυτου Ιησους κληθεν υπο αγγελου"

Jesus, the name given by the angel   111 × 22
Lk 2:21 Ιησους το κληθεν υπο αγγελου

Jesus, the name given by the angel before   111 × 45
He was conceived in the womb
Lk 2:21 Ιησους το κληθεν υπο αγγελου προ συλλημφθηναι αυτον εν κοιλια

We will now focus our attention on some of the more specific references that speak directly of the child Jesus. In Luke 2:17 the shepherds referred to Jesus as "this child."

This child   111 × 26
Lk 2:17 του παιδιου τουτου'

Ten verses later Joseph and Mary are spoken of as bringing "the child Jesus" to the temple as was the custom of the law.

The child Jesus   111 × 12
Lk 2:27 το παιδιον Ιησουν'

An outstanding feature which ties in perfectly with the above two features is found in the book of The Acts. Here it states that, "Signs and wonders are performed through the name of the holy child of thee Jesus."

Name of the holy child Jesus   111 × 28
Acts 4:30 ονοματος του αγιου παιδος Ιησου

This last feature will best speak for itself. "And she [Elizabeth] cried out with a loud voice and said, 'Blessed art thou amongst women, and blessed is the fruit of thy womb.' "

The fruit of thy womb   111 × 14
Lk 1:42 ο καρπος κοιλιας σου"

Luke, chapter 2, describes how Caesar Augustus made a decree, that all the world should be taxed. Because Joseph was from the house of David, he took his wife Mary, who was pregnant with child, to Bethlehem. "And it came to pass, that while they were there, the days were accomplished that she should give birth."

While they were there, the days were accomplished   111 × 48 (888)
that she should give birth
Lk 2:6 εν τω ειναι αυτους εκει επλησθησαν αι ημεραι του τεκειν αυτην'

One of the most popular stories during the Christmas season is where the baby Jesus was laid in a manger, because there was no room in the inn. Verse 7, which immediately follows the last feature we looked at, gives the account of this:

She bore the son of her, the firstborn, and wrapped Him   111 × 76
in swaddling clothes, and laid Him in a manger
Lk 2:7 ετεκεν τον υιον αυτης πρωτοτοκον και εσπαργανωσεν αυτον και
      ανεκλινεν αυτον εν φατνη"

From the opening clause of this phrase come the following words:

She bore the son, the firstborn   111 × 25
Lk 2:7 ετεκεν υιον πρωτοτοκον

When the shepherds were out tending their flocks, the angel of the Lord appeared unto them, saying, "And this will be a sign for you":

You will find the babe wrapped in swaddling clothes,   111 × 41
and lying in a manger
Lk 2:12 ευρησετε βρεφος εσπαργανωμενον και κειμενον εν φατνη'

The babe wrapped in swaddling clothes   111 × 21
Lk 2:12 βρεφος εσπαργανωμενον'

"And it came to pass, as the angels were gone away from them into heaven, the shepherds said one to another, 'Let us now go even unto Bethlehem, and see this thing which is come to pass, which the Lord has made known unto us.' "

This thing which is come to pass, which the Lord   111 × 39
has made known unto us
Lk 2:15 ρημα τουτο το γεγονος ο ο κυριος εγνωρισεν ημιν"

But after the angel had spoken, it says, "They went with haste, and found Mary and Joseph, and the babe lying in the manger."

And the babe lying in the manger   111 × 22
Lk 2:16 και το βρεφος κειμενον εν φατνη

The first verse in Matthew, chapter 2, begins with the following words:

Jesus was born in Bethlehem of Judea   111 × 55
in the days of Herod the king

Mt 2:1 Ιησου γεννηθεντος εν Βηθλεεμ Ιουδαιας εν ημεραις Ηρω̣δου του Βασιλεως"

But the most famous reference concerning the little town of Bethlehem is found in Matthew 2:6: "And thou Bethlehem, in the land of Juda, art not the least among the rulers of Juda: for out of thee shall come forth a governor, who will shepherd my people Israel."

For out of thee shall come forth a governor 111 × 24 (888)
Mt 2:6 εκ σου γαρ εξελευσεται ηγουμενος"

When the wise men came from the east, they inquired of King Herod where the Christ was to be born.

For we have seen His star in the east, 111 × 52
and have come to worship Him
Mt 2:2 ειδομεν γαρ αυτου αστερα εν τη ανατολη και ηλθομεν προσκυνησαι αυτω

In verse 9 of the same chapter, it is stated: "Lo, the star, which they had seen in the east, went before them, until. . . ."

It came and stood over where the child lay 111 × 28
Mt 2:9 ελθων εσταθη επανω ου ην παιδιον"

As the story goes, Herod after conferring with the wise men sent them to Bethlehem with the following instructions: "Go and search diligently for the child: and when you have found Him, bring me word again, that I may come and worship Him also."

Go and search diligently for the child 111 × 43
Mt 2:8 πορευθεντες εξετασατε ακριβως περι του παιδιου'

After the wise men had visited the child Jesus, they did not return to King Herod but departed into their country another way. "And after they were departed, behold, the angel of the Lord appeared to Joseph in a dream, saying, 'Arise, and take thou the child, and His mother, and flee into Egypt.' "

Take thou the child 111 × 4
Mt 2:13 παραλαβε παιδιον'

In the last portion of this verse, the angel told Joseph to "remain there until I tell you":

For Herod will seek the child to destroy Him 111 × 35
Mt 2:13 μελλει γαρ Ηρωδης ζητειν παιδιον του απολεσαι αυτο"

After fleeing into Egypt and remaining there, the angel again appeared unto Joseph. "But when Herod died, behold, an angel of the Lord appeared in a dream to Joseph in Egypt, saying, 'Rise, take thou the child and His mother, and go to the land of Israel, for have died the ones seeking the life of the child.' "

The life of the child 111 × 21
Mt 2:20 ψυχην παιδιου"

Finally, after returning to Nazareth, it states that "the child grew and became strong, filled with wisdom; and the grace of God was upon Him."

The child grew and became strong 111 × 19
Lk 2:40 παιδιον ηυξανεν και εκραταιουτο"

There is one other reference of outstanding significance in Luke, chapter 2: "And Simeon blessed them and said to Mary His mother, 'Behold, . . .' "

This child is set for the fall and rising again of many 111 × 60
in Israel; and for a sign spoken against
Lk 2:34 ουτος κειται εις πτωσιν και αναστασιν πολλων εν Ισραηλ και
εις σημειον αντιλεγομενον"

The words from Galatians 4:4 read as follows:

When the time had come, God sent forth His Son 111 × 64 (888)
born of a woman
Gal 4:4 οτε ηλθεν πληρωμα χρονου εξαπεστειλεν Θεος τον υιον αυτου
γενομενον εκ γυναικος

In the book of Revelation, there are five features of absolutely incredible significance. Chapter 12 describes how the woman brought forth the man child, and the dragon sought to destroy her child. "And there appeared a great sign in heaven; a woman clothed with the sun, and the moon under her feet, and upon her head a crown of twelve stars":

And she was with child and she cried out in her 111 × 41
birth pangs, in anguish for delivery
Rev 12:2 και εν γαστρι εχουσα και κραζει ωδινουσα και βασανιζομενη
τεκειν'

"And there appeared another sign in heaven; and behold a great red dragon, having seven heads and ten horns, and seven crowns upon his heads. And his tail drew a third part of the stars of heaven, and did cast them to earth: and the dragon stood before the woman who was about to bear, that he might devour the child of her when she brought it forth."

The child of her   111 × 16 (888)
Rev 12:4 το τεκνον αυτης"

But the first portion of verse 5, which immediately follows, states:

And she brought forth the man child Who is about   111 × 37
to shepherd all nations with a rod of iron
Rev 12:5 και ετεκεν υιον αρσεν ος μελλει ποιμαινειν παντα τα εθνη εν ραβδω σιδηρα'

The man child   111 × 8 (888)
Rev 12:5 υιον αρσεν"

The concluding portion of this verse reads as follows:

But the child of her was caught up to God,   111 × 47
and to His throne
Rev 12:5 και ηρπασθη το τεκνον αυτης προς τον Θεον και προς θρονον αυτου'

What Is the Chance?

We have now examined thirty-two references to the birth and coming of Christ and the child Jesus. All of these references contained one or more features that were multiples of 111. In order for one to fully appreciate the significance of this, he must first of all realize that the possibility or probability of these features having these numerical values by chance is very unlikely. In fact, the chance that what has happened could happen is only 1 chance in 31,608,834,580,000,000,-000,000,000. That's right, one chance in thirty-one septillion, six hundred and eight sextillion, eight hundred and thirty-four quintillion, five hundred and eighty quadrillion.

If this number sounds unrealistic, we might add that this figure was calculated by professional statisticians. Their calculations will be in the last chapter, dealing with the science of statistics and probability.

Pick a Dot, Any Dot

Now let's imagine that one of these 5,000 dots was secretly marked, but you didn't know which one. With only one guess possible, what do you think your chances would be of picking that one? Pretty slim, huh?

But the 32 scriptural references we just looked at had only 1 chance in 31,608,834,580,000,000,000,000 of occurring by chance. To some readers, this may seem like just another big number. However, the significance of its size can be illustrated in the following example: These 5,000 dots that we have just shown cover an area of approximately five inches by five inches on the page. If a person were to fill up a square mile with these five-inch-by-five-inch squares, he would find that a square mile contains 160,579,584 squares. Since there are 5,000 dots in each square, we then multiply 160,579,584 times 5,000, which gives us a total of 802,897,920,000 dots in each square mile.

Now if we divide this number, 802,897,920,000, into the number of the probability, 31,608,834,580,000,000,000,000,000, we would then have a total of 39,368,435,010,000 square miles of dots.

The total surface of the earth is only 197 million square miles. If we were to divide this figure into 39,368,435,010,000, it would take approximately 199,840 earths, their surfaces completely covered with dots, as far apart as these 5,000, to equal this number of probability.

Now, let's imagine that one of these earths contained one dot that was secretly marked, but you didn't know which one. The first thing you would have to do is guess which one of the 199,840 earths contained the magic dot. The chance of doing this would be 1 chance in 199,840. But if you were lucky and guessed the right earth, you would then have to find the right dot. Good luck!

So it is with every theomatic design in the Bible. Each mathematical design has only one chance in so many thousands, millions, billions, and trillions of occurring by chance. Keep in mind, too, as you read from one topic to the next, that these probabilities are continually mounting and multiplying themselves. In fact, the number becomes so large eventually that there would be no way of expressing it.

Before we present more theomatic features, there is probably a question that has been going through the reader's mind. You have just seen how the many references to the birth of Christ all contained features that were multiples of 111. But what is the significance of these secondary factors, you may ask? In other words, all of the features are working out to being multiples of 111, but sometimes it's 111 × 28, or 111 × 8, or 111 × 11. Do these second numbers, 28, 8, and 11, have any significance?

Yes. They have tremendous significance, and it all fits into the overall design of God's Word. Many times the meaning is quite clear. At other times, we must admit that we do not fully understand it. However, in this book we have declined to speculate or make mention of these secondary factors. Our only purpose at this time is to establish an overall consistency, and show you, the reader, how everything comes out to 111.

Why Does Jesus Equal 888?

Eight is the number that is symbolic and typical of the Lord Jesus, who is the head of the new order. However, before a person can understand the significance of the number eight, he must first of all understand the number seven.

Seven is God's perfect number. Everything to do with God's law is based on the number seven. Throughout Scripture, the number seven is extremely significant whenever it refers or speaks of perfection, fullness, or God's perfect law.

Man was incapable of keeping the law, and this is why the Savior had to come. Eight follows seven, and starts everything over again. Therefore, eight is the number of the new order and the number of Jesus.

The best way to illustrate the relationship between seven and eight is by the following example. The theomatic value of the words "the law" in Greek is 700. This is extremely significant because any time you have a number followed by zeros, the zeros serve only to amplify and add clarity to that number. Therefore, the number 700 is emphasizing the number 7, which speaks of God's law and God's perfect perfection. Here now are the Greek words for "the law."

The law 700
Eph 2:15 τον νομον

The Bible plainly teaches that Christians are not saved by works of law but rather that salvation comes through faith. What the law could not accomplish was accomplished through faith. This is why the theomatic value of the word *faith* is 800. Eight follows seven, and if a person is trusting by faith (800) instead of by works of law (700), then he is a new creation in Christ Jesus. For this reason, Jesus has a theomatic value of 888. Here now is the Greek word for *faith*.

Faith 800
Mt 9:22 πιστις

In the Old Testament, the Jews always kept the Sabbath, or seventh day of the week. But when Christ came all this changed. This is why the number eight speaks of Sunday and also of resurrection. An absolutely amazing theomatic feature that brings forth this fact is found in Matthew 20:19: "And they will deliver Him to the nations to be mocked and scourged and crucified, and on the third day He will be raised up."

The day He will be raised up   800
Mt 20:19 ημερα εγερθησεται

Mark 16:2 again refers to the first day of the week and Christ's resurrection:

Very early at sunrise, on the first day   888 × 9
of the week, they came to the tomb
Mk 16:2 λιαν πρωι τη μια των σαββατων ερχονται επι το μνημα ανατει-
λαντος του ηλιου

This verse states that the women came to the tomb at the rising of the sun. This is very significant, because the sunrise bespeaks the new day, or the new age, of which 888 is symbolic. If we go to the book of Revelation, we will find a perfect feature that brings forth this truth. Verse 5 of chapter 21 refers to the new heaven and earth: "And He Who sat upon the throne said, 'Behold, I make all things new.'"

New   80
Rev 21:5 καινα"

Because the number 8 speaks of faith, resurrection, and the new order, this is why Christians—or those who have put their trust in Jesus by faith—meet on Sunday instead of Saturday. The early church met on Sunday, and the number 888 clearly establishes this fact in theomatics. In The Acts 20:7 we find the following words:

And on the first day of the week, we   888 × 7
were gathered together to break bread
Acts 20:7 Εν δε τη μια των σαββατων συνηγμενων ημων κλασαι αρτον

There is another topic related to the number eight, which is also highly significant. It was on the eighth day after birth that a child was circumcised. When the flesh was removed a new life began, but that new life could not begin on the seventh day. It had to begin on the eighth day. The story concerning the birth of Christ says: "When were completed eight days to circumcise Him, His name was called Jesus, the name given by the angel, before He was conceived in the womb." From this passage come the following Greek words:

Eight days to circumcise Him   888 × 4

Lk 2:21 ημεραι οκτω του περιτεμειν αυτον"

The most amazing reference to the number eight is found in 1 Peter 3:20, which refers to "an ark in which a few, that is, eight souls were saved by water." In this passage we read how God destroyed the ancient wicked world and started a new creation with eight souls, Noah, his wife, his three sons, and their wives. Notice that the eight souls had to be in the ark in order to be saved. And of what is the ark a type? Christ, Who is our ark of safety. The only way Noah and his family could be saved was to be in Christ. This brings us to our next feature:

An ark in which a few, that is, eight   888 × 10
souls were saved by water

1 Pet 3:20 κιβωτου εις ην ολιγοι τουτ εστιν οκτω ψυχαι διεσωθησαν δι
υδατος

Jesus and the Number 37

At the beginning of this chapter we showed how the many references to the birth of Christ were all structured on multiples of 111. The number 111, of course, speaks of Jesus. But there is another number which also speaks of Jesus. It is the number 37. Thirty-seven is a prime number, which means that it can only be divided by itself or 1. It is also the base number on which all of the references to Christ are structured. If we were to divide 111 by 3, the result would be 37. In other words, 37 × 3 = 111. For this reason, many of the features to be presented in the remainder of this chapter will only be divisible by 37 and not by 111. However, everything that is divisible by 111 is also divisible by 37. You will understand this perfectly as you read.

An excellent example of a design using the number 37 is found in those verses that speak of the Messiah. Twice in the New Testament, reference is made to the Messiah. Here are those features:

When Jesus was speaking to the woman by the well, she said to Him: "I know that Messiah is coming, the one called Christ."

Messiah is coming, the one called Christ   37 × 100
Jn 4:25 Μεσσιας ερχεται ο λεγομενος Χριστος

In John, chapter 1, Andrew declared to Simon Peter:

We have found the Messiah   37 × 42
Jn 1:41 ευρηκαμεν τον Μεσσιαν'

But the important fact is that if you take just the word *Messiah* by itself, it produces the same 37.

The Messiah   37 × 25
Jn 1:41 τον Μεσσιαν'

Before moving on let us show one more example involving the number 8. The name *Jesus*, which has a theomatic value of 888, breaks down to 37 × 8 × 3; and the word *Christ* breaks down to 37 × 8 × 5. Notice that both of these names are not only multiples of 37 but also of 8. The most interesting fact is that the name *Jesus Christ* has a theomatic value of 2,368, or 37 × 8 × 8. No matter how you add it up, everything comes up eights.

Jesus   37 × 8 × 3 (888)
Ιησους

Christ   37 × 8 × 5
Χριστος

Jesus Christ   37 × 8 × 8
Ιησους Χριστος

JESUS AND THE GODHEAD

There are two references to the Godhead in the New Testament. Since every aspect of the fullness of the Godhead dwells in Christ, the following two features will confirm this fact:

His eternal power and Godhead   37 × 84
Rom 1:20 τε αιδιος αυτου δυναμις και Θειοτης'

For in Him dwells all the fullness of the Godhead   37 × 146
Col 2:9 οτι εν αυτω κατοικει παν το πληρωμα της Θεοτητος

The most important fact is that when you take just the word *Godhead* by itself, it produces the same 37.

Godhead   37 × 26
Col 2:9 Θεοτητος

What is probably the most outstanding reference to Christ being a part of the Godhead is found in 2 Corinthians, chapter 4. Here Christ is referred to as being the image of God.

Christ, Who is the image of God   111 × 35
2 Cor 4:4 Χριστου ος εστιν εικων Θεου΄

The number 111, of course, speaks of Jesus. As we mentioned earlier, 37 divides evenly into 111. Therefore, anything that is divisible by 111 is also a multiple of 37.

The most distinct portion from the above feature is the words "image of God." These words have a theomatic value of 1,369, or 37 × 37.

Image of God   37 × 37
2 Cor 4:4 εικων Θεου

Stop and think a minute. Of all the names in the Bible that have to do with the Godhead, which four do you think would be the most outstanding, clear-cut, and distinct? We think that everyone would agree that the following are:

Jesus   111 × 8 (888)
Ιησους

Christ   111 × 12
Χριστου"

God   111 × 5
τον Θεου΄

Lord   111 × 9
κυριου

There are two features of great significance, both of which are multiples of 888. We have already seen how Jesus, Christ, God, and Lord work out to being multiples of 111. But Revelation 15:3 talks about the "Lord God."

Lord God 111 × 8 (888)
Rev 15:3 κυριε ο Θεος'

Then when one turns to the book of Mark, he will read of how Jesus cried out, "Hear, Oh Israel":

The Lord God is one Lord 111 × 24 (888)
Mk 12:29 κυριος Θεος κυριος εις εστιν

Colossians 3:24 talks about "the Lord Christ." This will be followed by a quotation from Luke, chapter 2.

The Lord Christ 111 × 40 (888)
Col 3:24 τω κυριω Χριστω

Christ the Lord 111 × 21
Lk 2:26 Χριστον κυριου'

Finally, the next to the last verse of the Bible speaks about the "Lord Jesus."

Lord Jesus 111 × 11
Rev 22:20 κυριε Ιησου"

NAME OF JESUS

Whenever the word *name* is used in reference to Jesus there is special significance. Throughout this chapter many of the features will contain the word *name*. At this time we will show just a portion of these. The following three references will best speak for themselves:

Name of Jesus 111 × 18
Acts 5:40 ονοματι του Ιησου'

Name of the Lord Jesus 111 × 30
1 Cor 5:4 τω ονοματι κυριου Ιησου'

Name of Christ 111 × 20
1 Pet 4:14 ονοματι Χριστου'

Here are the words of Jesus from Matthew 19:29: "And everyone who has left houses or brothers or sisters or father or mother or children or lands, for the sake of My name, will receive a hundredfold, and inherit eternal life."

For the sake of My name   111 × 20
Mt 19:29 ενεκεν του εμου ονοματος'

In Revelation Jesus sent the following message to the church in Pergamum: "I know where you dwell, where Satan's throne is; and you held fast My name, and did not deny My faith."

And you held fast My name   111 × 16 (888)
Rev 2:13 και κρατεις το ονομα μου"

My name   111 × 10
Rev 2:13 το ονομα μου'

When the apostles were preaching in the book of The Acts, the elders and scribes inquired: "By what power or by what name did you do this?"

By what name   111 × 14
Acts 4:7 εν ποιω ονοματι"

One of the most famous references in the Bible using the word *name* is found in The Acts 4:12: "And there is salvation in no one else, for there is no other name under heaven given among men by which we must be saved." This complete passage, as we have quoted it, is a multiple of 111. Here now is the most distinct portion:

For there is no other name under heaven given among men   111 × 51
Acts 4:12 ουδε γαρ ονομα εστιν ετερον υπο τον ουρανον το δεδομενον εν ανθρωποις"

Here are the words from Philippians 2:9: "Wherefore God also highly exalted Him, and gave Him a name which is above every name." Like the last feature, this complete passage is a multiple of 111. Here now is the most distinct portion of this verse:

And gave Him a name which is above every name   111 × 36
Phil 2:9 και εχαρισατο αυτω ονομα υπερ παν ονομα'

Note. At this point in the book, we would like to mention something to the reader that is of utmost importance. The theomatic designs in the Bible are so numerous that there is no way they can all be shown. We could fill up an entire book with features of 37 and 111, related to the topic of Jesus. Besides, there are other key numbers and other designs flowing through the references to Christ. The ones to be presented are only a sampling of those that can be found. For this reason we have limited ourselves to Scripture passages that are best known and that people are familiar with. This makes the reading more interesting.

ONLY BEGOTTEN SON OF GOD

Perhaps no other term in Scripture concerning Christ is better known than the name "Son of God." There are so many references to Christ as the Son that we are only able to show a few of the more outstanding ones.

For our first feature let us examine a very famous and well-known quotation, where the Father speaks concerning His Son: "This is My beloved Son, in Whom I am well pleased." Notice how this phrase divides itself up mathematically:

This is My beloved Son 111×37
2 Pet 1:17 ο υιος μου ο αγαπητος μου ουτος εστιν'

My beloved Son in Whom I am well pleased 111×34
2 Pet 1:17 ο υιος αγαπητος μου εις ον εγω ευδοκησα

From Luke 20:13 come the simple words:

My beloved Son 111×14
Lk 20:13 υιον μου αγαπητον'

In John 1:18 Jesus is referred to as the:

Only begotten Son, Who is in the bosom of the Father 111×37
Jn 1:18 μονογενης Θεος ων εις τον κολπον του πατρος'

In 1 John, chapter 4, there are two features within one phrase that have outstanding significance.

God sent His only begotten Son into the world 111×40 (888)
1 Jn 4:9 οτι υιον αυτου μονογενη απεσταλκεν Θεος εις τον κοσμον"

His only begotten Son 111×18
1 Jn 4:9 υιον αυτου μονογενη'

"For God so loved the world, that He gave the only begotten Son, that whosoever believeth in Him, should not perish, but have everlasting life."

The only begotten Son 111 × 15
Jn 3:16 τον υιον τον μονογενη'

Here are the words from John 3:18: "He that believeth on Him is not condemned: but he that believeth not is condemned already, because he hath not believed in the name of the only begotten Son of God."

Name of the only begotten Son of God 111 × 23
Jn 3:18 ονομα μονογενους υιου Θεου

In his epistle the apostle John said the following: "These things I have written unto you who believe in the name of the Son of God, in order that you may know that you have eternal life."

Believe in the name of the Son of God 111 × 44
1 Jn 5:13 τοις πιστευουσιν εις ονομα υιου του Θεου'

Name of the Son 111 × 10
1 Jn 5:13 ονομα υιου'

In John, chapter 11, Jesus was explaining to Martha that He was the resurrection and the life. Martha replied by saying: "Yes Lord: I believe that Thou art the Christ, the Son of God."

Yes Lord, I believe that Thou art the Christ, 111 × 56 (888)
the Son of God
Jn 11:27 ναι κυριε εγω πεπιστευκα οτι συ ει ο Χριστος υιος Θεου"

Thou art the Christ, the Son of God 111 × 30
Jn 11:27 συ ει ο Χριστος υιος Θεου'

Christ, the Son of God 111 × 96 (888)
Jn 11:27 ο Χριστος ο υιος του Θεου"

Not only is Jesus called "Christ, the Son of God," but, in Mark 14:61, He is referred to as the "Son of the blessed."

Christ, the Son of the blessed 111 × 38
Mk 14:61 Χριστος υιος του ευλογητου"

John, chapter 1, tells how Phillip went and found Nathaniel and then brought him to Jesus. When Nathaniel saw Jesus, he said the following:

Rabbi, Thou art the Son of God 111 × 24 (888)
Jn 1:49 ραββι συ ει υιος του Θεου

To culminate this theme, we will show only seven more features.

During His ministry on earth Jesus was constantly routing demons. "And whenever the unclean spirits beheld Him, they fell down before Him and cried out, 'Thou art the Son of God.' "

Thou art the Son of God   111 × 27
Mk 3:11 οτι συ ει ο υιος του Θεου"

From 1 John 4:15 come these words:

Jesus is the Son of God   111 × 27
1 Jn 4:15 οτι Ιησους εστιν υιος Θεου

In John 1:34, John says, concerning Jesus: "I have seen and I have borne witness that this is the Son of God."

That this is the Son of God   111 × 29
Jn 1:34 οτι ουτος εστιν ο υιος Θεου

Without the word for "of God," this verse contains an even further design:

That this is the Son   111 × 24 (888)
Jn 1:34 οτι ουτος εστιν υιος'

When Jesus hung on the cross, it says that after He expired, the centurion cried out: "Truly this man was the Son of God."

Was the Son of God   111 × 11
Mk 15:39 υιος Θεου ην'

And here now is the most outstanding feature possible:

The Son of God   111 × 22
Gal 2:20 τη υιου του Θεου

For the concluding feature, we will let the Lord speak for Himself.

I am the Son of God   111 × 18
Jn 10:36 υιος του Θεου ειμι'

SON OF MAN

Perhaps the second most common name in reference to Christ is the title "Son of Man." Earlier in this chapter we mentioned that many of the designs worked out to be only divisible by 37. Such is the case with "Son of Man." Later on, in Chapter 5 we will be examining a detailed design on the "Son of Man." For now, however, let us confine our attention to only two features.

Son of Man   37 × 80
Lk 22:22 υιος του ανθρωπου

In the second chapter of Mark's gospel, Jesus refers to Himself as the "Lord of the Sabbath": "Therefore the Son of Man is Lord also of the Sabbath."

Lord of the Sabbath   111 × 8 (888)
Mk 2:28 κυριος σαββατου

JESUS CHRIST, THE NAZARENE

There is tremendous power and significance in the many references to Jesus of Nazareth, Jesus the Nazarene, and so on. To start off, here are some of the many phrases on this topic that are multiples of 111:

Jesus, the Nazarene, Who was a prophet mighty   111 × 81
in deed and word in the sight of God
Lk 24:19 Ιησου του Ναζαρηνου ος εγενετο ανηρ προφητης δυνατος εν
    εργω και λογω εναντιον του Θεου'

Jesus, the Nazarene, a man approved to you by   111 × 63
God with miracles, wonders, and signs
Acts 2:22 Ιησουν τον Ναζωραιον ανδρα αποδεδειγμενον απο του Θεου
    εις υμας δυναμεσι και τερασι και σημειοις'

Jesus of Nazareth, how God anointed Him   111 × 57
with the Holy Spirit
Acts 10:38 Ιησουν τον απο Ναζαρεθ ως εχρισεν αυτον ο Θεος πνευματι
    αγιω

This is the prophet Jesus from Nazareth of Galilee   111 × 40 (888)
Mt 21:11 ουτος εστιν ο προφητης Ιησους απο Ναζαρεθ Γαλιλαιας'

Jesus came from Nazareth of Galilee   111 × 19
Mk 1:9 ηλθεν Ιησους απο Ναζαρεθ της Γαλιλαιας'

Jesus, the son of Joseph from Nazareth   111 × 28
Jn 1:45 Ιησουν υιον Ιωσηφ απο Ναζαρεθ"

"As he drew near to Jericho, a blind man was sitting by the roadside begging; and hearing a multitude going by, he inquired what this meant. And they told him: 'Jesus of Nazareth is passing by.'"

Jesus of Nazareth is passing by   111 × 30
Lk 18:37 Ιησους Ναζωραιος παρερχεται'

The same design that exists in these complete thoughts also carries down to the key words and phrases. The Greek words for "Jesus, the Nazarene" vary throughout the English translations. In some versions it is rendered "Jesus of Nazareth" and in others as "Jesus, the Nazarene."

Jesus of Nazareth (or Jesus, the Nazarene)   111 × 13
Mk 10:47 Ιησους ο Ναζαρηνος"

But look at this next feature!

Nazarene   111 × 2
Lk 4:34 Ναζαρηνε

To top the whole design off, here are the words found in The Acts 3:6. "And Peter said, silver and gold have I none; but such as I have give I thee: In the name of Jesus Christ, the Nazarene, rise up and walk."

The name of Jesus Christ, the Nazarene   111 × 56 (888)
Acts 4:10 τω ονοματι Ιησου Χριστου του Ναζωραιου"

JESUS IS JACOB'S WELL

Jesus is Jacob's well. Perhaps you never heard of Christ being referred to as such in Scripture, but the following features will unveil an impressive design: In John, chapter 4, Jesus meets with the Samaritan woman by Jacob's well. Here He refers to Himself as the "gift of God": "If you knew the gift of God, and who is the one saying to you, 'Give me a drink,' you would have asked Him, and He would have given you living water."

Gift of God   111 × 13
Jn 4:10 δωρεαν Θεου'

The one saying to you, Give me a drink   111 × 16 (888)
Jn 4:10 ο λεγων σοι δος μοι πειν'

Existing inside this story, there are six features, all of them divisible by 37. These will show an amazing consistency.

The well   37 × 11
Jn 4:6 τη πηγη

Jacob's well   37 × 46
Jn 4:6 πηγη του Ιακωβ

Fountain of water   37 × 29
Jn 4:14 πηγη υδατος'

This water   37 × 68
Jn 4:13 υδατος τουτου'

The water which I shall give him   37 × 171
Jn 4:14 του υδατος ου εγω δωσω αυτω'

Water I will give   37 × 84
Jn 4:14 υδωρ δωσω

In verse 14 of this story, Jesus makes a profound statement. Here now is one of the most famous passages in the Bible:

The water which I shall give him shall become   111 × 96 (888)
in him a fountain of water springing up to life eternal
Jn 4:14 υδωρ ο δωσω αυτω γενησεται εν αυτω πηγη υδατος αλλομενου
          εις ζωην αιωνιον"

And then in verse 15 of this story, the Samaritan woman answered and said:

Sir, give me this water that I may never thirst   111 × 45
Jn 4:15 κυριε δος μοι τουτο υδωρ ινα μη διψω'

SHEPHERD AND DOOR OF THE SHEEP

Jesus is also the shepherd and the door of the sheep. Existing in this topic, there is another outstanding design with the number 37. Here now are six features that are self-explanatory:

I am the good shepherd   37 × 43
Jn 10:11 εγω ειμι ο ποιμην ο καλος'

I say to you that I am the door of the sheep　37 × 153
Jn 10:7 λεγω υμιν οτι εγω ειμι η θυρα των προβατων'

The door of the sheep　37 × 83
Jn 10:7 η θυρα των προβατων

The door　37 × 14
Jn 10:7 η θυρα

Shepherd of the sheep　37 × 76
Jn 10:2 ποιμην των προβατων'

Shepherd　37 × 7
Jn 10:2 ποιμην'

Finally, in the book of Hebrews, Christ is referred to as:

The great shepherd of the sheep　111 × 30
Heb 13:20 ποιμενα των προβατων τον μεγαν"

CHRIST, THE SAVIOR

Since Christ is God, and the only means of salvation, the following two features will have perfect meaning:

God, the savior　111 × 30
Lk 1:47 Θεω τω σωτηρι"

Christ, the savior　111 × 26
Lk 2:11 σωτηρ Χριστος"

When Jesus met the woman by the well, the Samaritans came to Him from the city, and believed in Him. "And they said unto the woman, 'Now we believe, not because of the saying: for we have heard Him ourselves, and know that this man is truly the savior of the world.' "

This man is truly the savior　111 × 40 (888)
Jn 4:42 οτι ουτος εστιν αληθως σωτηρ'

The words "savior of the world" from the above verse contain another design relevant to the topic of salvation. For this reason, the feature ends at the word *savior*.

THE WORD

Since Jesus is God come in the flesh, He is also the spoken Word of God. This fact is unequivocally confirmed by the following features. The first of these tells how the word became flesh and dwelt among us.

The word became flesh, and dwelt among us 111 × 25
Jn 1:14 ο λογος σαρξ εγενετο και εσκηνωσεν εν ημιν'

Jesus is the word, and word in Greek, spelled two different ways, produces the following:

Word 111 × 2
Jn 8:55 λογου'

The word 111 × 4
Jn 1:14 ο λογος'

Jesus is also the living word of God. In Hebrews 4:12 it states: "For the word of God is living and powerful and sharper than any two-edged sword."

Living word of God 111 × 23
Heb 4:12 Ζων ο λογος του Θεου'

In 1 Peter 1:23 the living word of God is again spoken of. Here, the two words "living word" produce the same design.

Living word 111 × 18
1 Pet 1:23 λογου ζωντος"

The first verse of 1 John describes Jesus in a beautiful manner. This complete passage is saturated with multiples of 111; however, only the last portion, concerning the word, will be given as the feature: "That which was from the beginning, which we have heard, which we have seen with our eyes, which we have looked upon and touched with our hands, concerning the word of life."

Concerning the word of life 111 × 23
1 Jn 1:1 περι του λογου ζωης

In the book of Revelation, John describes how he was the one "who bore witness to the word of God."

Bore witness to the word of God 111 × 28
Rev 1:2 εμαρτυρησεν τον λογον του Θεου″

And now we present another one of those features using the word *name:* "He is clad in a robe dipped in blood, and has been called the name of Him the word of God."

The name of Him [is] the word of God 111 × 21
Rev 19:13 ονομα αυτου ο λογος Θεου″

The name of Him [is] the word 111 × 16 (888)
Rev 19:13 ονομα αυτου λογος′

JESUS, THE LIGHT OF THE WORLD

Jesus is the light come into the world. This fact will be brought forth in the following three features, all of which are well-known quotations concerning Christ:

In Him was life, and the life was the light of men 111 × 71
Jn 1:4 εν αυτω ζωη ην και η ζωη ην φως των ανθρωπων

Here are the words of Jesus from John 8:12: "I am the light of the world: He that followeth Me shall not walk in darkness, but shall have the light of life."

The light of the world 111 × 31
Jn 8:12 το φως του κοσμου′

The light of life 111 × 26
Jn 8:12 το φως ζωης′

One of the more outstanding references to Christ is the term "morning star." In 2 Peter 1:19 it is spelled with one Greek word, which has a theomatic value of 2,440. But in Revelation 22:16 Jesus refers to Himself as the "bright morning star." This time there are three Greek words, but the theomatic value is still 2,440.

Morning star 111 × 22
2 Pet 1:19 φωσφορος″

Bright morning star 111 × 22
Rev 22:16 αστηρ λαμπρος πρωινος″

THE FIRSTBORN

There are six verses in the New Testament that refer to Christ as the firstborn. We examined the first of these in Luke 2:7, where Mary gave birth to the firstborn Son. Here are the remaining five:

Firstborn of all creation   37 × 109
Col 1:15 πρωτοτοκος πασης κτισεως'

Firstborn among many   37 × 65
Rom 8:29 πρωτοτοκον εν πολλοις

Firstborn of the dead   37 × 115
Rev 1:5 ο πρωτοτοκος των νεκρων

The firstborn into the world   37 × 87
Heb 1:6 τον πρωτοτοκον εις οικουμενην'

And the last feature is not only a multiple of 37, or 111, but also of 888.

He is the beginning, the firstborn   111 × 32 (888)
Col 1:18 ος εστιν αρχη πρωτοτοκος"

AUTHOR

Jesus is also referred to as the author. Here are three features that bring forth this truth:

The author of life   111 × 25
Acts 3:15 τον αρχηγον της ζωης

Author and finisher Jesus   111 × 28
Heb 12:2 αρχηγον και τελειωτην Ιησουν'

Author of eternal salvation   111 × 32 (888)
Heb 5:9 αιτιος σωτηριας αιωνιου'

SON OF DAVID

Tremendous significance attaches to the many references throughout Scripture concerning Christ coming from the family of David, being the son of David, and so on.

He raised a horn of salvation for us   37 × 139
in the house of David His servant
Lk 1:69 ηγειρεν κερας σωτηριας ημιν εν οικω Δαυιδ παιδος αυτου'

Of the house and family of David   37 × 48
Lk 2:4 εξ οικου και πατριας Δαυιδ'

Family of David   37 × 30
Lk 2:4 πατριας Δαυιδ'

Of the seed of David   37 × 70
Jn 7:42 οτι εκ του σπερματος Δαυιδ

This is the son of David   37 × 75
Mt 12:23 ουτος εστιν ο υιος Δαυιδ'

Christ is the son of David   37 × 75
Lk 20:41 τον Χριστον ειναι Δαυιδ υιον

Son of David   37 × 44
Mt 21:15 υιω Δαυιδ'

THE HIGH PRIEST

What is meant when Christ is referred to as the "high priest"? The term is not a name, but rather an office or position. It means that Christ is a mediator or a substitute on our behalf. In 1 Timothy 2:5 we find these words: "For there is one God, and one mediator between God and men, a man Christ Jesus." In going through this verse, we knew that there had to be a theomatic design present. Here is how it worked out:

The mediator, a man Christ Jesus   111 × 40 (888)
1 Tim 2:5 μεσιτης ανθρωπος Χριστος Ιησους'

Another passage that ties in with the above feature speaks of Jesus as "the advocate": "My little children, I am writing to you in order that ye sin not; but if any one does sin, we have an advocate with the Father, Jesus Christ the righteous."

Advocate with the Father, Jesus Christ   111 × 33
1 Jn 2:1 παρακλητον προς πατερα Ιησουν Χριστον"

Now that we understand what is meant by the term "high priest," here are some features that speak of Christ's position as such. In Hebrews 3:1 Jesus is referred to as "the apostle and high priest of the confession."

Jesus, the apostle and high priest of the confession   111 × 35
Heb 3:1 τον αποστολον και αρχιερεα της ομολογιας Ιησουν'

Here are the words from Hebrews 2:17: "Therefore He had to be made like His brethren in every respect, so that He might become a merciful and faithful high priest in the service of God."

A merciful faithful high priest   111 × 29
Heb 2:17 ελεημων πιστος αρχιερευς

Do you remember the features we noted earlier that spoke of the Son of God? Here now is a feature that ties together the priestly office of Christ with the name "Son of God": "Since then we have a great high priest Who has passed through the heavens, Jesus, the Son of God, let us hold fast our confession."

A great high priest Who has passed through the heavens,   111 × 63
Jesus, the Son of God
Heb 4:14 αρχιερεα μεγαν διεληλυθοτα τους ουρανους Ιησουν τον υιον
   του Θεου"

In Hebrews 10:21 Christ is referred to as a "great priest over the household of God."

Great priest   111 × 2
Heb 10:21 ιερεα μεγαν"

To those readers who are familiar with the Scriptures, the next four features will have great significance. Throughout the book of Hebrews Jesus is described as a priest after the order of Melchizedek. In Hebrews 7:1 we find these words: "For this Melchizedek, king of Salem, priest of the most high God, met Abraham returning from the slaughter of the kings and blessed him; . . ."

Melchizedek, king of Salem, priest of the   111 × 48 (888)
most high God
Heb 7:1 Μελχισεδεκ βασιλευς Σαλημ ειρευς Θεου υψιστου"

The next three features need no special introduction:

High priest after the order of Melchizedek   111 × 31
Heb 5:10 αρχιερευς κατα την ταξιν Μελχισεδεκ

For thou art a priest forever after the order   111 × 40 (888)
of Melchizedek
Heb 7:17 οτι συ ιερευς εις αιωνα κατα ταξιν Μελχισεδεκ΄

Entered Jesus, the one having become a high priest   111 × 56 (888)
forever after the order of Melchizedek
Heb 6:20 εισηλθεν Ιησους κατα την ταξιν Μελχισεδεκ αρχιερευς
γενομενος εις αιωνα

In order to be our priest Jesus had to bear our sins and give Himself in our behalf as our substitute. Two more features will be given which tie in with the priestly office of Christ.

Through this man forgiveness of sins   111 × 34
Acts 13:38 δια τουτου αφεσις αμαρτιων΄

The one having given Himself on behalf of sins   111 × 48 (888)
Gal 1:4 του δοντος εαυτον υπερ των αμαρτιων΄

THE HEAVENS

Throughout Scripture Jesus is constantly portrayed as the one through Whom heavens and earth were created: "For in Him all things were created, in heaven and on earth, visible and invisible, whether thrones or dominions or principalities or powers." This complete passage, as it has just been quoted, is a multiple of 111. Here now is the most distinct portion:

For in Him all things were created   111 × 29
Col 1:16 οτι εν αυτω εκτισθη τα παντα"

The following three features will add further confirmation to the feature we just looked at:

The one Who created the heavens and the earth   111 × 31
Rev 14:7 τω ποιησαντι τον ουρανον και την γην΄

The works of Thy hands are the heavens   111 × 41
Heb 1:10 εργα των χειρων σου εισιν οι ουρανοι΄

The one ascending far above all the heavens   111 × 51
Eph 4:10 ο αναβας υπερανω παντων των ουρανων″

Here are the words from John 3:13: "No one has gone into heaven but the one from heaven having come down, the Son of Man."

The one from heaven having come down, the Son of Man   111 × 49
Jn 3:13 εκ του ουρανου καταβας ο υιος του ανθρωπου″

The one from heaven   111 × 17
Jn 3:13 εκ του ουρανου′

In 1 Corinthians, chapter 15, the second Adam is spoken of, which is the second man, or Christ. Verse 47 states:

The second man is from heaven   111 × 32 (888)
1 Cor 15:47 δευτερος ανθρωπος εξ ουρανου″

When the apostle Paul wrote his epistle to the Colossians, he said the following:

For ye also have a Lord in heaven   111 × 37
Col 4:1 οτι και υμεις εχετε κυριον εν ουρανω

Revelation 11:13 tells of the great earthquake that took place during the tribulation period: "Seven thousand people were killed in the earthquake, and the rest were terrified and gave glory to the God of heaven."

The God of heaven   111 × 34
Rev 11:13 τω Θεω του ουρανου′

FEATURES FROM REVELATION

The book of Revelation contains many references to Christ. Some quotations from Revelation concerning Christ have been placed under other headings in this chapter. However, those which have not will be shown here.

Throughout the book of Revelation, Jesus refers to Himself as the alpha and the omega: "I am the alpha and the omega, the first and the last, the beginning and the end." This complete phrase, as it has just been quoted, is a multiple of 111. Let us now take the most distinct portions, and see what happens.

The alpha and the omega, the first and the last,   111 × 55
the beginning and the end
Rev 22:13 αλφα και ω πρωτος και ο εσχατος αρχη και το τελος

Alpha omega   111 × 12
Rev 22:13 αλφα ω

The first and the last, the beginning and the end   111 × 40 (888)
Rev 22:13 ο πρωτος και ο εσχατος αρχη και τελος"

Without question the most outstanding name in Revelation, in reference to Christ, is the name *lamb*. Before we examine a series of features from Revelation, let us first of all look at the most famous reference in the New Testament to the lamb: "The next day He saw Jesus coming toward him, and said, 'Behold, the lamb of God Who takes away the sin of the world.'"

The lamb of God Who takes away the sin of the world   111 × 28
Jn 1:29 αμνος Θεου αιρων αμαρτιαν κοσμου'

In Revelation 5:12 it states: "Worthy is the lamb Who was slain to receive power and wealth and wisdom and might and honor and glory and blessing."

Worthy is the lamb Who was slain   111 × 19
Rev 5:12 αξιος εστιν αρνιον εσφαγμενον"

The best reference is found in Revelation 7:17, which speaks about the 144 thousands and how the lamb in the midst of the throne will shepherd them.

The lamb in the midst of the throne   111 × 16 (888)
Rev 7:17 οτι αρνιον ανα μεσον θρονου'

The 144 thousands are also described as the ones following the lamb: "These are the ones following the lamb wherever He may go."

Following the lamb   111 × 24 (888)
Rev 14:4 οι ακολουθουντες αρνιω"

The book of Revelation also talks about those who are written in the lamb's book of life.

The lamb's book of life   111 × 37
Rev 13:8 τω βιβλιω της ζωης αρνιου'

In a later chapter of this book, we will be showing a complete design of the marriage supper of the lamb, the bride of the lamb, and so on. For now, however, let's examine a feature from Revelation 19:9: "And the angel said to me, 'Write this: Blessed are the ones having been invited to the marriage supper of the lamb.' "

The marriage supper of the lamb 111 × 23
Rev 19:9 το δειπνον του γαμου αρνιου'

At this point, you may be asking yourself the question: What does just the word *lamb* work out to? Earlier in this chapter we pointed out that the number seven bespeaks holiness, and God's perfect law, and so on. Throughout Scripture the lamb of God is always portrayed as unblemished, spotless, and without sin. Here now is a feature from 1 Peter 1:19: "For as ye know that ye were not redeemed from the futile ways inherited from your fathers, not with perishable things such as silver or gold, but with the precious blood of Christ, like that of a lamb without blemish or spot."

But with the precious blood of Christ, like that of a lamb 7,000
without blemish or spot
1 Pet 1:19 αλλα τιμιω αιματι ως αμνου αμωμου και ασπιλου Χριστου"

And if we go to the book of Revelation and take just the word *lamb* by itself, we find:

The lamb 700 × 2
Rev 22:1 του αρνιου'

Revelation 4:8 describes the four living creatures, each of them with six wings, full of eyes around and within: "And day and night they never cease to sing, ..."

'Holy, holy, holy, is the Lord God almighty, 111 × 56 (888)
Who was and is and is to come'
Rev 4:8 αγιος αγιος αγιος κυριος ο Θεος ο παντοκρατωρ ο ην και ο ων
και ο ερχομενος"

In Revelation 6:10 Jesus is described as the "holy master": "And they cried out with a loud voice, 'Holy master and true, how long before You will judge and avenge our blood on those who dwell on the earth?' "

Holy master 111 × 11
Rev 6:10 δεσποτης ο αγιος

The New Jerusalem is described in the following manner in Revelation 21:21–22: "And the twelve gates were twelve pearls: each of the gates was of one pearl: and the street of the city was pure gold, as it were transparent glass. And I saw no temple therein":

For the Lord God almighty and the lamb are 111 × 56 (888)
the temple of it
Rev 21:22 ο γαρ κυριος ο Θεος ο παντοκρατωρ ναος αυτης εστιν και
αρνιον'

The Lord God almighty 111 × 29
Rev 21:22 ο γαρ κυριος ο Θεος ο παντοκρατωρ'

When the seventh angel blew his trumpet, it says that "there were loud voices in heaven, saying, 'The kingdom of the world has become the kingdom of the Lord of us and His Christ.' "

The Lord of us and His Christ 111 × 50
Rev 11:15 κυριου ημων και του Χριστου αυτου

The following three features need no special introduction:

The one having the two-edged sword 111 × 30
Rev 2:12 εχων ρομφαιαν την διστομον'

The one sitting on the horse 111 × 19
Rev 19:21 καθημενου επι του ιππου'

And the one sitting on the throne 111 × 18
Rev 7:15 και καθημενος επι του θρονου

John describes in chapter 5 how one of the elders told him to "weep not, for the lion of the tribe of Judah, the root of David, has conquered."

The lion of the tribe of Judah, the root of David 111 × 29
Rev 5:5 ο λεων ο εκ φυλης Ιουδα η ριζα Δαυιδ'

In Revelation 22:16, Jesus refers to Himself in the following manner:

I am the root and offspring of David 111 × 16 (888)
Rev 22:16 εγω ειμι η ριζα και γενος Δαυιδ'

In Revelation 7:11 it describes how the four living creatures and the twenty-four elders "fell on their faces before the throne and worshiped God."

Worshiped God   111 × 18
Rev 7:11 προσεκυνησαν Θεω

An interesting parallel with the above feature is found in Revelation 13:6. Here it states that the beast "opened its mouth to utter blasphemy against God."

Blasphemy against God   111 × 18
Rev 13:6 βλασφημιας προς τον Θεου"

For our concluding feature from Revelation we will present the following: "And one of the four living creatures gave the seven angels seven golden bowls full of the wrath of God Who lives for ever and ever."

Of God Who lives for ever and ever   111 × 58
Rev 15:7 του Θεου του ζωντος εις αιωνας αιωνων'

In going through the book of Revelation, we found at least thirty to forty other references to Christ, all of which contained multiples of 111. The features you have seen are in no way exhaustive of those that can be found in the Apocalypse. As we cannot overemphasize, this is true with practically every single design to be presented in this book.

MISCELLANEOUS FEATURES

The following series of features has been placed under the heading "Miscellaneous." To conclude the New Testament portion of this chapter we will list and show some of the additional references to Christ that can be found.

In John 11:25 Jesus said: "I am the resurrection and the life."

Resurrection, life   111 × 16 (888)
Jn 11:25 αναστασις ζωη"

One of the most famous references to Jesus in the Bible is found in John 14:6: "I am the way and the truth and the life."

Way, truth, life 111 × 11
Jn 14:6 οδος αληθεια ζωη"

Because of the fact that Jesus is the "resurrection and the life," we have the following testimony of the early apostles, when Peter referred to Christ as "the author of life Whom God raised from the dead, of which we are witnesses." We have already seen how "author of life" was a multiple of 111. Here now is the concluding portion of this verse:

Whom God raised from the dead, of which 111 × 35
we are witnesses
Acts 3:15 ον ο Θεος ηγειρεν εκ νεκρων ου ημεις μαρτυρες εσμεν'

After the resurrection took place, Mary Magdalene went and said to the disciples:

I have seen the Lord 111 × 18
Jn 20:18 εωρακα τον κυριον'

Here are two very outstanding references, in which God the Father places His approval on His Son:

This is the Christ of God, His chosen one 111 × 38
Lk 23:35 ουτος εστιν Χριστος Θεου εκλεκτος'

On Him hath God the Father set His seal 111 × 28
Jn 6:27 τουτον πατηρ εσφραγισεν ο Θεος'

When Jesus was teaching in the synagogue in Capernaum, a man with an unclean spirit cried out: "Have you come to destroy us? I know Who Thou art, the holy one of God."

Thou art, the holy one of God 111 × 14
Mk 1:24 ει αγιος του Θεου'

In The Acts 3:14, Jesus is also described as "the holy one."

The holy one 111 × 5
Acts 3:14 τον αγιον'

The parable of the ten virgins refers to Jesus as "the bridegroom": "Then the kingdom of heaven shall be likened to ten virgins who took their lamps and went forth to a meeting of the bridegroom."

To a meeting of the bridegroom 111 × 32 (888)
Mt 25:1 εις υπαντησιν του νυμφιου"

When the Pharisees sent the officers to seize Jesus, they returned saying:

No man ever spoke like this man   111 × 70

Jn 7:46 ουδεποτε ελαλησεν ουτως ανθρωπος ως ουτος λαλει ανθρωπος'

The Scriptures also refer to Christ as the head. Here are three features that bring this out:

Christ, Who is the head   111 × 26

Eph 4:15 ος εστιν η κεφαλη Χριστος'

Head of the church, He Himself being savior of the body   111 × 57

Eph 5:23 κεφαλη της εκκλησιας αυτος σωτηρ του σωματος'

He is the head of all rule and authority   111 × 34

Col 2:10 ος εστιν κεφαλη πασης αρχης και εξουσιας

Jesus is not only the "head of all rule and authority," but He is also the appointed heir of all things." "But in these last days, He spoke to us through a Son, Whom He appointed heir of all things."

But in these last days, He spoke to us through a Son   111 × 67

Heb 1:2 επ εσχατου των ημερων τουτων ελαλησεν ημιν εν υιω'

Appointed heir of all things   111 × 17

Heb 1:2 εθηκεν κληρονομον παντων'

When Jesus rode into Jerusalem on a donkey before His crucifixion, the multitudes cried out, "Blessed is the one coming, the king in the name of the Lord."

The king in the name of the Lord   111 × 22

Lk 19:38 βασιλευς εν ονοματι κυριου"

John 12:14 again refers to Jesus riding into Jerusalem on the donkey: "Blessed is the one coming in the name of the Lord, even the king of Israel."

Even the king of Israel   111 × 18

Jn 12:13 και βασιλευς του Ισραηλ

Verse 15, which immediately follows says this: "Fear not daughter of Zion; behold the king of thee is coming, sitting on the foal of an ass."

Behold the king   111 × 12
Jn 12:15 ιδου βασιλευς

In 1 Timothy 1:17 Jesus is referred to as being:

The king of the ages   111 × 38
1 Tim 1:17 τω βασιλει των αιωνων'

And now, for the concluding feature from the New Testament, we proudly present the most outstanding one of all:

King of kings and Lord of lords   111 × 73
1 Tim 6:15 βασιλευς των βασιλευοντων και κυριος των κυριευοντων'

Now the God Who wrote the New Testament is also the God Who wrote the Old Testament. For this reason we would naturally expect to find that the design present in the Greek could also be found in the Hebrew.

JESUS IS THE JEHOVAH GOD OF THE OLD TESTAMENT

Jesus is the Jehovah God of the Old Testament. In almost all English translations, "Jehovah God" is translated as "Lord God." We have already seen how in the Greek Jesus is both God and Lord. Here now is the most outstanding feature possible from the Old Testament:

Jehovah God   111
Gen 3:9 יהוה אלהים'

When the Lord called forth the Jews as His chosen people, He made them a promise: "Then I will take you for My people, and I will be your God; and you shall know that I am Jehovah your God."

I am Jehovah your God   111 × 2
Ex 6:7 כי אני יהוה אלהיכם'

Another amazing confirmation of this same design occurs when Abraham says to the king of Sodom:

I have sworn by Jehovah God most high,   111 × 16 (888)
possessor of heaven and earth
Gen 14:22 הרמתי ידי אל יהוה אל עליון קנה שמים וארץ'

Here are the most important words from this phrase:

Jehovah God most high   111 × 2
יהוה אל עליון ' Gen 14:22

Hebrews 13:8 says: "Jesus Christ is the same yesterday and today and for ever." The Hebrew words from Malachi 3:6 read:

I am Jehovah, I change not   111 × 8 (888)
Mal 3:6 אני יהוה לא שניתי

John 1:3 states that through Christ all things were created. Thus we find in Genesis 2:4 from the creation story the words:

Jehovah God made   111 × 8 (888)
Gen 2:4 עשות יהוה אלהים

Probably the most outstanding reference to God in the Old Testament, besides "Jehovah God," is "Lord of hosts."

Lord of hosts   111 × 5
1 Sam 1:3 ליהוה צבאות

In Malachi 4:2 there is another messianic prophecy:

Unto you that fear My name, there shall arise   111 × 20
a son of righteousness, with healing in His wings
Mal 4:2 וזרחה לכם יראי שמי שמש צדקה ומרפא בכנפיה

After the Lord revealed the mystery unto Daniel, Daniel replied by saying:

Blessed be the name of God for ever and ever   111 × 10
Dan 2:20 שמה די אלהא מברך מן עלמא ועד עלמא

Genesis 22:8 refers to a "lamb for a burnt offering."

Lamb for a burnt offering   111 × 4
Gen 22:8 אלהים יראה לו שה לעלה '

Of all the features presented in this book none is more significant than this one. In Isaiah 52:10 it states that "all the ends of the earth shall see the salvation of our God."

Salvation of our God   111 × 8 (888)
Is 52:10 ישועת אלהינו

4

The 153 Fishes in the Net

One of the most fascinating passages of Scripture is John 21:11, wherein the disciples go fishing, and "Simon Peter went up, and drew the net to land, full of great fishes, a hundred and fifty-three; and although there were so many, the net was not being torn."

This number 153 has taxed the ingenuity and minds of some of the greatest Bible students over the centuries. All have felt that there must be something deeply significant and important about this number. Why would the number of fishes caught be such a strange number? Why not a nice even number, like 100 or 150? Many commentators have seen in this number some reference to the saved as being of a definite and particular number, even down to the last one; thus, they make up not a large round number but a smaller and odd number—153.

Theomatics will bring out many spiritual truths concerning this passage of Scripture. In the last chapter, we saw how 888 was a key number on which many different references to Christ were structured. The exciting thing you are about to discover is that many times the key numbers are given right in the text. In fact, every single number in the Bible is part of the overall theomatic design on which God has built His Word. This will then prove that the numbers we are using, are not those we thought up ourselves, but those placed right in the text by God Himself. It's as if God were to say: Here's the number to use. The story of the 153 fishes will bring this truth out perfectly.

The first feature we will be examining is from the passage in which this story took place. John 21:11 states that "Simon Peter went up, and drew the net to land, full of great fishes, a hundred and fifty-three."

Drew the net to land full of great fishes, 153 × 54
a hundred and fifty-three
Jn 21:11 ειλκυσεν δικτυον εις την γην μεστον ιχθυων μεγαλων εκατον
πεντηκοντα τριων'

But the most important word possible related to this story is the word for *fishes* in Greek, which has a theomatic value of 1,224, or 153 × 8.

Fishes 153 × 8 (1,224)
Lk 9:13 ιχθυες

This is an amazing number for two reasons. First of all, it is a multiple of 153 and it specifically states in John 21:11 that they caught 153 fishes. But that is not all. The number 1,224 is 153 × 8, and 8, as we discussed in the last chapter, is typical of the new order. Therefore, it is not surprising to find that with the most important word possible *(fishes)*, the theomatic value would be 1,224, or 153 × 8.

Let's not stop here, but move on to the next most important feature, which we find in the story of John 21:11. The net, which actually caught the 153 fishes, has been commonly accepted as being typical of the kingdom of God. It also has a theomatic value of 1,224, or 153 × 8.

The net 153 × 8 (1,224)
Jn 21:11 το δικτυον

In Scripture, the sea has always been understood to represent mankind, or the human race as a whole. This metaphor is well expressed in the book of Revelation. The 153 fishes (a specific amount) are brought out of humanity into the net and carried safely to shore. The fact that both "fishes" and "the net" have the same number values of 153 × 8 shows that their purpose is unified and one in the same. It is the net that draws the fishes out of the sea and protects them as they are carried to land.

Many are the references to fishes and fishing throughout the gospels that work out to multiples of 153. For the purpose of illustration we will show only a few of them; all of these are extremely significant. The first comes from Matthew's gospel, where it says that the disciples were:

Casting a net into the sea 153 × 20
Mt 4:18 βαλλοντας αμφιβληστρον την εις θαλασσαν

For they were fishermen 153 × 4
Mt 4:18 ησαν γαρ αλεεις"

At the beginning of the fish story in John, chapter 21, Jesus meets the disciples by the side of the lake. "Then Jesus said unto them, 'Children, have ye any meat?' They answered Him, 'No.' And He said unto them,"

Cast the net on the right side of the ship and ye shall find 153 × 27
Jn 21:6 βαλετε εις δεξια μερη του πλοιου δικτυον και ευρησετε"

The words that follow in the same verse say that "They cast therefore: . . ."

And they were not able to haul it in because of 153 × 47
the multitude of fishes
Jn 21:6 και ουκετι αυτο ελκυσαι ισχυον απο του πληθους ιχθυων'

Then again, Luke 5:6 states that the disciples caught a "multitude of fishes." These words by themselves are a multiple of 153. Notice, however, that they are divisible not only by 153, but also by 1,224, just as were "fishes" and "the net."

Multitude of fishes 153 × 16 (1,224)
Lk 5:6 ιχθυων πολυ'

The most powerful reference anywhere in the Bible related to fishes and fishing is found in the gospel according to Mark: "And Jesus said to them, follow Me, and I will make you to become fishes of men."

Follow me 153 × 12
Mk 8:34 ακολουθειτω μοι'

Why did Jesus say to the disciples to come and follow Him? So that He could make them to become "fishers of men." Here is the best-known and the most significant feature related to fishes and fishing in the entire Bible:

Fishers of men 153 × 14
Mk 1:17 αλεεις ανθρωπων'

Again, let's not stop here, but go directly to verse 18. Here's what the disciples did after Jesus had called them.

And immediately leaving the nets, they followed Him 153 × 36
Mk 1:18 και ευθυς αφεντες τα δικτυα ηκολουθησαν αυτω'

There is one other passage of Scripture related to this theme that shows the same design. It occurs in Matthew 4, where James and John were in the boat with Zebedee, their father, mending the nets. Jesus walked by, and here's what happened:

He called them, and they immediately left the   153 × 64
boat, and their father, and followed Him
Mt 4:21–22 εκαλεσεν αυτους οι δε ευθεως αφεντες το πλοιον και τον
πατερα αυτων ηκολουθησαν αυτω

Before moving on, let's examine the probability on just five of the previous features given.

Fishes   153 × 8
The net   153 × 8
Casting a net into the sea   153 × 20
Multitude of fishes   153 × 16
Fishers of men   153 × 14

I think almost everyone would agree that these five are unquestionably the most outstanding, popular, and clear-cut features possible as they relate to fish and fishing in the Bible. The chance that these five could all work out to be multiples of 153 is only 1 chance in 254,646. That's two hundred and fifty-four thousand, six hundred and forty-six. If you remember the page having the 5,000 dots mentioned in Chapter 1, this means you would have only one chance in over fifty such pages of dots. And this probability is only for these five key features mentioned above, not taking into consideration any of the others.

To top it all off the most exciting thing about the number 153 is that it states right in the text that the disciples caught 153 fishes. This bears out the marvelous truth that nothing occurs in God's Word by chance. Every word has been carefully placed in the text and has perfect meaning. Many times it is so easy to zip right by a verse such as John 21:11 and not realize its complete spiritual significance. However, with theomatics what was once meaningless and just a number takes on new spiritual importance. As a result, our hearts are blessed and filled with joy.

Jesus, the Way and the Door

Many wonderful and blessed spiritual truths are to be found throughout Scripture that relate to the number 153. God has woven together the design of His Word in such a way that all of the meanings flow together systematically like a stream winding through a forest. One such stream begins back in Mark 1:17, where Jesus said, "Follow me, and I will make you to become fishers of men." Why did Jesus say to the disciples to come and follow Him? The answer is found in John 14:6, where the Lord says, "I am the way, and the truth, and the life."

I am the way   153 × 8 (1,224)
Jn 14:6 εγω ειμι η οδος´

The reason Jesus said this is that He is "the way, and the truth, and the life." Earlier, in the last chapter, we saw how the leading three words (*way, truth,* and *life*) were a multiple of 111. Here now are the same three words again.

Way, truth, life   153 × 8 (1,224)
Jn 14:6 οδος αληθεια ζωη´

Since Jesus is the way and the only means of entrance into heaven, He is also spoken of in Scripture as being the "door," or the "door of the sheep."

I say to you that I am the door of the sheep   153 × 37
Jn 10:7 λεγω υμιν οτι εγω ειμι η θυρα των προβατων´

In verse 1 of John 10 we find the following words: "Verily, verily, I say unto you, 'He that does not enter by the door into the sheepfold, but climbeth in some other way, the same is a thief and a robber.' "

Enter by the door into the sheepfold   153 × 41
Jn 10:1 ο εισερχομενος δια της θυρας εις την αυλην των προβατων

In the last chapter we showed how the number 37 speaks of the many different references to Christ. If you will remember, we also showed three distinct features of 37, all from one line in John 10:7:

I say to you that I am the door of the sheep   37 × 153
The door of the sheep   37 × 83
The door   37 × 14

In the second chapter, which dealt with the definition of the theomatic structure, it was shown that some words in Greek have several possible spellings. We explained that each of these spellings had a particular place in the overall design of God's Word.

Since Jesus is the door, then it is not surprising to find that "the door" is a multiple of 37. But "the door" also speaks of Jesus as being "the way," "the door of the sheepfold," and so on. Here then is another spelling of "the door":

The door 153 × 6
Lk 13:25 την θυραν

So with one word two different spiritual truths can be brought out. Jesus is the door, and the door is the way.

Another confirmation of this truth is found in Matthew 7:13, where Jesus said to "enter through the narrow gate."

The narrow gate 153 × 13
Mt 7:13 της στενης πυλης

To conclude this theme two of the most significant verses in the Bible will be shown which have to do with Christ being the door. The first is from John 10:9:

I am the door; if anyone enters through Me, 153 × 28
he will be saved
Jn 10:9 εγω ειμι η θυρα δι εμου εαν τις εισελθη σωθησεται"

The second verse comes from the book of Revelation: "Behold I stand at the door and knock; if anyone hears My voice and opens the door, I will come in to him and eat with him and he with Me." This verse contains three features, all multiples of 153. For the sake of illustration, we will present only one of these. Here, now, is the most distinct portion of this verse possible, as it relates to Christ being the door:

If anyone hears My voice and opens the door, 153 × 39
I will come in
Rev 3:20 εαν τις ακουση της φωνης μου και ανοιξη την θυραν
        εισελευσομαι"

When Del began his research in theomatics, he thought that surely these 153 fishes were symbolic and typical of all the redeemed saints. After many hours of frustrating research, he realized that this original premise was wrong. Later on in his research, he discovered that there was indeed a number symbolic of all the redeemed, but it was not the number 153.

In a sense, however, the number 153 does speak of the redeemed, but the implications of this number go much deeper than that. Even though some marvelous designs can be shown with it, we will readily admit that, of all the numbers to be presented in this book, this is by far the one we least understand. The reason for this is that it flows through so many different topics, which on the surface do not appear related to each other, but in essence are related. For example, we have uncovered a complete design of 153 related to the topic of resurrection. There is also a design of 153 flowing through the passages that refer to the seed of Abraham. Much research remains to be done, however, before all of the pieces of this design fit together.

The Acid Test

As our research developed, we realized that it was going to be necessary for us to obtain a statistical method, which would unequivocally prove that God had written His entire Word mathematically—by the number values of the Hebrew and Greek letters. Up to that time we had gone through several rather complicated methods of proving probability, some of which were quite effective. However, we realized that there was another method needed that we could label the "acid test," in proving the existence of theomatics.

One day while Del was meditating, he remembered a statement made to him sometime earlier by a dear friend. This friend had told him about a famous inventor who made the declaration that "to be a true genius was having the ability to discover something simple that works!"

Here was our answer! We needed something simple that worked. It was not long after Del remembered the inventor's statement that the Lord placed into our hands a method for proving theomatics that is so simple and so effective that even a little child can understand it. Yet there is not a scientist or mathematician who can refute it. It is impregnable. It is the acid test for proving the existence of theomatics.

Earlier, in Chapter 2, we showed that each letter in the Hebrew and Greek alphabets has a number or theomatic value assigned to it by God. But wait a minute, somebody may say. How do you know for sure that God had anything to do with it? Or why is there anything so special about the letters given as numbers in the papyrus? In other words, why does *alpha* have to have a value of 1, or *beta* 2, or *gamma* 3, and so on?

Here was our answer! *Why not just rearrange the assignment of the numbers to the letters of the alphabet?* In order to do this, we turned to a professional statistician by the name of Dr. Laverne Stanton of California State University. Dr. Stanton wrote a report for us in which he established this acid test method as a valid means to prove or disprove theomatics. His report is in Chapter 10, which deals with the science of statistics and probability, p. 256. In this report Dr. Stanton randomly rearranged the number values for the letters of the Greek alphabet. (See chart on following page.)

We can explain what is meant by *random* this way: There are twenty-six letters in the Greek alphabet. A person could take twenty-six recipe cards and write each number value on a card, then throw all of the cards into a box. Reaching into the box blindfolded, he could draw out a card. Let's say that the first card he drew said 700. He could then assign the number 700 to the letter *alpha*. The next card he drew said 40. This would then be assigned to *beta*. And so on.

Since each letter in this random selection has a different number value, then each word would also have a different number value. We have already seen how *Jesus* works out to 888. Using Dr. Stanton's random selection, *Jesus* would work out to 1,113. A new value could also be worked out for every single word in the Bible. If you will turn back to Chapter 2, to the page showing the number values from the Greek-English New Testament, p. 31, you can see that by comparison the numbers over all the words would be different.

And here is the crux of the whole matter! If there is nothing special about the assignment of numbers as given in Webster's dictionary and the papyrus, then we can readily assume that any other alphabetical number arrangement should product the same results we have been able to produce. Why not? If God had nothing to do with the assignment of numbers to the letters of the Hebrew and Greek alphabets, then the numbers we are using would simply be one great big conglomeration of random numbers. Any other random assignment should produce the same results.

This means that in order for a person to disprove theomatics, all

Assignment Given in Webster's Dictionary and the Papyrus	Random Assignment
α 1	α 700
β 2	β 40
γ 3	γ 800
δ 4	δ 5
ε. 5	ε. 1
ς′ 6	ς′ 8
ζ. 7	ζ. 70
η 8	η 50
θ 9	θ 200
ι. 10	ι. 600
κ 20	κ 60
λ 30	λ 30
μ 40	μ 100
ν 50	ν 7
ξ. 60	ξ. 10
ο 70	ο 3
π 80	π 4
ο 90	ο 9
ρ 100	ρ 400
σ–ς . . 200	σ–ς . . . 80
τ 300	τ 90
υ 400	υ 300
φ 500	φ 6
χ 600	χ 500
ψ 700	ψ 2
ω 800	ω 20

he would have to do is show that he could build complete designs—equal to ours—by using another set of number values. This would prove that there is nothing at all special about the features that we have found.

In trying to build these designs, this individual would have to find *as many* features as we have found, of the *same significance,* and from the *same specific topic.* Also, his features would have to cluster around multiples of numbers of the *same general magnitude,* not smaller numbers.

Before presenting the truth of theomatics to God's people, we made sure that it was totally impossible for anyone to disprove theomatics in this manner. For this reason, we spent hundreds of hours on the calculator, in order to prove that no other number-letter equivalencies could produce a consistent design except those that God placed in the papyrus. When other number-letter equivalencies are used, there is no design present other than what may occur from sheer randomness. This fact will be demonstrated in greater detail in Chapter 10, on the science of statistics and probability.

We realize the extreme importance of scientifically proving that God wrote His entire Word mathematically. This means that many times we must give the mathematical proof that establishes this and which at the same time refutes any arguments or criticism given by those who are opposed to the existence of theomatics.

In doing so, we may sometimes give the impression that we are going forth with the attitude that "this will prove it to you," or "this will show you." Let the reader understand that our purpose and our goal are not to challenge or debate the critics. The purpose of theomatics is to glorify the Lord Jesus, and at the same time bless the hearts of God's people and build up their faith. This then is our intention: to glorify God and share with all those who have an open mind the beautiful mathematical design that God has placed in His Word.

Other Works of Literature

One question that has been repeatedly asked of the authors is the following: Can these mathematical designs be found in any other works of literature? In other words, could a person take the Apocrypha, or some of Josephus's works, or Shakespeare, or even the Book of Mormon, and find mathematical designs such as those found in the Bible?

The answer to this question is: *Absolutely not!* There is no other work of literature anywhere that can produce these designs except the Hebrew Old Testament and the Greek New Testament. And the way of proving it is simple.

Let us suppose that someone took another work of literature, and from it he discovered ten words or phrases that had number values which clustered around multiples of seventy-five (or any other number). This work of literature, let's say, was in Greek, and the number-letter equivalencies that this individual used were the same as ours, from Webster's dictionary and the papyrus.

Now in order for us to disprove his theory that other works of literature contain a design, all we would have to do is randomly reassign the numbers to the letters of the Greek alphabet or any other alphabet that he was using, and then show where we could produce at least ten features related to the same topic using a number as large as seventy-five.

For us to do this would be a cinch. If there is no design present in this other work of literature, then any random assignment of numbers to the letters of the alphabet should produce the same results as any other arrangement. This is a mathematical fact that cannot be denied. If a person could build a design with another work of literature that no other number-letter equivalencies could produce, then he would have performed a miracle that defies science and the laws of probability.

One question that some readers may ask us is this: Have you checked out other works of literature to see if they contain a design? The answer is no, and the reason is simple. Which work of literature are we going to examine? In order for us to prove that no other work of literature contains a design, we would have to check every piece of literature ever written in the history of man. Furthermore, which multiple factors would we use, and which number-letter equivalencies? As the reader can see, the number of numerical combinations is immeasurable. The amazing fact is that the Bible is the only book in the world where these designs can and do exist. And the only equivalencies that will produce them are those found in Webster's dictionary and the papyrus. Strange, isn't it?

Theomatics vs. Numerology

As Jerry and Del have presented theomatics to different church groups and organizations throughout the country, a few individuals have come up and accused us of promoting the occult science of numerology. Quite frankly, this accusation is so ridiculous that it almost causes us an embarrassment to bring it up in this book. But in order to leave no question in any reader's mind, we will make the following clarifications.

Webster's dictionary defines the word *numerology* as "a system of occultism built around numbers, especially those giving birth dates; those which are the sum of the letters of one's name, etc.; divination by numbers." And the word *divination* is defined by Webster's as "the act or practice of trying to foretell the future or the unknown by occult means."

Existing among all of the satanic cults of the modern day, there are certain psychics, among others, who use the number values of a person's name to predict his future. The system and arrangement of number values used is completely different from those found in Webster's dictionary and the papyrus. Along with the number value of a person's name, these clairvoyants also bring in astrology, tarot cards, crystal balls, and other devices too numerous to mention.

Now, what the writers of this book would like to know is, What relationship does theomatics have to fortune telling or the occult? Numerology glorifies Satan. But theomatics, as you will see in the forthcoming chapters, exposes the devil for what he is: a deceiver, a liar, and the enemy of all righteousness. Therefore, if theomatics is numerology, then this means that what we are presenting in this book has come from Satan, which also means that the devil must have written the Bible!

If a person will stop and think about it logically, there is absolutely *no way* that theomatics can possibly be associated with the occult. If theomatics is untrue, then at the very worst it would be nothing more than a complete fallacy. A big joke. And if it is a fallacy and a joke, then it could be disproven in an instant by the laws of statistics and probability.

The purpose of this book is not to glorify Satan, but rather to glorify Jesus. If there is any one truth that the theomatic design in God's Word brings forth, it is the following: Man is a sinner, held captive by the power of Satan. The only way of salvation is through faith in the saving blood of Jesus Christ.

No, theomatics is not numerology.

Science, the Holy Spirit, and Faith

Earlier in this chapter we presented the scientific method by which it was possible to prove theomatics. Here it was shown that in order for a person to disprove theomatics, all he would have to do is equal our findings with a random assignment of numbers to the letters of the Greek alphabet. As it will be demonstrated in the last chapter on statistics and probability, this is totally impossible to do.

Now, as convincing as this may be, would you believe that it still does not prove theomatics. Scientifically it does, but there is yet another ingredient necessary, which must also be included.

Theomatics must have the witness and the confirmation of the Holy Spirit to the hearts of God's people. This will be the ultimate test.

The scientific proof along with the witness of the Holy Spirit are the two ingredients that must be present if theomatics is to have credibility. What good would it be if a person had all of the scientific or intellectual proof, but was completely void of any spiritual understanding? Or what good would it be if someone said that he had the witness of the spirit but it could be proven that the theomatic features in this book were simply created out of random numbers?

Even after all of the mathematical facts have been established and confirmed, this still does not fulfill God's ultimate purpose in making this truth known to His people. God is not the least bit interested in proving to the atheist that He wrote the Bible. His ultimate objective with theomatics is what it will accomplish in the hearts of His people. God is preparing His church for the closing days of history, and theomatics will no doubt be a means used by the Holy Spirit to more fully unite the body of Christ. The only way this scientific evidence can be received is by the witness of the Holy Spirit.

In the first sentence to the introduction of this book, we wrote, "Theomatics scientifically proves that God wrote the Bible." While this statement is absolutely true, it is really incomplete. To be completely accurate, we should have said, "Theomatics scientifically proves that God wrote the Bible—to those who accept it by faith."

While this may seem like a contradiction of terms, it really is not. God's principle is that anything that comes from Him must be accepted by faith, and theomatics is no exception. Faith is God's security system, because God's spiritual truths are only reserved for those who come to Him with childlike faith and simplicity.

And here is something else. Theomatics will never become a system whereby we can go out and use it to make automatic Christians. Many unbelievers to whom the authors have related theomatics, including several statisticians, have confirmed that it is absolutely true. But that did not make them Christians. The only way a person can be born again is through faith in Jesus. Theomatics will never become anything more than just a tool in leading a soul to Christ. It is no different from a sermon by Billy Graham or a Christian teen-ager sharing the four spiritual laws with a friend. Theomatics is only a tool to be used by the Holy Spirit. Salvation comes through faith.

5

Light, Darkness, and Power

You are about to see a design that will confirm and establish the existence of the theomatic structure of the Bible in a way you never thought possible. So consistent is it that after seeing it there should be no question in anyone's mind that God has designed and constructed His entire Word to fit together by the number values of the individual letters and words.

With the exception of this chapter, all of the numbers to be presented in this book are uneven numbers. We have already looked at 37, 111, and 153, but now a completely different phenomenon appears. Here all of the numbers are what we will term "clear numbers." For example, 200 is an even, outstanding, and clear number, while the number 187 is not. Likewise, 1,300 stands out clearly, while 1,243 does not. In this chapter, the number 1,500 is the most important number, for it is the theomatic value of the word *light* in Greek. Furthermore, 1,500 can be divided evenly by 100 (100 × 15 = 1,500), and it can also be divided evenly by 150 (150 × 10 = 1,500). Therefore, each and every feature in this chapter will be presented in one of two ways. Practically 100 percent of the features will be direct multiples of 100. Those that are not multiples of 100 will work out to the number 2,250, or 150 × 15.

During the process of compiling our research, we observed that if the theomatic value was not a multiple of 100, it would invariably be 2,250 or 150 × 15. At first we thought this was rather strange, but then we discovered the reason why. Light has a theomatic value of 1,500, which is 15 followed by two zeros. The number 2,250, or 150 × 15, is the concentration of the number 15 squared. Therefore, all of the features to be presented in this chapter will be either direct multiples of 100, or 150 × 15. You will understand this perfectly as you read. The many passages related to light and darkness work out to multiples of these even, clear numbers. Light is bright and clear and stands out, and that is why God depicts it in this manner.

But why would everything having to do with darkness also work out to be multiples of these same even numbers? Darkness is the exact opposite of light, and sometimes in theomatics exact opposites will have the same number values. The features presented in this chapter are the only major examples of this that we have found to date. When light is present there can be no darkness, and in darkness there can be no light. These two are so opposed to each other that God depicts them with the same theomatic values. Light and darkness are complete diametric opposites.

This chapter has been entitled "Light, Darkness, and Power," but it will have many other related headings and subtopics. These will be self-explanatory as you progress through this design.

Light and Darkness

Here, now, is the theomatic value for the word *light* in Greek:

Light   1,500
Lk 11:35 φως

To begin, let's examine three verses from John, chapter 3. Verse 19 states: "Light has come into the world, and men loved darkness rather than light."

Light has come into the world   100 × 27
Jn 3:19 φως εληλυθεν εις κοσμον″

Men loved darkness   100 × 27
Jn 3:19 ηγαπησαν ανθρωποι το σκοτος′

Men loved darkness rather than light   100 × 48
Jn 3:19 ηγαπησαν ανθρωποι μαλλον το σκοτος η το φως

The next verse states: "For everyone who does evil hates the light, and does not come to the light."

Everyone doing evil hates the light,   100 × 79
and does not come to the light
Jn 3:20 πας φαυλα πρασσων μισει φως και ουκ ερχεται προς φως´

By eliminating the Greek word for *everyone* from this passage, there is even further design present. The meaning in Greek is emphatic.

Doing evil hates light   1,500 × 3
Jn 3:20 φαυλα πρασσων μισει το φως˝

The last feature in John 3 comes from verse 21, where it states:

But the one doing the truth comes to the light   100 × 49
Jn 3:21 ο δε ποιων την αληθειαν ερχεται προς το φως˝

Since Christ is spoken of as being the light coming into the world, we are going to discover a precious truth brought out by these numbers. John, chapter 1, depicts the world as being in darkness and Jesus as the light of the world. The words *darkness* and *world* have the same theomatic values of 100 × 6.

Darkness   100 × 6
Jn 1:5 σκοτια´

World   100 × 6
Jn 1:10 κοσμος

Because the world is full of darkness, the following will have perfect meaning:

Light of the world   100 × 23
Jn 8:12 φως κοσμου

In Philippians, Christians are reckoned to "appear as lights in the world."

Lights in the world   100 × 33
Phil 2:15 φωστηρες εν κοσμω˝

And, interestingly enough, the word *light* in the plural is also a multiple of 100.

Lights   100 × 16
Acts 16:29 φωτα´

Next we will examine nine features, all from a few verses in John, chapter 1. In fact, every single reference to light in this passage works out to even multiples. The statistical probability of this occurring by chance is so astronomical that it does not even bear mentioning. In fact, there is hardly a single major reference in the New Testament related to the topics in this chapter that does not work out to multiples of these even numbers. The features which we will be presenting in this chapter are only a sampling. Dozens upon dozens of other features could have easily been shown, but time and space would not permit us to do so. The thing that makes this evidence so insurmountable is the fact that the key words and phrases always work out, thus setting the stage for the consistency that follows. If the key words themselves didn't add up, the rest would be meaningless.

The first feature from John, chapter 1, is where he speaks of Jesus as the "light of men." "In Him was life, and the life was the light of men."

And the life was the light of men   100 × 43

Jn 1:4 και η ζωη ην φως ανθρωπων"

Was the light of men   100 × 46

Jn 1:4 ην φως των ανθρωπων"

Verse 5, which follows, says: "The light shines in the darkness; and the darkness did not comprehend it."

The light shines in the darkness   100 × 31

Jn 1:5 το φως εν σκοτια φαινει"

The next reference to light is found in verse 7. "He [John] came for a witness, that he might bear witness of the light." Here are the simple words with the proper meaning from this passage:

He came for a witness of the light   5,000

Jn 1:7 ουτος ηλθεν εις μαρτυριαν του φωτος'

Since John was a witness to the light, it would only follow that the word *witness* by itself should fit into the same design.

Witness   1,000

Jn 1:7 μαρτυριαν"

The last reference in John, chapter 1, to light is found in verse 9. The Greek words in this passage are arranged in a completely different order from that of the English. We will show three distinct features, all from the same verse: "There was the true light which, coming into the world, enlightens every man."

There was the true light coming into the world   100 × 43
Jn 1:9 Ην το φως αληθινον ο ερχομενον εις τον κοσμον'

The true light which enlightens   100 × 38
Jn 1:9 φως το αληθινον ο φωτιζει

Which enlightens   100 × 17
Jn 1:9 ο φωτιζει"

The true light   100 × 21
Jn 1:9 φως το αληθινον"

Now we will turn and focus our attention on a series of features that give a more direct reference to God Himself being light. The first comes from 1 John 1:5:

For God is light, and in Him there is no darkness at all   100 × 65
1 Jn 1:5 οτι Θεος φως εστιν και σκοτια εν αυτω ουκ εστιν ουδεμια"

For God is light   100 × 28
1 Jn 1:5 οτι ο Θεος φως εστιν'

James refers to God as the "Father of lights": "Every good thing bestowed and every perfect gift is from above, coming down from the Father of lights."

Father of lights   100 × 32
Jas 1:17 πατρος φωτων'

In Ephesians 5:14 we find the words, "Awake, sleeper, and arise from the dead, and Christ will shine on you."

And Christ will shine on you   1,500 × 2
Eph 5:14 και επιφαυσει σοι Χριστος"

Next we shall examine a reference from 1 John which brings out a precious spiritual truth: "But if we walk in the light, as He is in the light, fellowship we have with one another."

But if we walk in the light 100 × 43
1 Jn 1:7 εαν δε εν τω φωτι περιπατωμεν'

As He is in the light 100 × 53
1 Jn 1:7 ως αυτος εστιν εν τω φωτι'

But God is also referred to as:

The one having called you out of darkness 100 × 7
into His marvelous light
1 Pet 2:9 του εκ σκοτους υμας καλεσαντος εις το θαυμαστον αυτου φως

In the Greek language there is a very emphatic word, εκ, which carries great significance. It means "to come out," or "to come out of" something. Hidden inside the above feature is another feature of great significance. It ties together in a beautiful way the relationship between light and darkness.

Out of darkness into light 1,500 × 2
1 Pet 2:9 εκ σκοτους εις φως

Another feature using the word εκ and having the same theomatic value comes from Colossians 1:13: "He has delivered us out of the power of darkness, and translated us into the kingdom of His beloved Son."

Out of the power of darkness 1,500 × 2
Col 1:13 εκ εξουσιας του σκοτους'

Here are the words of Jesus from John, chapter 12: "For a little while longer the light is among you. Walk while you have the light, lest the darkness overtakes you; and he who walks in darkness does not know where he is going." This complete passage is a multiple of 100, but here are two of the more outstanding portions:

You have the light, lest the darkness overtakes you 1,500 × 3
Jn 12:35 το φως εχετε ινα μη σκοτια υμας καταλαβη'

And he who walks in darkness does not know 100 × 41
where he is going
Jn 12:35 και περιπατων εν τη σκοτια ουκ οιδεν που υπαγει'

One of the most relevent passages of Scripture which speaks of darkness is found in the book of 1 John. Connect these next features now with the last two from John 12:35:

The one who hates his brother is in   100 × 55
darkness and in the darkness walks
1 Jn 2:11 ο μισων αδελφον αυτου εν σκοτια εστιν και εν σκοτια
περιπατει

The one who hates his brother   1,500 × 2
1 Jn 2:11 ο μισων αδελφον αυτου'

The darkness walks   1,500
1 Jn 2:11 τη σκοτια περιπατει

The theme of light also carries over into another spiritual truth
which will be brought out by the next three features. The first feature
does not speak directly of light, but after reading all three, you will see
the meaning perfectly.

For nothing is covered that will not be revealed   100 × 73
or hidden that will not be known
Mt 10:26 ουδεν γαρ εστιν κεκαλυμμενον ο ουκ αποκαλυφθησεται και
κρυπτον ο ου γνωσθησεται'

All things exposed by the light are made manifest   100 × 54
Eph 5:13 τα παντα ελεγχομενα υπο φωτος φανερουται'

Exposed by the light   4,000
Eph 5:13 ελεγχομενα υπο του φωτος'

The words "works of darkness" are extremely significant, and we
find a reference to them in Ephesians 5:11: "Do not participate in the
unfruitful works of darkness, but instead reprove them."

The unfruitful works of darkness   100 × 29
Eph 5:11 εργοις ακαρποις του σκοτους

Works of darkness   1,500 × 2
Eph 5:11 τοις εργοις του σκοτους"

Here are the words from Matthew 4:16: "The people sitting in
darkness saw a great light; and to those who sat in the land of the
shadow of death light has dawned."

The people sitting in darkness   1,500
Mt 4:16 ο λαος ο καθημενος εν σκοτια

To those who sat in the land of the shadow   1,500 × 4
death light has dawned

Mt 4:16 καθημενοις εν χωρα και σκια θανατου φως ανετειλεν αυτοις'

The next feature is a perfect example of the many dozens of lesser known ones that we could have shown. Ephesians 5:9 states: "The fruit of the light is found in all that is good and right and true." Most everyone has heard of the expression "light of the world," but how many Christians know of this verse?

For the fruit of the light is found in all   1,500 × 4
that is good and right and true
Eph 5:9 ο γαρ καρπος του φωτος εν παση αγαθωσυνη και δικαιοσυνη και αληθεια

The spiritual message from the following will be quite obvious:

Satan transforms himself into an angel of light   100 × 58
2 Cor 11:14 αυτος Σατανας μετασχηματιζεται εις αγγελον φωτος'

Ephesians 6:12 refers to the "worldrulers of this darkness."

This darkness   100 × 28
Eph 6:12 σκοτους τουτου

Revelation 16:10 states that the kingdom of the beast "was full of darkness."

Darkness   1,500
Rev 16:10 εσκοτωμενη"

The Lamp

One of the minor problems encountered in writing this chapter and book was on how to divide, separate, and show the features. All of the topics relevant to light are so many and so interrelated that it sometimes poses the problem of which features should be shown with which others. The only thing that we could do was simply divide everything according to general headings and then place them in the best sequence possible.

Along with the many different references to light in the New Testament, there are a few verses which speak of "the lamp." The word *lamp* in Greek is different from the word *light*. In some translations it is translated as "light" and in others as "candle." Basically the meaning is the same, but since the passages referring to the lamp are somewhat different, they will shown under this heading.

To begin, here is one verse from Luke's gospel: "No one after lighting a lamp places it in a cellar or under a bushel, but on the lampstand, that those who enter may see the light." This complete verse, as we have just quoted it, is a multiple of 100, but here is how the first portion breaks down:

No one after lighting a lamp places it in a cellar 100×79
or under a bushel, but on the lampstand
Lk 11:33 ουδεις λυχνον αψας εις κρυπτην τιθησιν ουδε υπο τον μοδιον
      αλλ επι την λυχνιαν'

Lighting a lamp 100×21
Lk 11:33 λυχνον αψας"

Lamp 100×12
Lk 11:33 λυχνον

Place it under a bushel 100×18
Lk 11:33 τιθησιν υπο τον μοδιον'

The lampstand   1,500
Lk 11:33 την λυχνιαν'

Now the chance that in the above verse these features would all work out to being multiples of 100 is only 1 chance in 16,410. That's sixteen thousand, four hundred and ten.

This consistency exists everywhere in the passages related to light, darkness, and the other topics you are about to see presented. This brings us to something else that should be explained to the reader. Many times we will show a feature from one of the gospels, and sometimes the verse from which it was taken can also be found in some of the other gospels. The question naturally arises: Does the design work out there also? In almost every single instance we have encountered where there was a harmony of the gospels, the same design was found, even if the words were spelled differently in Greek.

Many times when two quotations from two gospels work out to the same number values, we will not mention it simply because an overdose of these facts would only slow down the flow of thought in the reader's mind.

To illustrate what we mean by a harmony of the gospels several examples will be given in reference to placing a light under a bushel. Not only did Jesus speak of this in the example we just saw (Luke 11:33), but also in Matthew and Mark. Each time the phrase is expressed in completely different Greek words.

Place it under a bushel or under the couch   100 × 22
Mk 4:21 υπο μοδιον τεθη η υπο την κλινην

Place it under a bushel   100 × 22
Mt 5:15 τιθεασιν αυτον υπο μοδιον

We reserved one of the more impressive quotations in the light design for now, because it occurs right after Matthew 5:15, from the above two features. Here it is:

Let your light so shine before men   100 × 104
Mt 5:16 ουτως λαμψατω το φως υμων εμπροσθεν των ανθρωπων'

Let your light so shine   100 × 68
Mt 5:16 ουτως λαμψατω το φως υμων"

Here is another one of those verses that is loaded with design: "If therefore your whole body is full of light, with no dark part in it, it shall be wholly illumined, as when the lamp illumines you with its rays." This passage contains five distinct features, all of which are clear in the Greek wording of the verse. The first clause gives us two features. Here is the first one:

If your whole body is full of light   100 × 41
Lk 11:36 ει το σωμα σου ολον φωτεινον'

Next it says: "With no dark part in it." The words "dark part" mean basically the same as the term *darkness*.

Dark part (or *Darkness*)   1,500
Lk 11:36 μερος τι σκοτεινον

The following clause of the verse reads: "It shall be illumined wholly, as when the lamp illumines you with its rays."

It shall be illumined   100 × 23
Lk 11:36 εσται φωτεινον'

As when the lamp illumines you with its rays   100 × 56
Lk 11:36 ως οταν λυχνος τη αστραπη φωτιζη σε'

And here is the word *illumine* by itself:

Illumine   1,000
Lk 11:36 τη αστραπη"

In the book of John, Jesus refers to John the baptist as:

The lamp burning and shining   100 × 34
Jn 5:35 ο λυχνος ο καιομενος και φαινων"

The last portion of the book of Revelation tells how the New Jerusalem will not need the light from the sun or the moon to shine on it for:

The lamp is the lamb   2,000
Rev 21:23 λυχνος το αρνιον'

The next feature is rather interesting, and you will quickly see the spiritual truth being brought out by the numbers: "Or what woman, if she has ten silver coins and loses one coin, does not light a lamp and sweep the house and search carefully until she finds it?" As it has been previously shown, the words *lamp* and *lighting a lamp* worked out to multiples of 100.

Search carefully   1,500
Lk 15:8 ζητει επιμελως

Our last feature under this heading is in no way related to the lamp topic, but we decided to show it at this time anyway. This feature is one of the most fascinating possible.

When the wise men came to see the baby Jesus, they first went to old King Herod. "When they had heard the king they went their way; and lo, the star which they had seen in the east went before them."

The star in the east   1,500
Mt 2:9 ο αστηρ εν τη ανατολη"

Eyes and Blindness

The thing which makes the theomatic design of God's word so overwhelming is that the evidence keeps piling up and piling up. If we were to show a small design here and then a small design over there, that would be one thing, but when each design covers the complete spectrum of a topic, and then relates directly to its subtopics, the whole issue becomes indisputable. As a result, God receives His due praise and glory, and our hearts are filled with joy.

The features from this category—eyes and blindness—will only serve to amplify the truths from the light, darkness, and lamp series we just looked at. We have already seen how *light* has a theomatic value of 1,500. Do you see any connection between light and this next feature?

Eyes 1,500
Acts 9:18 οφθαλμων

Both the words *light* and *eyes* have the theomatic value of 1,500. These next two verses from Matthew, chapter 6, will tell us why: "The lamp of the body is the eye; if therefore your eye is clear, your whole body will be full of light. But if your eye is evil, your whole body will be full of darkness. If therefore the light in you is darkness, how great the darkness." Since the lamp of the body is the eye, the first feature will consist of Christ's first words.

The lamp of the body 100 × 38
Mt 6:22 ο λυχνος του σωματος ́

The next words of Jesus are: "If therefore your eye is clear."

Clear eye 100 × 17
Mt 6:22 οφθαλμος απλους ́

Jesus said, if the eye is clear:

Your whole body will be full of light 100 × 46
Mt 6:22 ολον το σωμα σου φωτεινον εσται ̋

But the words "will be full of light" produce still further design.

Will be full of light 100 × 23
Mt 6:22 φωτεινον εσται ́

The next words Jesus spoke were: "But if your eye is evil, your whole body will be full of darkness."

Evil eye 1,500
Mt 6:23 οφθαλμος πονηρος ̋

Your whole body will be full of darkness   100 × 36
Mt 6:23 η ολον το σωμα σου σκοτεινον εσται

Without the word *whole* there is even further design.

Your body will be full of darkness   1,500 × 2
Mt 6:23 σωμα σου σκοτεινον εσται"

And to top the whole thing off, here are the Lord's last words: "If therefore the light in you is darkness, how great the darkness."

The light in you is darkness   4,000
Mt 6:23 το φως το εν σοι σκοτος εστιν

How great the darkness   100 × 17
Mt 6:23 το σκοτος ποσον

The same account can also be found in Luke 11:34–35. The same total consistency exists in this passage also, even though it is expressed in different words in Greek.

So far we have seen how God depicts everything related to light with clear numbers. Darkness is the exact opposite of light, and it also is depicted in the same clear numbers. *Light* has a theomatic value of 1,500, and *darkness* is also 1,500. Since the light of the body is the eye, then it was not surprising to find that *eyes* also worked out to 1,500. And what is the exact opposite of eyes or sight?

Blindness   1,500
Mt 15:14 τυφλος

Two verses that bear out this truth appear in Romans 11:8 and 11:10. Verse 8 says: "God gave them a spirit of stupor, eyes to see not and ears to hear not."

Eyes to see   1,500
Rom 11:8 οφθαλμους βλεπειν"

See not   1,000
Rom 11:8 του μη βλεπειν

Two verses later the text says: "Let their eyes be darkened to see not, and bend their backs forever."

Eyes darkened to see not   100 × 39
Rom 11:10 σκοτισθητωσαν οφθαλμοι του μη βλεπειν"

Darkened eyes 100 × 29
Rom 11:10 σκοτισθητωσαν οφθαλμοι"

John 10:21 refers simply to:

Blind eyes 100 × 34
Jn 10:21 τυφλων οφθαλμους

John 12:40 states: "He hath blinded their eyes, and hardened their heart."

Blinded the eyes 100 × 47
Jn 12:40 τετυφλωκεν τους οφθαλμους

Here is the most famous quote concerning blindness in the entire Bible. These two features came from different gospels, and each was spelled differently in Greek, but the number values are the same.

Blind leading the blind 1,500 × 2
Mt 15:14 τυφλος τυφλον εαν οδηγη'

Blind leading the blind 1,500 × 2
Lk 6:39 τυφλος τυφλον οδηγειν

The following verse from John 9:39 contains the same design: "And Jesus said, for judgment I came into this world, that those who do not see may see, and that those who see may become blind."

And that those who see may become blind 100 × 33
Jn 9:39 και βλεποντες τυφλοι γενωνται'

A cross reference to the above is found in Matthew, which says that the people have closed their eyes.

They have closed their eyes 100 × 46
Mt 13:15 τους οφθαλμους αυτων εκαμμυσαν"

Remember the verse from 1 John about the one walking in darkness because he hates his brother. Here is the complete verse, which will be followed by two features relevant to blindness: "But the one who hates his brother is in darkness and walks in darkness, and does not know where he is going, for the darkness has blinded the eyes of him."

For the darkness hath blinded the eyes 100 × 46
1 Jn 2:11 οτι η σκοτια ετυφλωσεν οφθαλμους'

The darkness hath blinded   100 × 29
1 Jn 2:11 η σκοτια ετυφλωσεν'

We shall now turn to those verses that speak of blind eyes being opened and of Jesus healing the eyes of the blind. To lead off this sequence, here is an outstanding feature from the gospel of John:

Opening the eyes of the blind so that he should not die   7,000
Jn 11:37 ο ανοιξας τους οφθαλμους του τυφλου ποιησαι ινα και ουτος μη αποθανη

Here are three features from two passages concerning the opening of blind eyes:

Open eyes of the blind   4,000
Jn 9:32 ηνεωξεν οφθαλμους τυφλου"

Open blind eyes   100 × 36
Jn 10:21 τυφλων οφθαλμους ανοιξαι"

Open   100 × 2
Jn 10:21 ανοιξαι"

After the two disciples from Immaus had followed Jesus and finally recognized Him, it says that:

Their eyes were opened   100 × 33
Lk 24:31 αυτων διηνοιχθησαν οφθαλμοι'

In Mark 8:25 there is a precious design contained in four explicit features. "Then again He laid His hands upon the eyes of him; and he looked steadily and was restored, and saw clearly all things."

Then again He laid His hands upon the eyes   1,500 × 2
Mk 8:25 ειτα παλιν επεθηκεν χειρας επι οφθαλμους

Hands upon the eyes   100 × 33
Mk 8:25 χειρας επι τους οφθαλμους'

The one Greek word preceding the above (επεθεκεν) is translated as "lay on" or "laid." Some translations of the Bible use the word *anoint.* This translation is much more beautiful and brings forth a spiritual meaning not found in the word *laid.*

We have already seen two features concerning the Lord placing His hands upon, or anointing, the eyes of the blind man. For a further confirmation of this truth, here are the two words *anoint* and *eyes*.

Anoint eyes   1,500
Mk 8:25 επεθηκεν οφθαλμους″

But notice what happened when Jesus anointed the eyes of the blind man.

He looked steadily and was restored and saw   100 × 42
clearly all things
Mk 8:25 διεβλεψεν και απεκατεστη και ενεβλεπεν τηλαυγως απαντα

One of the most precious stories in Scripture is how the blind man in John, chapter 9, received his sight. He tried every way he could to explain his healing to the scribes and Pharisees questioning him. The only way he could describe it was by the following words:

One thing I know, whereas once I was blind, now I see   100 × 42
Jn 9:25 εν οιδα οτι τυφλος ων αρτι βλεπω″

In order to conclude the blindness theme, three features will be shown from Luke 7:21–22.

And to many that were blind He gave sight   100 × 35
Lk 7:21 και τυφλοις πολλοις εχαρισατο βλεπειν

Many that were blind   2,000
Lk 7:21 τυφλοις πολλοις

Verse 22 says: "And He [Jesus] answered and said to them, 'Go and report to John what you have seen and heard: the blind receive sight, the lame walk.'"

Receive sight   100 × 9
Lk 7:22 αναβλεπουσιν′

Volumes alone would hardly begin to exhaust the theomatic design present in the Word of God. In preparing this book, we had to reject many outstanding features simply for lack of space. Also, we wanted to show only those designs which best fit into the sequence of thought being brought to the reader's attention.

Before moving on to the next aspect of this design, let's examine just a few more quotations concerning eyes. One of the best-known references to eyes is when Jesus talks about judging one another: "And why beholdest thou the mote that is in thy brother's eye, but perceivest not the beam that is in thine own eye?"

Thy brother's eye 5,000
Lk 6:41 τω οφθαλμω του αδελφου σου

Beam that is in thine own eye 4,000
Lk 6:41 δοκον την εν τω ιδιω οφθαλμω'

Both Matthew and Mark give an account of the following: "And if thine eye offend thee, pluck it out: it is better for thee to enter into the kingdom of God with one eye, than having two eyes to be cast into hell fire." The following two features are from different gospels, and they are spelled differently in Greek.

And if thine eye offends thee 150 × 15
Mt 18:9 και ει ο οφθαλμος σου σκανδαλιζει σε'

If thine eye offends thee 150 × 15
Mk 9:47 εαν ο οφθαλμος σου σκανδαλιζη σε"

Here is a reminder. At the very beginning of this chapter we mentioned that all of the features to be presented would be either multiples of 100 or work out to the number 2,250, which is 150 × 15. This number is extremely significant throughout the theomatic structure. Another example of it is found in Matthew 5:38. Here now is the most famous quotation in the Bible concerning eyes: "An eye for an eye, and a tooth for a tooth."

An eye for an eye 150 × 15
Mt 5:38 οφθαλμον αντι οφθαλμου'

Here is a well-known quotation from 2 Peter:

Eyes full of adultery 100 × 48
2 Pet 2:14 οφθαλμους εχοντες μεστους μοιχαλιδος

Paul tells us in Ephesians that slaves are to be obedient, "not by way of eyeservice as men-pleasers, but as slaves of Christ."

Not by way of eyeservice as men-pleasers 100 × 41
Eph 6:6 μη κατ οφθαλμοδουλιαν ως ανθρωπαρεσκοι

Colossians also states that slaves are to be obedient "not with eyeservice as men-pleasers."

With eyeservice   1,500
Col 3:22 εν οφθαλμοδουλιαις

In 1 John the apostle refers to Jesus as:

What we have seen with our eyes   100 × 35
1 Jn 1:1 ο εωρακαμεν τοις οφθαλμοις ημων

In Revelation the Lord's eyes are described in a little different manner.

Jesus in Revelation is found telling the Laodicea church to buy eyesalve, with which to anoint their eyes so they can see.

Eyesalve to anoint the eyes   4,000
Rev 3:18 κολλυριον εγχρισαι τους οφθαλμους'

Do you remember from a few pages ago the feature from Mark 8:25, where "anoint eyes" had a number value of 1,500. In this passage "anoint eyes" is spelled completely different in Greek, but look what happens:

Anoint eyes   150 × 15
Rev 3:18 εγχρισαι οφθαλμους'

After Jesus finished speaking in Matthew about the blindness of unbelievers, he turned to his disciples and said:

Blessed are your eyes because they see   100 × 35
Mt 13:16 υμων μακαριοι οφθαλμοι οτι βλεπουσιν'

Of all the features presented in this chapter, this one is the most precious, because it has to do with our Christian faith. We believe even though we do not see with our physical eyes.

Blessed are the ones not seeing and believing   100 × 28
Jn 20:29 μακαριοι οι μη ιδοντες και πιστευσαντες'

The next topic in this chapter is entitled "Power and the Coming of the Son of Man." In Matthew, chapter 24, when he speaks of Christ's second return, he says that "they will see the Son of Man coming on the clouds of heaven with power and great glory."

See 100 × 12
Mt 24:30 οψονται'

In Revelation it declares: "Behold, He is coming with clouds, and every eye will see Him."

Every eye 100 × 12
Rev 1:7 πας οφθαλμος'

Power and the Coming of the Son of Man

Have you ever heard someone say, "Turn on the power," when they wanted you to turn on the lights in a room? Of course, we all have. Light and power are inseparable. Webster's dictionary defines power in many different ways. It means having "great ability to do, act, or affect control over others; have authority." It is also described as meaning "physical force or energy, such as electric power."

Throughout the rest of this chapter, you are going to find another great truth revealed by these numbers. Everything to do with power, authority, rulership, thrones, dominions, lordship, and glory, all work out to multiples of these clear numbers. Light stands out and so does power; thus, God depicts both of them in the same manner.

Power 1,500
Lk 21:27 δυναμεως

There is probably no topic in Scripture that can better express this truth than the one which speaks of "the coming of the Son of Man," or as it is better known the second coming of Christ. Every single passage that speaks of the Son of Man coming is loaded with theomatic features, each of which will bring out the design in the Word of God. So, without further hesitation, let's begin by examining a few of the passages that will describe in a brand-new way the glorious and powerful second return of our Lord Jesus Christ.

The coming of the Son of Man is described and portrayed in Scripture by lightning, which lights up the sky from one end to the other. So, in the first feature to be examined, there will be a definite connection made with the term *light* as it relates to the coming of the Son of Man and power.

For as the lightning flashes and lights up the sky from   14,000
one end to the other, so will be the Son of Man in His day
Lk 17:24 ωσπερ γαρ αστραπη αστραπτουσα εκ της υπο τον ουρανον εις
          την υπ ουρανον λαμπει ουτως εσται υιος ανθρωπου εν τη
          ημερα αυτου

Lightning   100 × 7
Lk 17:24 η αστραπη"

There are approximately sixteen direct references in the New Testament to the coming of the Son of Man. Every single one, without exception, is absolutely loaded with multiples of 100. In each reference, the complete sentence worked out, and then portion after portion of that phrase also came out to clear multiples, including in almost every instance, all of the key words.

"And then will appear the sign of the Son of Man in heaven, and all the tribes of the earth will mourn, and they will see the Son of Man coming on the clouds of heaven with power and great glory."

Then will appear the sign of the Son of Man in heaven   6,000
Mt 24:30 τοτε φανησεται σημειον υιου ανθρωπου εν ουρανω'

They will see the Son of Man coming   5,000
Mt 24:30 οψονται υιον του ανθρωπου ερχομενον'

See   100 × 12
Mt 24:30 οψονται'

Son of Man coming   100 × 38
Mt 24:30 υιον του ανθρωπου ερχομενον'

This verse also tells us that the Son of Man is coming on the "clouds of heaven" with "power" and great glory.

Clouds of heaven   100 × 33
Mt 24:30 νεφελων του ουρανου'

Power   1,500
Mt 24:30 δυναμεως

Let us now connect the word *power* to the second return of Christ. 2 Peter refers to "the power and coming of our Lord Jesus Christ." The word *power* and the next feature both have theomatic values of 1,500.

Power and coming   1,500
2 Pet 1:16 δυναμιν και παρουσιαν″

The following feature is one of the most important in this entire design: "As were the days of Noah, so will be the coming of the Son of Man."

The coming of the Son of Man   100 × 48
Mt 24:37 η παρουσια του υιου του ανθρωπου

Here now is another feature with the same exact theomatic value as "the coming of the Son of Man." Matthew 25:31 states that "when the Son of Man comes in His glory, and all the angels with Him, then He will sit on His glorious throne."

When the Son of Man comes in His glory   100 × 48
Mt 25:31 οταν ελθη υιος του ανθρωπου εν δοξη αυτου′

In Matthew's gospel, there is another verse that brings out the same consistency:

Ye will see the Son of Man sitting on the right hand of   13,000
power and coming with the clouds of heaven
Mt 26:64 οψεσθε τον υιον του ανθρωπου καθημενον εκ δεξιων της δυ-
      ναμεως και ερχομενον επι των νεφελων του ουρανου′

Mark 8:38 states: "For whoever is ashamed of Me and My words in this adulterous and sinful generation, the Son of Man will also be ashamed of him when He comes in the glory of His Father with the holy angels."

When He comes in the glory of His Father with the holy angels   5,000
Mk 8:38 οταν ελθη εν τη δοξη πατρος αυτου μετα αγγελων αγιων″

When He comes in the glory of His Father   100 × 25
Mk 8:38 οταν ελθη εν τη δοξη του πατρος′

Glory of His Father   100 × 12
Mk 8:38 τη δοξη πατρος′

With the holy angels   100 × 21
Mk 8:38 μετα αγγελων αγιων″

There is tremendous significance to Christ's coming in a cloud or with the clouds of heaven, and many have speculated about what this means. Surely these must be more than just the everyday clouds we see in the sky. Some people have even proposed that these clouds might be some kind of UFOs, but all of this is just wild speculation. Theomatics throws light on what they might be, and this will be discussed in Chapter 8. Anyhow, the same design of power exists in these references to clouds, and the next feature will bear this out.

They will see the Son of Man coming   100 × 75
in a cloud with power
Lk 21:27 οψονται υιον του ανθρωπου ερχομενον εν νεφελη μετα δυναμεως

Let's see how this number 7,500 divides itself up.

They will see the Son of Man coming   5,000
Lk 21:27 οψονται υιον του ανθρωπου ερχομενον'

See   100 × 12
Lk 21:27 οψονται'

Son of Man coming   100 × 38
Lk 21:27 υιον του ανθρωπου ερχομενον

In a cloud with power   100 × 25
Lk 21:27 εν νεφελη μετα δυναμεως'

Cloud   100 × 6
Lk 21:27 νεφελη"

Power   1,500
Lk 21:27 δυναμεως

We have seen that "clouds of heaven" has a number value of 3,300, and the word *cloud* from the last feature had a value of 600. Mark 13:6 refers to "clouds" in the plural.

Clouds   100 × 8
Mk 13:26 νεφελαις'

In Luke, chapter 17, Jesus is found telling His disciples that as it was in the days of Noah, and in the days of Lot:

So it will be on the day the Son of Man is revealed   6,000
Lk 17:30 τα αυτα εσται ημερα ο υιος του ανθρωπου αποκαλυπτεται'

Revealed 100 × 13
Lk 17:30 αποκαλυπτεται

In Luke 18:18 we find these words:

When the Son of Man comes, will He find faith on the earth 6,000
Lk 18:8 υιος του ανθρωπου ελθων αρα ευρησει την πιστιν επι γης"

The following parable in Luke produces an outstanding feature: "But and if that servant says to himself, 'My lord delayeth his coming'; and shall begin to beat the menservants and maidens, and to eat and drink, and to be drunken; the lord of that servant will come in a day when he looketh not for him, and at an hour when he is not aware, and shall cut him in sunder."

That servant says to himself, 'My lord delayeth his coming' 6,000
Lk 12:45 ειπη δουλος εκεινος εν τη καρδια αυτου χρονιζει κυριος μου ερχεσθαι'

From 2 Thessalonians, chapter 1, come the following words: "And to give relief to you who are afflicted and to us as well when the Lord Jesus shall be revealed from heaven." This passage, like all others, is loaded with theomatic design. Here then are its most distinct words:

When the Lord Jesus shall be revealed from heaven 5,000
2 Thess 1:7 εν αποκαλυψει του κυριου Ιησου απ ουρανου"

Here are the words from Philippians 3:20: "For our citizenship is in heaven, from where also a savior we await, the Lord Jesus Christ."

Also a savior we await, the Lord Jesus Christ 5,000
Phil 3:20 και σωτηρα απεκδεχομεθα κυριον Ιησουν Χριστον"

And from 2 Peter, chapter 3, come these words: "Knowing this first of all, that in the last days mockers will come with their mocking, following after their own lusts, and saying, 'Where is the promise of His coming?' "

Where is the promise of His coming 4,000
2 Pet 3:4 που εστιν η επαγγελια της παρουσιας αυτου"

2 Timothy 1:10 refers to the:

Appearing of Jesus Christ 4,000
2 Tim 1:10 επιφανειας του Χριστου Ιησου

If there is any feature that should work out, this is the one. Nothing could be more outstanding than the following:

The coming of the Lord Jesus Christ 5,000
1 Thess 5:23 παρουσια του κυριου Ιησου Χριστου

At this time we would like to slow the pace down a little, in order to open things up for discussion. Our purpose in writing this book has been twofold. The first thing we are endeavoring to accomplish is to prove beyond doubt that God has unequivocally written His entire Word mathematically—through the number, or theomatic, values of the Hebrew and Greek languages; and that in the last days this may be one of the means used by God to help unlock the true meaning of Scripture.

Second, in making this truth known, it will give all of God's people a common cause to rejoice and as a result be more united in their views. This will provide a solid front to the world and be testimony of Christ's resurrection. Only the people of God, who have spiritual discernment, will understand the significance of these numbers. To the ungodly they will have no meaning. All Scripture, particularly the book of Revelation, has been locked up in symbolism. But now God has provided a means whereby His Word can be better understood.

It was with mixed emotions that Jerry and Del began writing this book some months ago. This subject is so vast that to do it justice would require years of research by many people along with the use of a large computer system. Steps are already being made in this direction. The theomatical structure of the Bible is as complex as the universe. In fact, it is inexhaustible. Even though the designs presented herein are outstanding, much more remains to be found. When we decided to go ahead and write this book, we asked the Lord how He would have us present this truth to His body, and what approach should be taken in proving the theomatic design in the Word of God.

The answer came back loud and clear. The first thing that would have to be done was to prove that *it is there, that theomatics exists!* This book would have to be a John-the-baptist book, a forerunner of all that was to come about from the disclosure of this truth. What did this mean?

The first and one thing of utmost importance was the fact that in this book the designs presented would have to show a consistency. Let us explain this another way. Suppose that in one of the passages pertaining to light, there appeared a feature that was a multiple of a certain number, but over in another passage of Scripture related to light, there existed another design. How many people would accept our theory if we showed a different design for every passage? Not many, and rightly so. So the crucial issue at hand was that a consistency would have to be shown, flowing through the many passages related to a particular topic. Thanks be to God that He has provided His people with this kind of evidence.

For this reason, our book is limited to approximately half a dozen designs, each of which will provide the reader with overwhelming consistency. All of these designs are building toward one thing, and one thing only—the last chapter, dealing with the science of statistics and probability. It is here that the whole issue will be decided once and for all.

Power and Authority

In the Greek language there are two words that mean *power:* δυναμις and εξουσια. As a general rule, δυναμις is translated as *power* and εξουσια as *authority*, but these meanings are interchangeable. The various translations take their own liberty on these two words, so we will do likewise. Power means authority, and authority means power.

In going through the New Testament, we discovered that the two Greek words for *authority* and *power* occurred a total of 213 times.[1] We also discovered that practically every one of these references was a multiple of 100 or 150 × 15, *i.e.*, 2,250. For obvious and practical reasons, it would be impossible to show all of them, so in order to give the reader a sampling of the consistency that exists throughout these passages, we will take from the New Testament the first five passages using the word *authority* (εξουσια) and the first five passages using the word *power* (δυναμις).

The first passage using the word *authority* is found in Matthew 7:29: "For He taught them as one having authority, and not as the scribes."

For He taught as one having authority 1,500 × 3
Mt 7:29 ην γαρ διδασκων ως εξουσιαν εχων"

[1]Moulton and Geden, *Concordance to the Greek Testament* (Edinburgh, Ltd.: T. & T. Clark).

Having authority   150 × 15
Mt 7:29 εξουσιαν εχων'

The second passage using the word *authority* comes from Matthew 8:9. Here the two words used for "having authority" are the same as in the last passage: εξουσιαν εχων.

Having authority   150 × 15
Mt 8:9 εξουσιαν εχων'

The third feature is self-explanatory.

For the Son of Man has authority on earth to forgive sins   100 × 68
Mt 9:6 οτι εξουσιαν εχει υιος του ανθρωπου επι της γης αφιεναι αμαρτιας

Authority on earth   100 × 11
Mt 9:6 εξουσιαν επι γης"

The fourth feature is from verse 8 of the same chapter: "But when the multitudes saw this, they were filled with awe, and glorified God, Who had given such authority unto men."

Given such authority unto men   100 × 41
Mt 9:8 τον δοντα εξουσιαν τοιαυτην ανθρωποις

The verse for the fifth feature contains several distinct multiples of 100. We will limit ourselves to just the first portion of the verse: "And He called forth His twelve disciples, and gave them authority over unclean spirits."

And He called forth His twelve disciples   100 × 73
and gave them authority
Mt 10:1 και προσκαλεσαμενος τους δωδεκα μαθητας αυτου εδωκεν
αυτοις εξουσιαν"

The first feature using the word *power* is found in verse 22 of Matthew 7: "Lord, Lord, did we not prophecy in Your name, and cast out demons in Your name, and do many powerful works in Your name?"

Powerful works in Your name   150 × 15
Mt 7:22 σω ονοματι δυναμεις'

The second, third, and fourth features using the word *power* all come from three verses in chapter 11 of Matthew. Here is verse 20: "Then He began to reproach the cities in which were done the many powerful deeds of Him, because they did not repent."

Were done the many powerful deeds   100 × 19
Mt 11:20 εγενοντο πλεισται δυναμεις´

Verse 21, which follows, says: "Woe to you, Chorazin! woe to you, Bethsaida! for if the powerful works done in you had been done in Tyre and Sidon, they would have repented long ago in sackcloth and ashes."

Powerful works done in you   1,500
Mt 11:21 δυναμεις γενομεναι εν υμιν´

Two verses later power is mentioned again: "And you, Capernaum, will you be exalted in heaven? You shall be brought down to hades. For if the powerful works done in you had been done in Sodom, it would have remained until this day."

Powerful works done in you   100 × 13
Mt 11:23 αι δυναμεις αι γενομεναι εν σοι´

The fifth and last feature to be presented is found in Matthew 13:54: "And coming to His own country He taught them in their synagogue, so that they were astonished, and said, 'Where did this man get His wisdom and powerful works?' "

His wisdom and powerful works   150 × 15
Mt 13:54 η σοφια αυτη και αι δυναμεις

POWER OF THE HOLY SPIRIT

Many times in Scripture the Holy Spirit is described as being powerful in function and effect. Those passages that speak of the power of the spirit show an amazing theomatic design. One such passage is found in The Acts 4:31:

They were all filled with the Holy Spirit   1,500 × 4
and spoke the Word of God with boldness
Acts 4:31 επλησθησαν απαντες του αγιου πνευματος και ελαλουν
λογον Θεου μετα παρρησιας´´

Boldness   100 × 7
Acts 4:31 παρρησιας

These next two are undoubtedly two of the most outstanding features in this chapter. We think you will agree. "And behold, I am sending forth the promise of the Father upon you; but you are to stay in the city until you are clothed with power from on high."

Clothed with power   1,500
Lk 24:49 ενδυσησθε εξ δυναμιν'

From The Acts 1:8 comes: "Ye will receive power after the Holy Spirit is come upon you."

Ye will receive power after the Holy Spirit is come   4,000
Acts 1:8 λημψεσθε δυναμιν επελθοντος αγιου πνευματος'

Since the Holy Spirit bespeaks power, then it is not surprising to find that it is divisible by 100. In compiling our research, we discovered that "spirit of God" had the same theomatic value.

Holy Spirit   100 × 24
Acts 1:8 του αγιου πνευματος

Spirit of God   100 × 24
1 Cor 2:14 πνευματος του Θεου

POWER OF SATAN

The Bible teaches that Satan is powerful, but not all-powerful. It was on the cross of Calvary that Christ defeated His foe and took over his position of authority. Satan will be allowed to exercise his power on a limited basis, at least until the day of judgment when he is to be bound and cast into the bottomless pit.

When the devil took Jesus up on a high mountain and showed Him all the kingdoms of the world and their glory, the Lord did not deny the fact that these powers had been given and delivered into Satan's hand. "And the devil said to Him, 'I will give You all this power and its glory; for to me it has been been delivered, and I give it to whomever I will. If You, then, will worship me, it shall all be yours.'" The first clause, after the opening statement in this verse, contains several features of 100. Here is one of them:

Power I will give   100 × 26
Lk 4:6 δωσω εξουσιαν

The concluding portion of verse 6 along with verse 7 produces an absolutely phenomenal design that is loaded with spiritual truth. Here it is, right out of the text:

For to me it has been delivered, and I give it to whomever I   10,000
will. If You, then, will worship me, it shall all be yours
Lk 4:6–7 οτι εμοι παραδεδοται και ω εαν θελω διδωμι αυτην συ ουν εαν
προσκυνησης ενωπιον εμου εσται σου πασα'

But Jesus replied to Satan in verse 12 by saying:

Thou shalt not tempt the Lord thy God   1,500 × 2
Lk 4:12 ουκ εκπειρασεις κυριον τον Θεον σου

In the first portion of this chapter, we mentioned that the key words, as a rule, always work out, thereby setting the stage for the consistency that follows. *Light* is 1,500, *darkness* 1,500, *eyes* 1,500, *blindness* 1,500, *power* 1,500, and now:

Power of Satan   1,500
Acts 26:18 εξουσιας σατανα'

There is even further truth in the book of Revelation. Here Satan is called "the prince of the power of the air." We were rather surprised to see how the following two features divided themselves up:

Prince of the air   1,500
Eph 2:2 αρχοντα αερος"

Power of the air   100 × 26
Eph 2:2 της ενοξσιας του αερος

Because Satan is the prince of the power of the air, the following passage has perfect meaning. Here are the words from Ephesians 3:10: "In order that the manifold wisdom of God might now be made known through the church to the principalities and powers in the heavenlies."

Principalities and powers   100 × 19
Eph 3:10 αρχαις και εξουσιαις'

Powers in the heavenlies   100 × 31
Eph 3:10 ταις εξουσιαις εν τοις επουρανιοις"

One of the Scriptures that speaks of Satan's power is found in Luke's gospel: "Behold, I have given you authority to tread upon serpents and scorpions, and over all the power of the enemy."

Authority to tread upon serpents and scorpions, 100 × 87
and over all the power of the enemy
Lk 10:19 εξουσιαν του πατειν επανω οφεων και σκορπιων και επι πασαν δυναμιν του εχθρου'

All the power of the enemy 100 × 32
Lk 10:19 την πασαν δυναμιν του εχθρου'

When Jesus was crucified, it was our sins that nailed Him to the tree. The powerful forces of evil were also instrumental in bringing about Christ's death on the cross. Theomatics brings out another great truth in the book of John, when Jesus stands before Pilate the governor. In verse 10 of chapter 19, Pilate said to Jesus:

Knowest Thou not that I have power to release 100 × 88
You, and power to crucify You
Jn 19:10 ουκ οιδας οτι εξουσιαν εχω απολυσαι σε και εξουσιαν εχω σταυρωσαι σε"

I have power 100 × 22
Jn 19:10 εξουσιαν εχω'

Even though Pilate claimed to be innocent in passing sentence on Christ, he was still an instrument of Satan. Before the crucifixion, the text says that the scribes and chief priests sent out spies, who pretended to be sincere, "that they might take hold of what He said, so as to deliver Him up to the rule and power of the governor."

Rule and power of the governor 100 × 27
Lk 20:20 αρχη και εξουσια του ηγεμονος"

Power of the governor 1,500
Lk 20:20 τη εξουσια ηγεμονος

POWER OF GOD

So far in this chapter we have shown how exact opposites work out to the same theomatic values. *Light* is 1,500, *darkness* 1,500, *blindness* 1,500, *power* 1,500, *power of Satan* 1,500. We would expect "power of God" to be 1,500, since it is the exact opposite of "power of Satan." But guess what? It isn't. "Power of God" works out to the number 2,000.

Power of God   2,000
Rom 13:2 εξουσια του Θεου

And in 2 Corinthians 4:7, these words are found:

Power belongs to God   100 × 25
2 Cor 4:7 της δυναμεως η Θεου

In The Acts 8:10 we find the words:

Power of God called great   100 × 19
Acts 8:10 δυναμις Θεου καλουμενη μεγαλη

Here is a verse with which everyone is familiar:

The gospel is the power of God   100 × 27
Rom 1:16 το ευαγγελιον δυναμις Θεου εστιν'

Paul, in Ephesians, chapter 3, states that he was "a minister, according to the gift of God's grace, which was given to me according to the operation of His power."

Operation of His power   100 × 29
Eph 3:7 ενεργειαν δυναμεως αυτου

From the first chapter of Ephesians, there comes another one of those verses that is loaded with design: "the unexcelling greatness of His power in us who believe, according to the operation of the might of His strength." This complete verse, as it was just quoted, has a number value of 12,500. Here then is how it divides itself up:

The unexcelling greatness of His power in us who believe   100 × 77
Eph 1:19 το υπερβαλλον μεγεθος της δυναμεως αυτου εις ημας τους
πιστευοντας'

Unexcelling greatness of power   100 × 26
Eph 1:19 υπερβαλλον μεγεθος δυναμεως

Unexcelling greatness   100 × 11
Eph 1:19 υπερβαλλον μεγεθος

And here is the second phrase from this verse:

According to the operation of the might of His strength   100 × 48
Eph 1:19 κατα ενεργειαν κρατους της ισχυος αυτου'

According to the operation of might   2,000
Eph 1:19 κατα την ενεργειαν κρατους

The operation of the might of His strength   100 × 51
Eph 1:19 την ενεργειαν του κρατους ισχυος αυτου'

Operation of the might of strength   100 × 28
Eph 1:19 ενεργειαν κρατους ισχυος

All Christians should do the following:

Be ye empowered in the Lord and in the strength   100 × 74
of His might
Eph 6:10 ενδυναμουσθε εν κυριω και εν τω κρατει της ισχυος αυτου

Here now are two more features that show the same design:

Everlasting power   1,000
Rom 1:20 αιδιος δυναμις

Signs and wonders   1,000
Acts 6:8 τερατα και σημεια"

In relation to the subject of power and authority, there is one verse in Revelation that demonstrates an amazing truth as it pertains to the design in this chapter. In speaking to the seven churches, Jesus said: "And to the one overcoming, and keeping My words until the end, to him I will give power over the nations."

The one overcoming   1,000
Rev 2:26 ο νικων

I will give him power   100 × 41
Rev 2:26 δωσω αυτω εξουσιαν'

Almost all of the key numbers to be presented in this book can be found somewhere in the text of the Word of God. The number 153, from the last chapter, is a perfect example of this. The book of Jude, verse 14, states that Christ is coming with 10,000 of His saints. Obviously, the number has to be symbolic, since there will be more than 10,000 people in heaven. The number 10,000 indicates that the saints will be coming in power to reign with Christ. A feature that brings out this truth is found in Revelation 22:5: "And there shall no longer be any night; and they shall not have need of the light of a lamp nor the light of the sun, because . . ."

The Lord God will shed light on them, and they   10,000
shall reign for ever and ever
Rev 22:5 κυριος ο Θεος φωτισει επ αυτους και βασιλευσουσιν εις τους
    αιωνας αιωνων"

Probably the most popular reference to a clear number is where Christ is described as having a hundred sheep. This number shows ordinal perfection, and the number, or theomatic, value of "one hundred sheep" is 1,000, which is also $10 \times 10 \times 10$.

One hundred sheep   1,000
Mt 18:12 εκατον προβατα

Glory of God

The definition of the word *glory* is "to give great honor, to worship, give adoration and praise, to have splendor, to be exalted to the highest degree." Perhaps no other term can best describe God as the word *glory*. The same design that exists in the verses related to power can also be found in the passages that speak of God's glory.

Glory of God   1,500
Rev 21:23 η γαρ δοξα του Θεου'

Glory to God   1,000
Lk 17:18 δοξαν Θεω'

Glorify God 100×9
Rom 15:9 δοξασαι τον Θεον

Father of glory 100×9
Eph 1:17 ο πατηρ δοξης'

The glory of the Father 100×12
Mt 16:27 τη δοξη πατρος'

In John, chapter 17, Jesus refers to the glory that the Father has given Him.

My glory, which Thou hast given Me   1,500
Jn 17:24 δοξαν εμην ην δεδωκας μοι'

Multiples of 100 proliferate throughout the references to glory in the New Testament. Here are a few of those references:

Heavenly glory   100 × 17
1 Cor 15:40 επουρανιων δοξα'

Unfading crown of glory   100 × 27
1 Pet 5:4 αμαραντινον της δοξης στεφανον'

His kingdom and glory   100 × 17
1 Thess 2:12 εαυτου βασιλειαν και δοξαν'

When His glory is revealed   100 × 37
1 Pet 4:13 εν τη αποκαλυψει της δοξης αυτου'

The eternal glory in Christ   100 × 36
1 Pet 5:10 την αιωνιον δοξαν εν Χριστω'

Glory of Christ   100 × 33
2 Cor 4:4 της δοξης του Χριστου'

The word *riches* ties in perfectly with *glory*, as in the following phrases:

Riches in glory in Christ Jesus   100 × 41
Phil 4:19 πλουτος εν δοξη εν Χριστω Ιησου

Riches of glory   2,000
Eph 3:16 πλουτος της δοξης

Riches   1,000
Rev 5:12 πλουτον

Riches of Christ   100 × 36
Eph 3:8 πλουτος του Χριστου

For this next feature, let's tie together the two words *glory* and *power*:

Glory of His power   100 × 35
2 Thess 1:9 δοξης της ισχυος αυτου'

Here now are eight outstanding features which will conclude this chapter. May the Lord bless them to your heart.

Lord   1,000
Lk 5:17 κυριου

Lord of glory   1,500
1 Cor 2:8 κυριον της δοξης

Name of the Lord   2,000
1 Cor 1:2 ονομα του κυριου'

Name of Jesus   2,000
Acts 5:40 ονοματι του Ιησου'

Name of the Lord Jesus   3,000
1 Cor 5:4 ονοματι του κυριου Ιησου'

And the name of the Lord Jesus was magnified   4,000
Acts 19:17 και εμεγαλυνετο το ονομα του κυριου Ιησου'

To Him be the glory for ever and ever, amen   5,000
Rom 16:27 ω η δοξα εις τους αιωνας αιωνων αμην

And He shall reign for ever and ever   6,000
Rev 11:15 και βασιλευσει εις τους αιωνας των αιωνων"

6

The Satanic Kingdom

Of all the chapters to be presented in this book this one is by far the most important. We will explain why shortly.

The theomatic value of the name *Satan* is as follows:

Satan   276 × 2
Mt 16:23 Σατανα'

In 1 John 5:19, Satan is referred to as:

The evil one   276 × 8
1 Jn 5:19 τω πονηρω

Here now is one of the most famous quotations of all concerning Satan to be found in the entire Bible:

The prince of the power of the air   276 × 15
Eph 2:2 τον αρχοντα της εξουσιας του αερος"

In the book of Revelation Satan is called:

The accuser of our brethren   276 × 13
Rev 12:10 ο κατηγωρ αδελφων ημων"

In various passages of Scripture, the scribes and Pharisees accused Jesus of casting out demons by Beelzebub. But in Matthew 12:28 Jesus replied to his accusers by saying: "And if I cast out demons by Beelzebub, by whom do your sons cast them out?"

Cast out demons by Beelzebub   276 × 6
Mt 12:27 εν Βεεζεβουλ εκβαλλω δαιμονια'

Then in Luke 11:15, the scribes and Pharisees accused Jesus again:

He casts out demons by Beelzebub, the ruler   276 × 11
of the demons
Lk 11:15 εν Βεεζεβουλ αρχοντι δαιμονιων εκβαλλει δαιμονια

When we take the most specific portions from the above, the following will result. "Beelzebub, the ruler of the demons" shows the following design:

Beelzebub, the ruler   276 × 6
Lk 11:15 Βεεζεβουλ αρχοντι'

The ruler of the demons   276 × 16
Lk 11:15 τω αρχοντι των δαιμονιων

We personally consider this next feature to be one of the most important possible—after the very name of Satan himself. All through the book of Revelation there are references to:

The dragon   276 × 6
Rev 13:4 τω δρακοντι'

The book of Revelation also states: "They have as king over them the angel of the bottomless pit; his name in Hebrew is Abaddon, and in Greek he has the name Apollyon." Interestingly enough, the translators have completely switched around the arrangement of the words in this passage. Here is how it appears in the original text:

A king, the angel of the bottomless pit, whose name   276 × 30
in Hebrew is Abaddon, and in Greek he has the name Apollyon
Rev 9:11 βασιλεα αγγελον της αβυσσου ονομα αυτω Εβραιστι Αβαδδων και εν τη Ελληνικη ονομα εχει Απολλυων'

Three times in the New Testament the text mentions the "ruler of this world." All three phrases are divisible by the number 276. In John 14:30 Jesus said: "I will not speak much more with you, for the ruler of this world is coming, and he has nothing in Me."

The ruler of this world is coming   276 × 15
Jn 14:30 ερχεται του κοσμου αρχων"

In John 16:10–11 Jesus said the following: "And concerning right-eousness, because I go to the Father, and you no longer behold Me;

and concerning judgment, because the ruler of this world has been judged."

Concerning judgment, because the ruler of this   276 × 22
world has been judged
Jn 16:11 περι δε κρισεως οτι ο αρχων κοσμου τουτου κεκριται"

The best one is the last one: "Now judgment is upon this world; now is the ruler of this world cast out."

Now is the ruler of this world cast out   276 × 24
Jn 12:31 νυν αρχων του κοσμου τουτου εκβληθησεται εξω

John, chapter 8, contains a line that is loaded with meaning: "When he speaketh a lie, he speaks according to his own nature, for he is a liar, and the father of lies." The Greek word for *lie* (ψευδος) means "an intentional or deliberate falsehood," in a broad sense, "whatever is not what it professes to be."

Lie   276 × 5
Jn 8:44 ψευδος'

Here is the last part of this verse:

He is a liar and the father of lies   276 × 15
Jn 8:44 ψευστης εστιν και ο πατηρ αυτου'

One of the better known verses concerning Satan is found in 1 Peter: "Your adversary the devil goes about as a lion seeking whom he may devour." Two distinct features are present in these words. Here they are:

Your adversary the devil goes about as a roaring lion   276 × 24
1 Pet 5:8 ο αντιδικος υμων διαβολος ως λεων ωρυομενος περιπατει'

Your adversary the devil goes about as a   276 × 31
roaring lion, seeking whom he may devour
1 Pet 5:8 αντιδικος υμων διαβολος ως λεων ωρυομενος περιπατει ζητων
        τινα καταπιειν

In Luke 10:18 Jesus said: "I beheld Satan fall from heaven as lightning."

I beheld Satan fall from heaven   276 × 14
Lk 10:18 εθεωρουν σαταναν εκ ουρανου πεσοντα

And now, from the Old Testament, from the book of Isaiah, comes what has to be the most famous and outstanding quotation in the entire Bible concerning Satan.

How art thou fallen from heaven, oh Lucifer,   276 × 6
son of the morning
Is 14:12 איך נפלת משמים הילל בן שחר

At this point you are probably asking yourself the question, Why the number 276? Before finishing this chapter, you will see one of the most revealing designs to be found in the Word of God. This chapter on the satanic kingdom is the most important chapter in this entire book in one respect. Here's the reason why.

In the third chapter on Jesus, we showed how everything to do with Jesus worked out to multiples of 111, with a few of the features only being divisible by 37. Chapter 4 demonstrated that the number 153 was quite prominent. And in the last chapter, the features for the most part were divisible by 100. But now the number being presented is 276. The reason it is the most important is that it unequivocally proves the existence of the theomatic design in the Word of God. A number as large as 276 presents a very low and unlikely probability of occurring by chance. In fact, any one of these features has an extremely low chance of even happening at all, much less all of them working out.

Furthermore, the consistency in this chapter is overwhelming. The consistency along with the size of the number 276 is what makes this chapter so impressive. Earlier, in Chapter 4, we showed how a person could disprove theomatics by making a random assignment of number values to the letters of the Greek alphabet and then building designs equal to those that we have been able to produce. To try and do this with any design in this book is totally impossible. To try and do it with a number the size of 276 is so totally impossible that it is ludicrous. We have tried it ourselves, and our calculations will be in the last chapter, on the science of statistics and probability. No other number values for the letters can produce these theomatic designs except those that God placed in the papyrus. Praise the Lord!

We shall now turn and focus our attention on a few general references to Satan. One of the best known is where Jesus makes the statement:

And if Satan also is divided against himself,   276 × 22
how shall his kingdom stand
Lk 11:18 ει δε και Σατανας εφ εαυτον διεμερισθη πως σταθησεται
      βασιλεια αυτου"

One of the most famous verses that speaks of Satan's kingdom is
found in Luke 10:19: "Behold I have given you authority to tread on
serpents and scorpions, and over all the power of the enemy."

Serpents and scorpions and all the power of the enemy   276 × 19
Lk 10:19 οφεων και σκορπιων και πασαν την δυναμιν εχθρου"

When Jesus rebuked Simon Peter, he said the following words:

Get thee behind Me, Satan: for thou savorest not the   276 × 29
things that be of God, but the things that be of men
Mk 8:33 υπαγε οπισω μου Σατανα οτι ου φρονεις του Θεου αλλα τα
      ανθρωπων

2 Thessalonians 2:9 speaks about the antichrist coming "according
to the operation of Satan, with all power and signs and wonders of a
lie."

According to the operation of Satan   276 × 4
2 Thess 2:9 και ενεργειαν Σατανα'

Paul said in 1 Timothy that "some have already turned aside to
follow Satan."

Follow Satan   276 × 9
1 Tim 5:15 οπισω του Σατανα'

In 2 Corinthians 11:14 we find the following words:

Satan transforms himself into an angel of light   276 × 21
2 Cor 11:14 αυτος Σατανας μετασχηματιζεται εις αγγελον φωτος"'[1]

One of the best-known passages concerning Satan is when he
tempts Christ in the wilderness for forty days.

And He was in the wilderness forty days being   276 × 20
tempted by Satan
Mk 1:13 και ην εν τη ερημω τεσσερακοντα ημερας πειραζομενος υπο
     του Σατανα"

[1]See footnote on p. 149.

In Matthew, chapter 4, the same account appears again, only in different words:

Then Jesus was led up by the spirit into   276 × 29
the wilderness to be tempted by the devil
Mt 4:1 τοτε ο Ιησους ανηχθη εις την ερημον υπο του πνευματος
     πειρασθηναι υπο του διαβολου″

A verse that ties in perfectly with resisting Satan is found in Ephesians 6:11: "Put ye on the whole armor of God that ye may be able to stand against the craftiness of the devil."

Against the craftiness of the devil   276 × 5
Eph 6:11 προς μεθοδειας διαβολου′

Connect this next feature with the last one we looked at: "Above all, taking the shield of faith, by which ye will be able to quench all the fiery darts of the evil one."

All the fiery darts of the evil one   276 × 13
Eph 6:16 παντα βελη του πονηρου πεπυρωμενα″

But praise God! The fiery darts of the evil one have no effect on us who know Jesus, and the words from 1 John 5:18 tell why: "We know that everyone born of God does not sin, but He Who was born of God keeps him, and the evil one does not touch him."

The evil one does not touch him   276 × 13
1 Jn 5:18 ο πονηρος ουχ απτεται αυτου″

In Ephesians Paul said:

Give no opportunity to the devil   276 × 11
Eph 4:27 μηδε διδοτε τοπον τω διαβολω′

In James 4:7 we find these words:

Be subject to God and resist the devil   276 × 34
and he will flee from you
Jas 4:7 υποταγητε τω Θεω αντιστητε δε τω διαβολω και φευξεται αφ
     υμων

This feature needs special comment. When we first found this feature, it puzzled us as to why the first portion in this phrase worked out to 276. Why would the words "be subject to God" be contained in this feature? Then we realized why. Being subject to God is the power that enables us to resist the devil so that he will flee. This phrase is one complete thought, and for this reason it works out to 276.

This next passage from Revelation is quite familiar to almost everyone:

The devil who had deceived them was thrown   276 × 20
into the lake of fire and sulfur
Rev 20:10 ο διαβολος ο πλανων αυτους εβληθη εις λιμνην του πυρος και
         θειου'

We think that the following is one of the best features in this series: "Those by the wayside are they that hear; then cometh the devil, and taketh away the word out of their hearts, lest they should believe and be saved."

Then cometh the devil, and taketh away   276 × 15
the word out of their hearts
Lk 8:12 ειτα ερχεται διαβολος και αιρει λογον απο καρδιας αυτων"

1 John 3:8 tell us that:

The one doing sin is of the devil;   276 × 21
for the devil has sinned from the beginning
1 Jn 3:8 ποιων αμαρτιαν εκ του διαβολου εστιν οτι απ αρχης ο διαβολος
         αμαρτανει'

But now look at the first portion of this verse, and watch what happens!

The one doing sin is of the devil   276 × 20
1 Jn 3:8 ο ποιων αμαρτιαν εκ διαβολου εστιν

Do you remember from the last chapter the feature that said: "Out of darkness into light?" The Greek word εκ means "out of" or "of" something. This word is extremely significant, and here it is from the verse above:

Of the devil   276 × 5
1 Jn 3:8 εκ του διαβολου"

There is one other multiple of 276 present in a feature found in 2 Corinthians 4:4. Here the text is referring to those whom the god of this age has blinded: "But if our gospel be hid, it is hid to them that are lost: in whom the god of this age has blinded the minds of them which believe not."

The god of this age has blinded 276 × 19
2 Cor 4:4 θεος αιωνος τουτου ετυφλωσεν'

The significance of these words in Greek is outstanding, for it is Satan who blinds the minds of those that are lost. This is why these words work out to multiples of 276.

If we take another portion of this verse, there is an even further design. This verse states that "the god of this age has blinded the minds of them which believe not":

Blinded the minds 276 × 10
2 Cor 4:4 ετυφλωσεν νοηματα

One of the more remarkable designs in the Bible with the number 276 occurs when the disciples come to Jesus and ask Him to explain the meaning of the parable He had just spoken to them: "Then He left the crowds and went into the house. And His disciples came to Him, saying, 'Explain to us the parable of the tares of the field.' "

The parable of the tares of the field 276 × 8
Mt 13:36 την παραβολην ζιζανιων αγρου'

Two verses later Jesus said:

The tares are the sons of the evil one 276 × 7
Mt 13:38 τα ζιζανια εισιν υιοι πονηρου"

The next verse says:

And the enemy sowing them is the devil 276 × 12
Mt 13:39 ο δε εχθρος σπειρας αυτα εστιν διαβολος'

This parable contains many features that are multiples of 276. Some will be shown later on in this chapter, but for now we will confine our attention to two more.

Back in verse 26, when Jesus had originally given the parable, the text states that when the grass sprouted,

Then also appeared the tares 276 × 6
Mt 13:26 τοτε εφανη και τα ζιζανια'

Two verses later after the servants told the master about what had happened, the master said:

An enemy has done this   276 × 14
Mt 13:28 εχθρος ανθρωπος τουτο εποιησεν"

The Dragon

One of the more important designs that speak of Satan is found in the book of Revelation, where Satan is called "the dragon." The dragon is mentioned twelve times in Revelation, and the design is overwhelming. The interesting fact is that the only place where Satan is called the dragon is in the book of Revelation. Because this one design is so revealing, we decided to place it under a separate heading.

As you will recall, "the dragon" by itself is 276 × 6.

The dragon   276 × 6
Rev 13:4 τω δρακοντι'

Revelation 12:7 states that Michael and his angels made war "with the dragon."

With the dragon   276 × 7
Rev 12:7 μετα του δρακοντος'

Next we shall look at one of those verses that is full of theomatic design. First of all, here is the complete verse:

The dragon was cast down, the great serpent of old   276 × 19
who is called the devil and Satan
Rev 12:9 εβληθη ο δρακων ο μεγας οφις αρχαιος καλυμενυς διαβολος
    και Σατανας'

In all of the English translations this passage reads "the great dragon was cast down, the serpent of old" instead of "the dragon was cast down, the great serpent of old." In the original Greek text, the words are arranged in such a manner that either two of these readings is possible. Everything fits together perfectly in theomatics when the latter is used.

Here now is one more distinct feature from within this verse:

The great serpent of old who is called the devil and Satan   276 × 16
Rev 12:9 ο μεγας ο οφις ο αρχαιος ο καλουμενος διαβολος και ο
       Σατανας"

When the dragon was cast down, he pursued the woman who had brought forth the man child. Verse 17 tells us: "Then the dragon was enraged with the woman, and went off to make war on the rest of her offspring."

Then the dragon was enraged   276 × 8
Rev 12:17 και ωργισθη ο δρακων"

The next section in this chapter deals with the subject of hell. The last five features on the dragon will lead us directly into this next topic. Revelation 20:1 tells about the angel who comes down out of heaven with a great chain in his hand. Verse 2 that follows says:

And he laid hold of the dragon, the serpent of old   276 × 19
who is the devil and Satan
Rev 20:2 και εκρατησεν δρακοντα ο οφις ο αρχαιος ος εστιν διαβολος
       και ο Σατανας

Now look at how these words divide themselves up:

And he laid hold of the dragon, the serpent of old   276 × 13
Rev 20:2 και εκρατησεν τον δρακοντα ο οφις ο αρχαιος

He laid hold of the dragon   276 × 6
Rev 20:2 εκρατησεν τον δρακοντα'

The angel who came down had a "great chain" with which to bind the serpent and cast him into the bottomless pit.

Great chain   276 × 3
Rev 20:1 αλυσιν μεγαλην

The passage then states that Satan will be bound for a thousand years, during which time the millenium will take place. After the thousand years have expired,

Satan will be loosed out of his prison   276 × 15
Rev 20:7 λυθησεται ο σατανας εκ φυλακης αυτου'

Hell

In the Greek language of the New Testament, there are two primary words used to express the term *hell*. The first and foremost is the word γεεννα (gehenna), and the second word is αδην (hades). Both of these words have the same basic meaning of "hell," and they occur with equal frequency in the New Testament.

To start off, let's examine a verse from Matthew 23:33. Here Jesus is speaking to the scribes and Pharisees: "You serpents, you brood of vipers, how shall you escape the judgment of hell?" The word *you* from the words "You serpents, you brood of vipers" does not appear in the original text. The translators have added it so that the verse will be easier to understand. Here is the first feature from this verse:

Serpents, brood of vipers   276 × 10
Mt 23:33 οφεις γεννηματα εχιδνων"

The last part of this verse says: "How shall you escape the judgment of hell?"

Judgment of hell   276 × 6
Mt 23:33 κρισεως γεεννης

Hell   276 × 3
Mt 23:33 της γεεννης'

The second word for hell is "hades." In The Acts 2:27 Simon Peter is preaching, and during the course of his sermon he quotes an Old Testament verse: "Moreover my flesh also will abide in hope. Because Thou wilt not abandon my soul in hades."

In hades   276
Acts 2:27 εις αδην"

In Revelation 1:18 Jesus said: "I was dead, and behold, I am alive forevermore, and I have the keys of death and of hades."

And I have the keys of death and hades   276 × 11
Rev 1:18 και εχω κλεις θανατου και αδου"

Jesus in Luke, chapter 16, gives the parable of Lazarus and the rich man. When the rich man died and was in hades, he looked up and saw father Abraham afar off and Lazarus in his bosom. "And he cried out and said, 'Father Abraham, have mercy on me, and send Lazarus, that he may dip the tip of his finger in water and cool off my tongue; for I am in agony in this flame.' "

This flame   276 × 7
Lk 16:24 τη φλογι ταυτη"

Four verses later the rich man cried out again: "For I have five brothers, so that he may warn them, lest they also come into this place of torment."

This place of torment   276 × 9
Lk 16:28 τοπον τουτον βασανου

Do you remember the parable of the wheat and the tares, from Matthew, chapter 13? In this parable the reapers are spoken of as "collecting the tares."

Collecting the tares   276 × 5
Mt 13:29 συλλεγοντες ζιζανια'

In the next verse it says that Jesus will say to the reapers: "Collect ye first the tares; and bind them in bundles to burn them."

Burn them   276 × 6
Mt 13:30 κατακαυσαι αυτα

In this passage of Scripture, Jesus continues explaining the parable to His disciples. Down in verse 41 there is another parallel made, which relates to the last two features we looked at. When the Son of Man comes, the text says that He will send forth His angels:

And they will collect out of His kingdom   276 × 27
all causes of sin and all evildoers
Mt 13:4 και συλλεξουσιν εκ της βασιλειας αυτου παντα τα σκανδαλα
       και τους ποιουντας την ανομιαν'

The next line says: "and will cast them into the furnace of fire." The following feature from this verse does not sound very good in English, but the meaning in Greek is quite clear. After the word "cast" come the words "them into the furnace of fire." These words are actually referring to those going into the furnace of fire, and for this reason the theomatic value is 276.

Them into the furnace of fire   276 × 11
Mt 13:42 αυτους εις την καμινον πυρος'

The line which immediately follows gives us an even more outstanding feature:

There will be weeping and gnashing of teeth   276 × 13
Mt 13:42 εκει εσται ο κλαυθμος και βρυγμος οδοντων"

Jesus said the following in Mark 9:43: "And if thine hand offend thee, cut it off: it is better for thee to enter crippled into life than having two hands to go into hell, into the fire unquenchable."

Hell fire unquenchable   276 × 7
Mk 9:43 την γεενναν πυρ ασβεστον"

Hell fire   276 × 4
Mk 9:43 την γεενναν πυρ"

Unquenchable   276 × 3
Mk 9:43 ασβεστον

It is beautiful the way the next feature fits in with the above features on the unquenchable fire of hell:

Where their worm dieth not, and the fire is not quenched   276 × 25
Mk 9:48 οπου σκωληξ αυτων ου τελευτα και πυρ ου σβεννυται'

Luke 12:5 also fits into the same design:

Fear him who, after he has killed, has power   276 × 15
to cast into hell
Lk 12:5 φοβηθητε μετα αποκτειναι εχοντα εξουσιαν εμβαλειν εις
γεενναν'

Power to cast into hell   276 × 4
Lk 12:5 εξουσιαν εμβαλειν γεενναν'

Woven inside the theomatic design of God's word, there exist thousands upon thousands of other designs, all flowing together to form the complete structure of the Bible. The next three features will demonstrate that along with the multiples of 276 there exist other number patterns.

When some people think of the word *hell*, they also think of the term "outer darkness." Three times in the New Testament Jesus spoke of casting the unprofitable servant, the sons of the kingdom, and so on, into outer darkness.

In the last chapter on light, darkness, and power, we mentioned the tremendous significance of the fact that many of the features were multiples of 150 × 15. The multiple 150 × 15 is one of the most significant number values to be found in the design dealing with light, darkness, and power. The expression "outer darkness" occurs three times in the New Testament, and each time it has a theomatic value of 150 × 15.

In Matthew 25:30 Jesus said: "Cast out the unprofitable servant into outer darkness."

Cast out the unprofitable servant   150 × 15
Mt 25:30 τον αχρειον δουλον εκβαλετε"

In Matthew 8:12 Jesus said: "But the sons of the kingdom shall be cast out into outer darkness."

The sons of the kingdom shall be cast out   150 × 15
Mt 8:12 οι υιοι της βασιλειας εκβληθησονται

Outer darkness   150 × 15
Mt 8:12 σκοτος εξωτερον

Many times in the New Testament the text speaks of useless, wicked, and unprofitable servants. The first of the above features says: "Cast out the unprofitable servant into outer darkness." Luke 17:10 talks about "unprofitable servants" in the plural.

Unprofitable servants   276 × 5
Lk 17:10 δουλοι αχρειοι

Matthew 25:26 talks about the "wicked and unprofitable servant."

Wicked and unprofitable servant   276 × 4
Mt 25:26 πονηρε δουλε και οκνηρε"

Of all the passages having to do with the topic of hell, the next three verses may be the most outstanding possible in this design of hell. First, we shall consider Matthew 7:23: "And then I will declare to them, 'I never knew you; depart from Me, ye that work iniquity.'"

I never knew you   276 × 9
Mt 7:23 ουδεποτε εγνων υμας'

Depart from Me, ye that work iniquity   276 × 13
Mt 7:23 αποχωρειτε απ εμου οι εργαζομενοι την ανομιαν

Second, we shall examine Matthew 25:41: "Then He will also say to those on His left, 'Depart from Me, ye cursed, into everlasting fire prepared for the devil and his angels.' " This complete verse as we have just quoted it is a multiple of 276; and watch what happens now.

He will also say to those on His left   276 × 10
Mt 25:41 ερει και εξ ευωνυμων'

Depart from Me, ye cursed, into everlasting fire prepared   276 × 36
for the devil and his angels
Mt 25:41 πορευεσθε απ εμου κατηραμενοι εις το πυρ το αιωνιον το ητοιμασμενον τω διαβολω και τοις αγγελοις αυτου

Cursed into everlasting fire   276 × 10
Mt 25:41 κατηραμενοι εις το πυρ αιωνιον'

Prepared for the devil and his angels   276 × 14
Mt 25:41 ητοιμασμενον διαβολω και τοις αγγελοις αυτου'

The third and last feature comes from verse 46 of this chapter:

These will go away into everlasting punishment   276 × 13
Mt 25:46 απελευσονται ουτοι εις κολασιν αιωνιον'

Everything to do with hell is structured on the number 276. During the process of compiling our research we found that the consistency was overwhelming, but when we went to the book of Revelation, and started researching the verses that spoke of the "lake of fire," a strange thing happened: The whole design of 276 collapsed. None of these verses had a design of 276 present in them. This, of course, surprised us and led to further investigation and research. As a result, a key was found that opened up a completely new design tying together the lake of fire with the second death. This design requires further research, which will be shown in a future publication.

However, one very interesting feature appeared in Revelation 20:14. This verse says: "Death and hades were cast into the lake of fire."

Hades was cast into the lake of fire   276 × 8
Rev 20:13 ο αδης εβληθησαν εις την λιμνην πυρος'

To conclude this basic topic, we will now look at a few more features, which will only serve to substantiate those already shown. Here now is a well-known passage from Matthew, chapter 5:

Whoever says, "Thou fool!" shall be in danger of hell fire   276 × 19
Mt 5:22 ος δ αν ειπη μωρε ενοχος εσται εις την γεενναν του πυρος'''[2]

Matthew, chapter 25, tells the parable of the ten virgins. Five were foolish, and five were wise. As the story goes, the five wise virgins went into the wedding feast, but the other five were locked out. When the foolish virgins tried to come in, Jesus declared that he did not know them. Here is verse 10: "And while they were going away to make the purchase, the bridegroom came, and those who were ready went in with him to the wedding feast; and the door was shut."

And the door was shut   276 × 3
Mt 25:10 και εκλεισθη θυρα

Here are the words from John 3:36:

He who does not believe the Son shall not see life;   276 × 23
but the wrath of God abides on him
Jn 3:36 απειθων υιω ουκ οψεται ζωην αλλ οργη Θεου μενει επ αυτον

Almost everyone has heard these words of Jesus from Matthew, chapter 7:

For wide is the gate, and broad is the way   276 × 23
leading to destruction
Mt 7:13 οτι πλατεια η πυλη και ευρυχωρος η οδος η απαγουσα εις
        απωλειαν'

Broad is the way leading to destruction   276 × 18
Mt 7:13 ευρυχωρος οδος απαγουσα εις απωλειαν'

Our last feature will best speak for itself:

For it has been appointed unto man once to die   276 × 17
and then the judgment
Heb 9:27 καθ οσον αποκειται ανθρωποις απαξ αποθανειν μετα δε τουτο
        κρισις''

[2]We have discovered that in rare instances the theomatic design clusters by threes. This is only true of super-large numbers such as 276 and 666. This feature is a perfect example. The probability of this happening is very low and is why this phenomenon occurs on extremely large numbers.

Demon Possession

Luke 4:33 says that there was a certain man in the synagogue,

Having the spirit of an unclean demon   276 × 13
Lk 4:33 εχων πνευμα δαιμονιου ακαθαρτου

Unclean   276 × 2
Lk 4:33 ακαθαρτου

And here is the most outstanding word possible:

Demon possession   276 × 3
Jn 10:21 δαιμονιζομενου'

But guess what the theomatic value of the word *expell*, or *cast out*, is. Same as Jesus—888.
Expell (or *Cast out*)   888
Lk 11:20 εκβαλλω

Praise the Lord! And why shouldn't it be? Jesus has power over all demons, and it is through His name that they are expelled and cast out.

The Law

The purpose of this chapter on the number 276 is to demonstrate that everything to do with Satan, hell, sin, evil, and so on contains designs that work out to multiples of 276. During the process of this research, an astounding thing occurred. It was discovered that everything to do with the law, or the Old Testament covenant under Moses, also worked out to 276. What resulted was a completely new design, which brought forth some marvelous truths.

So what we will now do is temporarily deviate from the general themes of Satan, evil, and so on, and show the design of the law.

Psalms 19:7 states that "the law of the Lord is perfect." There is nothing sinful about the law at all. The thing which made the law bad was that man was totally incapable of keeping the law. This is why Christ had to come—to deliver us out of the curse of the law.

Now the first feature we will be looking at is "the law" itself. The words "the law" are not a multiple of 276, and the reason is very simple.

The law is perfect, and as you should know by now, seven is God's perfect number. It bespeaks total perfection and completeness.

The law 700
Eph 2:15 τον νομον

The law has always been referred to by Christians as the "old covenant," or the "first covenant." The first covenant was the covenant of the law, and the second covenant was the one of grace. Romans 6:14 brings this out best when it says that we are "not under law, but under grace." The covenant of grace is the new covenant. Let's now begin by looking at two features from one verse in Hebrews, chapter 9: "And for this reason He is the mediator of a new covenant, in order that since a death has taken place for the redemption of the transgressions committed under the first covenant. . . ."

The transgressions committed under the first covenant   276 × 15
Heb 9:15 των επι τη πρωτη διαθηκη παραβασεων'

The first covenant   276 × 6
Heb 9:15 τη πρωτη διαθηκη

Luke 24:44 talks about:

All things written in the law of Moses   276 × 15
Lk 24:44 παντα γεγραμμενα εν νομω Μωυσεως

John 10:34 refers to the things:

Written in the law   276 × 9
Jn 10:34 γεγραμμενον εν τω νομω"

But look at this next feature. To illustrate the impact of its meaning, we will quote The Acts 6:13–14: "And they put forward false witnesses who said, 'This man incessantly speaks against this holy place, and the law; for we have heard him say that this Nazarene, Jesus, will destroy this place and alter the customs which Moses delivered to us.' "

The customs which Moses delivered   276 × 11
Acts 6:14 τα εθη α παρεδωκεν Μωυσης'

Ephesians 2:15 talks about:

The law of commandments in ordinances   276 × 13
Eph 2:15 τον νομον των εντολων εν δογμασιν

The next one is remarkable:

Stone tablets   276 × 2
2 Cor 3:3 πλαξιν λιθιναις'

Do you remember the feature that spoke of the transgressions under the first covenant? If we connect it with the stone tablets, we will find a feature from Hebrews 9:4 which talks about the:

Tablets of the covenant   276 × 4
Heb 9:4 πλακες της διαθηκης

We will allow the reader to figure out the significance of the following:

The Sabbath day   276 × 8
Lk 13:14 τη ημερα του σαββατου

The next feature will need no special introduction either:

The righteousness of the scribes and Pharisees   276 × 18
Mt 5:20 δικαιοσυνη των γραμματεων και φαρισαιων

The next series of features will demonstrate that the law was brought in simply to show that man was not capable of keeping the law. Romans 3:20 tells us: "By works of law no flesh will be justified in His sight; for through the law comes a full knowledge of sin." Later on we will examine the first part of this verse, but for now here is the second clause:

For through the law comes a full knowledge of sin   276 × 10
Rom 3:20 δια γαρ νομου επιγνωσις αμαρτιας

In Romans 5:13 we find that:

Until the law sin was in the world   276 × 11
Rom 5:13 αχρι νομου αμαρτια ην εν κοσμω'

Romans 4:15 says: "For the law brings about wrath, . . ."

But where there is no law, neither is there transgression   276 × 11
Rom 4:15 ου δε ουκ εστιν νομος ουδε παραβασις'

Here is a verse from James 2:11: "Now if you do not commit adultery, but do commit murder, . . ."

You have become a transgressor of the law   276 × 6
Jas 2:11 γεγονας παραβατης νομου'

This feature will explain perfectly why the law came into being. Paul, in Galatians 3:19, says:

Why the law? Because of transgressions it was added   276 × 13
Gal 3:19 τι ο νομος παραβασεων χαριν προσετεθη

Another one of those verses that fully expresses this design is the following: "For while we were in the flesh, . . ."

The sinful passions, which were aroused by the law,   276 × 40
operated in our members to bear fruit for death
Rom 7:5 παθηματα των αμαρτιων τα δια του νομου ενηργειτο εν τοις μελεσιν ημων εις το καρποφορησαι τω θανατω"

The sinful passions, which were aroused by the law   276 × 15
Rom 7:5 τα παθηματα των αμαρτιων τα δια νομου'

Paul, in Romans 7:23, talks about:

The law of sin in my members, taking me captive   276 × 31
Rom 7:23 αιχμαλωτιζοντα με εν τω νομω της αμαρτιας τω οντι εν τοις μελεσιν μου

We shall now turn and focus our attention on a few features that speak of justification, based on works of law. These will be listed in succession since they are quite easy to follow.

By works of law shall no flesh be justified   276 × 14
Rom 3:20 εξ εργων νομου ου δικαιωθησεται σαρξ"

A man is justified by faith, apart from works of law   276 × 21
Rom 3:28 δικαιουσθαι πιστει ανθρωπον χωρις εργων νομου"

Knowing that man is not justified by works of law   276 × 19
Gal 2:16 ειδοτες δε οτι ου δικαιουται ανθρωπος εξ εργων νομου"

By works of law   276 × 6
Gal 2:26 εξ εργων νομου'"

This should prove that works based on the law will not save you. Only a belief and faith in Jesus will.

The next sequence of thought deals with the two most important words in this entire design. Constantly throughout the New Testament the text talks about being "under law." We have included just a few of the features that speak of this, and they are quite outstanding. Here is the first one:

Now we know that whatever the law says,   276 × 9
it says to those who are under the law
Rom 3:19 οιδαμεν δε οτι οσα ο νομος λεγει εν νομω λαλει

Romans 2:12 refers to:

All those who have sinned under the law   276 × 7
Rom 2:12 οσοι εν νομω ημαρτον"

But the best feature is this one, from Galatians:

The ones who desire to be under the law   276 × 6
Gal 4:21 οι υπο νομον θελοντες ειναι'

And now the most outstanding feature possible in this entire design:

Under law   276 × 3
Gal 4:21 υπο νομον"

Another one of those verses that fits perfectly into this design is found in Galatians 3:10. The first portion of the verse reads: "For as many as are of the works of the law are under a curse." This verse is referring to the curse of the law, and the Greek words *curse* and *law* produce the following:

Curse of the law   276 × 4
Gal 3:10 νομου καταραν'

In the remaining portion of the verse there exist two other features of important significance:

It is written, cursed is every one who does not abide   276 × 29
by all things written in the law, to perform them
Gal 3:10 γεγραπται οτι επικαταρατος πας ος ουκ εμμενει πασιν τοις γεγραμμενοις εν βιβλιω του νομου ποιησαι αυτα'

Cursed is everyone who does not abide by all   276 × 17
things written in the law
Gal 3:10 επικαταρατος πας ος ουκ εμμενει πασιν γεγραμμενοις εν βιβλιω νομου'

To conclude this design, we will show only a few more features, each of which will pile more evidence on that which has already been given. We do not claim by any means to have shown all the features existing in this design. You might say that we randomly selected those we felt were the most outstanding, and which at the same time fit into the sequence of thought being given. Everything to do with the law is saturated with multiples of 276. It's like swimming in a sea of theomatics.

In Romans 7:11 Paul said the following: "Do you not know, brethren—for I am speaking to those who know the law—that the law is binding on a person only during his life?" This passage contains two Greek words that are very emphatic. They produce the following meaning:

The law is binding   276 × 5
Rom 7:1 νομος κυριευει

Here are the words from 1 Corinthians 14:34: "The women should keep silence in the churches. For they are not permitted to speak, but should be subordinate, as even the law says."

The law says   276 × 2
1 Cor 14:34 ο νομος λεγει'

Many times Christians use the expression "letter of the law." These words do not appear in the Bible, but there is an interesting passage of Scripture which brings forth the same design of 276. In 2 Corinthians 3:6 it says that "the letter killeth, but the spirit giveth life."

The letter killeth   276 × 4
2 Cor 3:6 το γραμμα αποκτεινει"

In Titus 3:9, Paul advises Christians to:

Shun disputes about the law   276 × 8
Tit 3:9 μαχας νομικας περιστασο'

One of the great spiritual truths of Christianity is the fact that Christians have been freed from the bondage and dictatorship of the law. One of the most famous verses that speaks of this is Romans 8:2: "For the law of the spirit of life in Christ Jesus has set me free from the law of sin and death."

Free from the law of sin and death   276 × 16
Rom 8:2 ηλευθερωσεν απο νομου της αμαρτιας και θανατου

Our next to the last feature comes from Romans 7:6. Here it says that Christians have been "discharged" from the law. This word means "to be free" from the law.

Discharged   276 × 2
Rom 7:6 κατηργηθημεν

Jerry Lucas has said many times that the last feature presented here is his favorite in this entire book. There is no doubt that it is one of the most significant. However, both of us would like to say that there really isn't any one feature that can be labeled as the most outstanding. They all are outstanding.

In The Acts 26:5, Paul states that, before becoming a Christian: "I lived as a Pharisee according to the strictest sect of our religion."

Both "Satan" and "religion" have the same theomatic values.

Satan   276 × 2
Mt 16:23 Σατανα'

Religion   276 × 2
Acts 26:5 θρησκειας'

Religion is of Satan, but Christianity is a new life and a personal relationship with Jesus Christ. Christianity is not religion. Praise God for this fact!

Sin and Evil

The two words *sin* and *evil* are perhaps the two most common terms used by Christians to express all that which is in opposition to God. The design of 276 is found in many of those passages of Scripture that speak of sin and evil. We will show only a few of the more outstanding ones.

The first word we shall examine is the word *sin*. In Greek the word for *sin* is αμαρτια, and it means "to miss the mark." However, in the Bible the word is used in a much broader sense. It implies rebellion, the breaking of God's law—as in the original sin of Adam, and the act of committing anything which is in opposition to God.

The Greek word for *evil* is πονηρος, but there are other Greek words which carry the same basic meaning of evil. One of these is κακος. The definition of the word *evil* is "to be malignant, destructive, injurious, or of a mind to practice such things." It also means "to be morally bad or wrong, wicked, depraved."

These two words, along with the many meanings and shades of meanings attached to them, appear so many times in the New Testament that to do the subject justice would require much time in research. For this reason, the features we will be showing are only a sampling of those to be found.

To begin, let's examine a verse that ties together the subject of sin with that of the law.

The sting of death is sin, and the power of sin is the law 276 × 15
1 Cor 15:56 το δε κεντρον θανατου η αμαρτια η δε δυναμις αμαρτιας ο νομος'

The sting of death is sin 276 × 11
1 Cor 15:56 το δε κεντρον του θανατου η αμαρτια

James 1:15 tells us that:

Lust having conceived brings forth sin 276 × 11
Jas 1:15 επιθυμια συλλαβουσα τικτει αμαρτιαν

Probably the most famous reference to sin is found in Romans 6:23: "The wages of sin is death." Needless to say, we were rather surprised at how this feature worked out. It is *the wages* of sin that is death. This is why they have a theomatic value of 276.

The wages 276 × 7
Rom 6:23 τα οψωνια

When Jesus forgave the woman caught in adultery, he said to her:

Sin no more 276 × 5
Jn 8:11 νυν μηκετι αμαρτανε

Jesus, in Luke, chapter 18, tells of the two prayers given by the Pharisee and the tax collector. The one was thanking God that he was not like other people, swindlers, unjust, adulterers, or even like the tax collector. "But the tax gatherer, standing some distance away, was even unwilling to lift up his eyes to heaven, but was beating his breast, saying, 'God, be merciful to me a sinner!' "

Be merciful to me a sinner!   276 × 10
Lk 18:13 ιλασθητι μοι αμαρτωλω

In Luke, chapter 24, Jesus tells his disciples that "the Son of Man must be delivered into the hands of sinful men, and be crucified, and the third day rise again."

The Son of Man must be delivered into the hands   276 × 33
of sinful men
Lk 24:7 τον υιον του ανθρωπου οτι δει παραδοθηναι εις χειρας
      ανθρωπων αμαρτωλων"

In Matthew, when Jesus was praying before going to the cross, the disciples were sleeping. "Then He came to the disciples, and said to them, 'Are you still sleeping and taking your rest? Behold, the hour is at hand and the Son of Man is being betrayed into the hands of sinners.' "

Hands of sinners   276 × 11
Mt 26:45 χειρας αμαρτωλων"

Hebrews 2:17 says that after Christ died He became a "merciful and faithful high priest in things pertaining to God, to make propitiation for the sins of the people."

The sins of the people   276 × 6
Heb 2:17 τας αμαρτιας λαου'

But Christ also gave of Himself on behalf of sins.

On behalf of sins   276 × 11
Gal 1:4 υπερ των αμαρτιων'

The term *evil* appears in the New Testament fewer times than the expression *sin;* but the design is just as good, if not more so. Here again, the features we will be showing are only a sampling of those to be found.

Evil   276 × 8
Mt 5:39 τω πονηρω

Probably the best-known reference to evil in the Bible is found in the Garden of Eden story, when it talks about the "tree of the knowledge of good and evil." Here the feature is from the Hebrew of the Old Testament:

Evil 276
Gen 2:9 וְרַע

Next we shall examine several verses that bring forth an important truth. Jesus had the following to say in Mark 7:23: "All these evil things come from within and defile the man."

These evil things come from within and defile the man 276 × 20
Mk 7:23 ταυτα τα πονηρα εσωθεν εκπορευεται και κοινοι τον
    ανθρωπον"

Evil things from within 276 × 5
Mk 7:23 πονηρα εσωθεν"

Two verses earlier Jesus said: "For from within, out of the heart of men, proceed the evil thoughts and fornications, thefts, murders, adulteries." Here again the Greek word εκ, meaning "out of," takes on tremendous significance.

Out of the heart of men 276 × 10
Mk 7:21 εκ της καρδιας ανθρωπων'

Another passage which brings forth the same truth is found in Luke 6:45. Notice the capitalized words. These do not appear in the Greek, but have been inserted by the translators so the passage will be easier to understand. "The good man out of the good treasure of his heart brings forth what is good; and the evil MAN out of the evil TREASURE brings forth what is evil."

Evil out of the evil 276 × 5
Lk 6:45 πονηρος εκ πονηρου'

This account is also found in Matthew's gospel. In Luke's account, which we just looked at, the word *treasure* as in "evil treasure" does not appear in the text. In Matthew's it does: "The good man out of his good treasure brings forth what is good; and the evil man out of evil treasure brings forth what is evil."

Out of evil treasure 276 × 10
Mt 12:35 εκ του πονηρου θησαυρου'

In Luke's account, the first feature said: "evil out of evil." This verse says: "the evil man out of evil." The next feature has exactly the same theomatic value as the above one:

The evil man out of evil   276 × 10
Mt 12:35 ο πονηρος ανθρωπος εκ πονηρου᾿

In the features we just examined, it was seen that evil is in the heart of man, and that the evil things from within are what defile the man. In Matthew 15:11 Jesus said the following: "Not that which goeth into the mouth defileth a man; but that which cometh out of the mouth, this defileth a man."

That which cometh out of the mouth   276 × 12
Mt 15:11 το εκπορευομενον εκ του στοματος᾿

In the epistle of James, the following words are found:

No human being is able to tame the tongue   276 × 19
a restless evil full of deadly poison
Jas 3:8 γλωσσαν ουδεις δαμασαι δυναται ανθρωπων ακαταστατον
    κακον μεστη ιου θανατηφορου᾿

No human being is able to tame the tongue   276 × 19
Jas 3:8 την γλωσσαν ουδεις δαμασαι δυναται ανθρωπων

Galatians 1:4 says the following: "Who gave Himself on behalf of sins, that He might deliver us out of this present evil age." We have already seen how the words "on behalf of sins" made a multiple of 276. Here now are two more features from this passage:

Deliver us out of the present evil age   276 × 22
Gal 1:4 εξεληται ημας εκ του αιωνος του ενεστωτος πονηρου

Out of the present evil age   276 × 14
Gal 1:4 εκ αιωνος ενεστωτος πονηρου

Jesus in Matthew talks about:

This evil generation   276 × 5
Mt 12:45 γενεα ταυτη πονηρα"

This generation   276 × 5
Mt 12:45 τη γενεα ταυτη

And in the gospel of Luke, Jesus said: "This generation is an evil generation."

This generation is evil   276 × 6
Lk 11:29 η γενεα αυτη πονηρα εστιν᾿

Ephesians 6:13 says: "Therefore take up the full armor of God, that you may be able to resist in the day of evil."

In the day of evil   276 × 3
Eph 6:13 εν τη ημερα πονηρα"

Paul, in writing his epistle to the Romans, gives some good advice: "Do not be overcome by evil, but overcome evil with good."

Do not be overcome by evil   276 × 10
Rom 12:21 μη νικω υπο του κακου'

One of the best-known verses that speak of evil is the following:

For we wrestle not against flesh and blood, but against   276 × 61
principalities, against powers, against the rulers of
the darkness of this world, against the spiritual hosts
of evil in the heavenlies
Eph 6:12 οτι ουκ εστιν ημιν η παλη προς αιμα και σαρκα αλλα προς τας
αρχας προς τας εξουσιας προς τους κοσμοκρατορας του
σκοτους τουτου προς τα πνευματικα της πονηριας εν τοις
επουρανιοις'

Spiritual hosts of evil   276 × 7
Eph 6:12 πνευματικα της πονηριας"

The spiritual hosts of evil in the heavenlies   276 × 14
Eph 6:12 τα πνευματικα της πονηριας εν τοις επουρανιοις"

The last two features come from Paul's second epistle to Timothy. In verse 17 he tells how he was "delivered out of the mouth of the lion." If you remember from earlier in this chapter, we showed the verse from 1 Peter 5:8, where the devil goes about as a roaring lion, seeking whom he may devour. Connect this now with Paul's words from 2 Timothy.

Out of the mouth of the lion   276 × 7
2 Tim 4:17 εκ στοματος λεοντος'

In verse 18, which follows, Paul said: "The Lord will deliver me from every evil work."

From every evil work   276 × 8
2 Tim 4:18 απο παντος εργου πονηρου

The Flesh, Corruption, and Man

Perhaps no portion of this book will be more revealing than this one. Man is a sinner and in total rebellion to God. The word *flesh* is used throughout Scripture to describe man, a sensuous, depraved, and corrupt creature, with cravings which excite to sin. One does not have to look far in this world to realize this fact. The closest radio, television, or newspaper leaves very little to the imagination.

The topic we shall now examine exposes man for what he is. To some readers this fact may not be pleasant. To the Christian, however, it will make him appreciate his salvation as never before. At the conclusion of this chapter, a beautiful design will be shown, which demonstrates that we who know Jesus have been saved from the satanic kingdom.

The story of Noah and the flood is a perfect example of what is to take place when Christ returns to destroy Satan and set up His own kingdom. In Chapter 3 we explained how God destroyed the ancient wicked world and started a new creation with eight people, Noah and his family. The ark in which the eight souls were saved is a type of Christ, Who is our ark of safety.

But let us now examine a verse from Genesis, chapter 6, which best describes the world situation as it was then and is today: "Now the earth was corrupt in the sight of God, and the earth was filled with violence. And God looked on the earth, and behold, it was corrupt; for all flesh had corrupted their way upon the earth."

Behold, it was corrupt; for all flesh had corrupted their way   276 × 10
Gen 6:12 הנה נשחתה כי השחית כל בשר את דרכו'

All flesh   276 × 2
Gen 6:12 כל בשר

Now when we come to the New Testament, we find that the theomatic value of the word *flesh* is also 276. Hebrews 12:9 speaks of the "fathers of our flesh." The theomatic value of the word *flesh* from this verse is also a multiple of 276.

The flesh   276 × 6
Heb 12:9 τους μεν σαρκος

The subject of circumcision is covered extensively throughout the Bible. Within this topic, there also emerges a design of 276, because circumcision involves the removal of the flesh. The word *uncircumcision* would apply to those who had not had the flesh removed. Here now is a feature of outstanding significance:

Uncircumcision   276 × 4
Rom 2:25 ακροβυστια

The next feature is one of the most significant possible. We think you will agree.

Lust of the flesh   276 × 6
1 Jn 2:16 επιθυμια της σαρκος"

Observe how the above feature fits in with the next feature: "Now those who belong to Christ Jesus have crucified the flesh with its passions and lusts."

The flesh with its passions and lusts   276 × 11
Gal 5:24 την σαρκα συν παθημασιν και ταις επιθυμιαις

Romans, chapter 8, says that God sent His own Son "in likeness of flesh sinful."

Likeness of flesh   276 × 7
Rom 8:3 ομοιωματι σαρκος

But Romans, chapter 8, also talks about:

Those who live according to the flesh   276 × 3
Rom 8:5 οι γαρ κατα σαρκα

Galatians 5:19 begins by saying: "Now the works of the flesh are manifest."

Manifest works of the flesh   276 × 6
Gal 5:19 φανερα τα εργα σαρκος"

During the process of compiling the features for this topic, many outstanding features on the flesh had to be rejected, simply for lack of space in the book. The number 276 prevails throughout the topic of the flesh. One particular aspect of the flesh which bears great significance is the one that speaks of being born of the flesh, being born in sin, and so on.

In John, chapter 3, Nicodemus comes to Jesus. Jesus explains to him that a man must be born again before he can see the kingdom of

God. Nicodemus then replied by asking: "How can a man be born when he is old?"

A man born when he is old 276×12
Jn 3:4 ανθρωπος γεννηθηναι γερων ων

A few verses later comes what has to be one of the most significant features possible in this entire design. Jesus replied to Nicodemus by saying:

That which is born of the flesh is flesh 276×10
Jn 3:6 το γεγεννημενον εκ της σαρκος σαρξ εστιν'

John 12:13 speaks of those "who were not born of blood, nor of the will of the flesh, nor of the will of man, but of God."

Born of blood 276×6
Jn 1:13 εξ αιματων εγεννηθησαν

This feature is powerfully significant, because the bloodline from Adam is what constitutes the curse on fallen humanity.

When Jesus healed the blind man in John, chapter 9, it says that the scribes and Pharisees were crossexamining him. The blind man responded by saying: " 'If this man were not from God, He could do nothing.' They answered and said to him, 'In sin you were born entirely, and you are teaching us?' "

In sin you were born 276×6
Jn 9:34 εν αμαρτιαις συ εγεννηθης

Adam and the Rebuilding of the Temple

In the first portion of this chapter, we explained that before finishing it you would see why the number 276 is used by God to depict the satanic kingdom. What you are about to see in the concluding portion of this chapter points out the significance of theomatics. God has put the number 276 right in the text. Twice it is referred to in the New Testament. The first reference is when Jesus makes the declaration that He will destroy the temple and rebuild it in three days.

As you have seen, the number 276 relates directly to the subject of the flesh. But what about man? The first man, or father of the human race, was Adam. It was because of his sin that death has passed onto all humanity.

Romans 5:12 tells us the following:

Wherefore, as through one man sin entered into   276 × 27
the world, and death by sin
Rom 5:12 Δια τουτο ωσπερ δι ενος ανθρωπου η αμαρτια εις τον κοσμον
εισηλθεν και δια αμαρτιας ο θανατος

As through one man   276 × 11
Rom 5:12 ωσπερ δι ενος ανθρωπου"

Romans 5:18 tells us the same thing, only in different words: "Therefore, as by one offense judgment came upon all men to condemnation."

As through one offense   276 × 12
Rom 5:18 ως δι ενος παραπτωματος

Verse 14 from the same chapter states that "death reigned from Adam to Moses."

Death from Adam   276 × 3
Rom 5:14 θανατος απο Αδαμ

We are now going to discover something of unique significance. In 1 Corinthians 15:22 we find these words: "For as in Adam all die, even so in Christ shall all be made alive." The word for *in* in the Greek is εν. Thus, we find it in this phrase: "As *in* Adam all die." But the interesting fact is that this little word is also the word for the number *one* in Greek. Therefore, this verse could have easily been translated: "As one Adam all die" instead of "As in Adam all die." Interestingly, when this word is removed from the Greek, the following presents itself:

As Adam all die   276 × 11
1 Cor 15:22 δωτερ Αδαμ παντες αποθνησκουσιν'

But the next feature from Romans 5:9 seems to definitely indicate that this is not a coincidence. "For as by the disobedience of one man, many were made sinners." Here again, when the word *one* was present in this phrase, it didn't add up either. When it was deleted, however, the next feature was discovered. The words "disobedience of man" have a theomatic value of 2,760, or 276 × 10. Nothing could be more significant than this.

Disobedience of man   276 × 10
Rom 5:19 παρακοης του ανθρωπου

The fact that these words only work without the number one seems to definitely indicate that the reference is to all mankind instead of one man. Adam, of course, represents all humanity, and for further confirmation we present the very feature that is the foundation to this complete design:

Man   276 × 5
Mt 26:24 ο ανθρωπος

Luke 13:4 refers to "all men."

All men   276 × 12
Lk 13:4 παντας τους ανθρωπους

The definition of the name *Adam* in Hebrew is simply "man." If one were to go to the text of the Old Testament, he would find that the Hebrew words are full of multiples of 276 throughout the text of the creation of man. For sake of illustration, we will show one verse containing two features. Here is Genesis 5:2, which has a number value of 2,760, or 276 × 10:

He created them male and female, and He blessed them   276 × 10
and called their name man, in the day when they were created
Gen 5:2 אדם'

The words "their name man" form the most distinct portion of the above verse. Here again, the same design is present:

Their name man   276 × 3   זכר ונקבה
Gen 5:2 בראם ויברך אתם ויקרא את שמם אדם ביום הבראם'

Now here is something remarkable. The name *Adam* in Hebrew has a theomatic value of 46, and in Greek it is also 46.

Adam (or *Man*)   46
Gen 5:2 את שמם אדם"

Adam (or *Man*)   46
Rom 5:14 Αδαμ

So in Greek the word *man* is 276, and *Adam* is 46 in both Hebrew and Greek. At this point you may be asking yourself the question, What relation does the number 46 have to the number 276? Watch!

$$46 \times 6 = 276$$

Now the number six has been universally accepted by Bible scholars as being the number of man. There are many instances in Scripture where this is brought out. It was on the sixth day of creation that God created man. So 46 (the number of *Adam* in both Hebrew and Greek) times 6 (the number of man) equals 276 (the number of flesh and sin).

When Jesus died on the cross, He took with Him man's sin. Scripture declares that Christ became sin for us, and it was in His body that He bore our sins. In John, chapter 2, Jesus goes into the temple, throws out the money-changers, and overturns their tables. "The Jews therefore answered and said to Him, 'What sign do You show to us, seeing that You do these things?' Jesus answered and said unto them, 'Destroy this temple, and in three days I will raise it up.' The Jews therefore said, 'It took forty-six years to build this temple, and You will raise it up in three days?' But He was speaking of the temple of His body."

It took forty-six years to build this temple 276×13
Jn 2:20 τεσσερακοντα και εξ ετεσιν οικοδομηθη ναος ουτος

Before Jesus was to die, He spoke a parable to His disciples which symbolized His taking the temple of His body into the ground, and then resurrecting it on the third day: "And Jesus answered them, saying, 'The hour has come for the Son of Man to be glorified. Truly, truly, I say to you, unless a grain of wheat falls into the earth and dies, it remains by itself alone; but if it dies, it bears much fruit.' "

A grain of wheat falling into the earth dies 276×15
Jn 12:24 κοκκος του σιτου πεσων εις την γην αποθανη"

Grain of wheat 276×5
Jn 12:24 κοκκος σιτου

Into the earth   276
Jn 12:24 εις γην

And from Mathew 26:35, the word *die* also supports this design:

Die   276
Mt 26:35 αποθανειν

Corruption, Incorruption, and Paul's Shipwreck

And now another great truth is going to be unveiled before our eyes. In the design of light and darkness, we saw how God depicts both light and darkness with the same number or theomatic values—because they are exact opposites.

One day while researching Romans, chapter 1, something rather unusual was noticed. The word *corruptible* had a number value of 1,380, or 276 × 5. We then looked and saw that the word *incorruptible* had the same number value of 1,380, or 276 × 5. This led to further investigation, and the results were staggering, until the whole thing was understood when in the book of The Acts the number 276 appeared right in the text of the Word of God.

Romans 1:23 talks about those who "exchanged the glory of the incorruptible God for an image in the form of corruptible man and of birds and four-footed animals and crawling creatures." The words "image of corruptible man" are a multiple of 276, but the important thing from this passage is the following:

Corruptible   276 × 5
Rom 1:23 φθαρτου

Incorruptible   276 × 5
Rom 1:23 αφθαρτου'

1 Corinthians 15:53 says the following:

For this corruptible must put on incorruption   276 × 16
1 Cor 15:53 Δει γαρ το φθαρτον τουτο ενδυσασθαι αφθαρσιαν'

Paul in the same chapter talks about the resurrection of the dead: "So also is the resurrection of the dead. It is sown in corruption; it is raised in incorruption."

It is sown in corruption; it is raised in incorruption   276 × 10
1 Cor 15:42 σπειρεται εν φθορα εγειρεται εν αφθαρσια"

Again Paul in the same chapter speaks of corruption and incorruption: "Now this I say, brethren, that flesh and blood cannot inherit the kingdom of God; neither doth corruption inherit incorruption."

Flesh and blood cannot inherit the kingdom of God; 276 × 20
Neither doth corruption inherit incorruption
1 Cor 15:50 σαρξ και αιμα βασιλειαν Θεου κληρονομησαι ου δυναται
ουδε η φθορα αφθαρσιαν κληρονομει

In the next verse Paul proceeds to explain how "we shall not all sleep, but we shall all be changed, in a moment, in the twinkling of an eye, at the last trumpet."

For a trumpet will sound, 276 × 10
and the dead will be raised incorruptible
1 Cor 15:52 σαλπισει γαρ και οι νεκροι εγερθησονται αφθαρτοι"

Jesus is described in 1 Timothy as He "Who alone has immortality." These words could have been translated as meaning "the only one having incorruption," because in Greek the words *immortality* and *incorruption* have the same meaning.

The only one having incorruption 276 × 8
1 Tim 6:16 μονος εχων αθανασιαν

The apostle Peter, in his epistle, talks about "an inheritance incorruptible, and undefiled, and that fadeth not away, reserved in heaven for you." Hidden inside these words is the same theomatic design that flows through the many different references to corruption and incorruption.

Inheritance incorruptible reserved in heaven 276 × 12
1 Pet 1:4 κληρονομιαν αφθαρτον τετηρημενην εν ουρανοις"

The following two features will only add more weight to the evidence already given. Paul in 1 Corinthians talks about many who run a race, but one who receives the prize. Paul then advises: "So run, that ye may obtain. And every man that striveth for the mastery is temperate in all things. Now they do it to obtain a corruptible crown; but we an incorruptible [crown]."

Corruptible crown 276 × 8
1 Cor 9:25 φθαρτον στεφανον"

Incorruptible crown 276 × 8
1 Cor 9:25 αφαρτον στεφανον'

In the book of Revelation the tree of life is spoken of. In His message to the seven churches, Jesus stated: "To him who overcomes, I will grant to eat of the tree of life, which is in the paradise of God." The tree of life bespeaks one thing, and one thing only—incorruption. Only those who inherit incorruption will be granted to eat from the tree of life. Thus, we have the following feature:

Tree of life 276 × 9
Rev 2:7 ξυλου της ζωης'

In the book of Revelation, "water of life" is also mentioned. "To the one thirsting I will give of the fountain of the water of life freely."

Water of life 276 × 10
Rev 21:6 του υδατος ζωης

Thus, from corruption, comes that which is incorruptible. God expresses this fact with the same number values. In three other examples this design is brought forth loud and clear. Let's examine them.

We have seen how the word *die* has a number value of 276. In Revelation 2:8, Jesus refers to Himself as being the one Who died and lived again. There is one word in Greek for "lived again," and it means exactly that.

Die 276
Mt 26:35 αποθανειν

Live again 276
Rev 2:8 εζησεν'

Earlier in this chapter, we showed the feature from Hebrews 2:17 in which Christ made propitiation for the sins of the people. The words "sins of the people" had a theomatic value of 276 × 6, but *propitiate* means to "reconcile or cancel out one's sins," placing that person in a favorable position. Let's now take the word *propitiation* from 1 John 2:2, and see what happens.

Propitiation 276 × 2
1 Jn 2:2 ιλασμος'

The sins of the people 276 × 6
Heb 2:17 τας αμαρτιας λαου'

One of the best examples is this one from Romans 5:18: "Therefore, as through one offense judgment came upon all men to condemnation; even so through one act of righteousness there resulted justification to all men."

As through one offense 276 × 12
Rom 5:18 ως δι ενος παραπτωματος

Condemnation 276 × 6
2 Cor 3:9 κατακρισεως

Justification 276 × 4
Rom 5:18 δικαιωσιν'

The reason why God describes corruption (the old) with incorruption (the new), by using the same number values, is that He is demonstrating that out of the old corrupt system He is bringing forth a new creation. In Galatians 6:15, believers are described as "a new creation." In 1 Peter, the apostle refers to believers as "newborn" babes. The two terms—"new creation" and "newborn"—have the same theomatic values.

New creation 276 × 3
Gal 6:15 καινη κτισις'

Newborn 276 × 3
1 Pet 2:2 αρτιγεννητα

In the last portion of the book of The Acts, Paul goes sailing on a ship. Aboard the ship there were a certain number of passengers, including a large number of prisoners, along with the crew. Before sailing, Paul advised the centurion not to sail, because he foresaw danger. But the centurion refused to heed Paul's advice and sailed anyway. As the story goes, a storm came about in the Mediterranean Sea, and the ship was in great danger. The story ended when the ship was wrecked, and all those aboard swam safely to shore.

In verse 23 of The Acts, chapter 27, Paul describes how the angel of the Lord stood before him and said: "Do not be afraid, Paul; you must stand before Caesar; and behold, God has granted you all those who are sailing with you." Later on, in verse 34, Paul tells those on board that "not a hair is to perish from the head of any of you."

"And when he had said this, he took bread, and giving thanks to God in the presence of all he broke it and began to eat. Then they were all encouraged and ate some food themselves. And we were in all two hundred and seventy-six persons in the ship."

And we were in all two hundred and seventy-six persons   276 × 11
Acts 27:37 ημεθα δε πασαι ψυχαι διακοσιαι εβδομηκοντα εξ

So right in the text of the Bible is another number that points to a great theomatic truth.

In this chapter, we have seen how God uses the number 276 to depict the satanic kingdom, hell, the curse of the law, sin, evil, the flesh, and so on. The number 276 is symbolic of all that is bad. Why then were there 276 souls saved? Let's answer this question by asking the Christian reader another question.

When you were saved, what were you saved from? The satanic kingdom, right? This is exactly why there were 276 souls saved in Paul's shipwreck. The number 276 symbolizes the fact that these souls were saved from Satan's power; and the Greek word from this story meaning "to be saved" also has a theomatic value of 276. This further substantiates why 276 souls were saved.

To be saved   276 × 5
Acts 28:4 διασωθεντα

7
The Number 666

No study on the subject of numbers in the Bible would be complete without mention of the number 666. It was in the later stages of this research that we began to look into the number 666, and what we found was truly exciting. Perhaps no other number in Scripture has fascinated students of the Word more than this one. Books on Bible prophecy are full of speculation as to what 666 means. We think that theomatics has partially unlocked its meaning.

As was shown in the second chapter, the number 666 appears with theomatic values ($\chi\xi\varsigma$) in the earliest known manuscript for the book of Revelation. In the Chester Beatty papyrus, in which this reading occurs, there exist other variations also. Throughout the text, there are a few Greek words here and there that are spelled differently from the Nestle text, which we used exclusively for this book.[1] These spelling variations are for the most part minor, but crucial to theomatics. If even one letter is different from the original text that God wrote, it would throw all of the number values off. The interesting thing we discovered, however, was that if the reading in the papyrus differed from that of Nestle's, the theomatics would often only work out in the papyrus. A perfect example of this is found in Revelation 13:18.

In the King James Version of the Bible, Revelation 13:18 reads as follows: "Here is wisdom. Let him that hath understanding count [calculate] the number of the beast: for it is the number of man; and his number is six hundred three score and six."

In the papyrus, this verse is expressed in completely different words.

[1] Please refer to p. 173 for textual information.

The Greek word for *understanding* is νουν, but in the papyrus a different word appears which eliminates the first letter, the result being ουν. The word ουν means "therefore." This changes the meaning of the verse somewhat. The biggest change comes at the end of the verse. The words "his number" do not appear in the papyrus. Here is how the verse reads: "Here is wisdom. The one therefore having [wisdom], let him calculate the number of the beast: for it is the number of man, and it is 666."

The amazing thing is that in the papyrus the number value of this verse after the opening sentence is 666×15. The probability of this happening by chance is very low and only serves to offer proof that this may be the correct reading. Here now is the verse with its number value —from the papyrus of the third century.

The one therefore having wisdom, let him calculate 666×15
the number of the beast: for it is the number of man, and it is   *666*
Rev 13:18 εχων ουν ψηφισατω αριθμον του θηριου αριθμος γαρ
         ανθρωπου εστιν εστιν δε χξς

When most people hear the number 666 mentioned, one thing invariably enters their mind.

Antichrist

Who is the antichrist? This one question has excited the minds of Christians since earliest times. The early church fathers were the first to try and identify the beast of Revelation by the number value of his name. In fact, many early Christians thought that the Roman empire was the world system described in Revelation, and that Nero was the antichrist. Much ingenuity was applied to try and make the number value of his name work out to 666. Since that time others have tried to do likewise, thus picking out their favorite candidate for antichrist, and trying to make the number value of his name work out to 666. A recent example of this will illustrate what we mean.

A few years ago there were some people who proposed the idea that Henry Kissinger might be the antichrist. One such individual, to prove this, devised a system of number values to fit the English alphabet. The letter *a* had a value of 6, *b* was 12, or 6×2, *c* was 18, or 6×3, and so forth. Each letter that followed was six more than the previous one. Using this method the following results were obtained.

66	54	114	114	54	84	42	30	108		
K	I	S	S	I	N	G	E	R	=	666

Quite frankly, we do not believe that Henry Kissinger is the antichrist. Many other examples could be shown, in which people have tried to make somebody's name work out to 666. In fact, if one tries hard enough arranging mathematic alphabets, he can make just about anyone's name add up to 666.

Throughout Christian church history, many scholars have accepted the idea that the verse in Revelation is speaking about the number value of someone's name. A perfect example of this is found in the paraphrased edition of the living Bible: "Here is a puzzle that calls for careful thought to solve it. Let those who are able interpret this code: the numerical values of the letters in his name add to 666!"

If the numerical values of the name of the antichrist are supposed to work out to 666, it poses some very interesting questions. In what language is his name? To coincide with theomatics, his name would have to be either a Hebrew or Greek name. Such would seem a very unlikely possibility. If his name was not in Hebrew or Greek, then how could it be identified? It would mean devising a number code based on the alphabet of the language of his name. But, here again, what number values would be used? In the example of Kissinger's name, the person who devised the code took his own liberty and started out his alphabet with the number 6. Why couldn't there have been another mathematical arrangement?

After many hundreds of hours of research in theomatics, we have come to the definite conclusion that Revelation 13:18 is not referring to the number value of someone's personal name. Let us state, however, that this is only an opinion, for nobody can be completely assured of anything in Bible prophecy until after it happens. The reasons we have come to this conclusion are several.

Throughout Revelation, chapter 13, one major translation that is in use today[2] refers to the beast as *he*. For example, verse 16 is translated: "He causes all, the small and the great . . . to be given a mark." Verse 17, which follows, is translated: "He provides that no one should be able to buy or sell."

[2]New American Standard Version.

The Greek of this passage does not necessarily refer to the beast as *he*, but rather as *it*. The translators in this particular case simply assumed that *it* was male. Verse 18 of the same translation reads as follows: "For the number is that of a man." The word *a* as in "a man" is an indefinite article, and in the Greek language there are no indefinite articles. The passage does not necessarily say that 666 is the number of a man, but rather that it is the "number of man." The Revised Standard Version translates this verse in the following manner: "Let him who has understanding reckon the number of the beast, for it is a human number." The King James Version refers to 666 simply as "the number of man."

As you can clearly see by now, the beast, and all that it stands for, is not necessarily male, but rather neuter (neither male nor female). Obviously there will be a world ruler, and this world ruler could be the beast that is talked about in Revelation 13:18, but we believe that here the beast spoken of is much more than just a man—even though a man must assuredly be involved. It is speaking of a system, a blasphemous system of antichrist, which incorporates much more than simply being the number value of someone's name. The number 666 bespeaks mankind, and its rebellion against God, all tied in and interlocked with the satanic kingdom. As will be shown later in this chapter, 276 also weaves its way through the passages that speak of 666 and the antichrist. In fact, you might say that 666 and 276 are brothers, because they always work together.

Before we examine some very exciting features, let's discuss for a moment the word *antichrist*. When we show theomatics to many of our friends, one question invariably arises. Does the word *antichrist* work out to 666? The answer to this question is no, and there is a definite reason for it. The word *antichrist* appears five times in the New Testament, all instances of which are found in 1 and 2 John. The remarkable thing that we discovered was that the Bible referred to the word in a broad sense rather than in a specific one. Antichrist is a spirit, a spirit of rebellion, and anyone who is not a Christian is an antichrist. 1 John 2:22 says: "This is the antichrist, the one who denies the Father and the Son." Here the word is used in a broad sense, as it applies to all those who deny the Father and the Son. Chapter 4, verse 3, says this: "And every spirit that does not confess Jesus is not from God; and this is the spirit of antichrist, of which you have heard that it is coming, and now it is already in the world." So, as you can see, antichrist is a spirit which is coming, meaning that it will increase, but it is already here. 2 John:7 throws even more light on the topic: "For many deceivers have gone out into the world, those who do not acknowledge Jesus Christ's coming in the flesh. This is the deceiver and the antichrist." The last two references to antichrist are found in 1 John 2:18: "Children, it is the last hour; and just as you heard that antichrist is coming, even now are there many antichrists; from this we know that it is the last hour."

Never once does the Bible specifically refer to the one world ruler in the book of Revelation as being the antichrist. Obviously he is the antichrist in the true sense of the word, but he is not referred to as such in Scripture. Christians have coined the expression, and it is definitely descriptive of the man, but even more so of the one world system, which is to prevail during the tribulation period. The spirit of antichrist is already in the world, but it is going to build up and increase even more as time passes. The number 666 definitely bespeaks antichrist, not only as the man, but also as the system. The system, the man, and the beast of Revelation all tie together to comprise the one world system that is to take the mark of the beast.

Of all the references to the antichrist, there is one that definitely seems to indicate the last days and points toward the one world ruler and the system of antichrist: "Children, it is the last hour; and just as you heard that antichrist is coming." The theomatic value of this phrase is 666 × 12, or 666 × 6 × 2.

Children, it is the last hour; and just   666 × 6 × 2
as you heard that antichrist is coming
1 Jn 2:18 παιδια εσχατη ωρα εστιν και καθως ηκουσατε οτι αντιχριστος ερχεται'

2 Thessalonians, chapter 2, is unquestionably the passage of Scripture that most clearly speaks of the antichrist, to be revealed in the last day. The next feature is the most outstanding possible in the entire design of antichrist: "Let no man deceive you by any means; for that day will not come, except there come a falling away first, and the man of sin is revealed, the son of perdition."

The man of sin, the son of perdition   666 × 6
2 Thess 2:3 ανθρωπος ανομιας υιος της απωλειας'

Let's now take the complete phrase that follows "the man of sin, the son of perdition," which are adjacent in the Greek, and see what happens.

The man of sin, the son of perdition, who opposeth and   666 × 22
exalteth himself above all that is called God, or that
is worshiped; so that he takes his seat in the temple
of God, showing himself as being God
2 Thess 2:3–4 ανθρωπος της ανομιας υιος της απωλειας ο αντικειμενος
και υπεραιρομενος επι παντα λεγομενον Θεον η
σεβασμα ωστε αυτον εις τον ναον Θεου καθισαι απ-
οδεικνυντα εαυτον οτι εστιν Θεος

The next most outstanding reference to the antichrist occurs in verse 8, which says:

Then the lawless one will be revealed whom the   666 × 13
the Lord Jesus will slay with the breath of His mouth
2 Thess 2:8 τοτε αποκαλυφθησεται ανομος ον κυριος Ιησους ανελει
πνευματι του στοματος αυτου

Finally it says that this man of sin and son of perdition is coming "according to the operation of Satan with all power and signs and wonders of a lie." In the Greek text, the words "of a lie" appear after the word "wonders." Interestingly enough, without the words "of a lie" an outstanding design is present. Watch!

According to the operation of Satan   666 × 6
with all power and signs and wonders
2 Thess 2:9 κατ ενεργειαν του Σατανα εν παση δυναμει και σημειοις
και τερασιν"

And to top this whole design off, here is the word *wonders* by itself:

Wonders   666
2 Thess 2:9 τερασιν

Next, we shall turn to the book of Revelation, which will occupy most of our attention for the rest of this chapter. In chapter 13, verse 2, the text states: "And the dragon gave to it [the beast] its power, and its throne and great authority." The following two features, taken from the above quotation, will explain why the beast is coming with all power and signs and wonders:

And the dragon gave to it its power and   666 × 6 × 2
its throne and great authority
Rev 13:2 και εδωκεν αυτω δρακων την δυναμιν αυτου και θρονον αυτου
        και εξουσιαν μεγαλην"

Its power and its throne and great authority   666 × 7
Rev 13:2 δυναμιν   αυτου   και   τον   θρονον   αυτου   και   εξουσιαν
        μεγαλην'

Since the word *antichrist* does not work out to 666, you are probably curious as to what it does work out to. At this time we have not researched the subject thoroughly, but we have uncovered an interesting design. One particular passage that has intrigued many scholars is found in 2 Thessalonians 2:7, where it talks about the "mystery of lawlessness." Here is that verse: "For already the mystery of lawlessness operates: only he who now letteth will let, until he is taken out of the way."

The mystery of lawlessness operates   2,040
2 Thess 2:7 μυστηριον ενεργειται ανομιας'

And the word "antichrist" has the same theomatic value.

Antichrist   2,040
1 Jn 4:3 αντιχριστου

Do you see any connection between the last two features and the following?

The great tribulation   2,040
Rev 7:14 θλιψεως μεγαλης'

At this time we do not fully understand the significance of the number 2,040, but there is obviously some connection among these three features. This only demonstrates that along with the numbers 276 and 666, there are many other key numbers that comprise the overall theomatic design of the Bible. This is why much research is needed to answer many of our questions.

In the above example, the word *antichrist* had a value of 2,040. However, in the New Testament this word is spelled two different ways. In the nominative case it has a value of 1,840. Here now are two features which bring forth further truth in the theomatic design. The word *antichrist* will be followed by a well-known term from the book of Revelation.

Antichrist   1,840
1 Jn 2:22 αντιχριστος'

The image of the beast   1,840
Rev 13:15 τη εικονι του θηριου

In the process of compiling the features for this book, many out-standing facts were discovered concerning 666. The number 666 weaves its way through many themes, topics, and subtopics. For this chapter, we have selected only those that showed consistency and bring out the true meaning of the number—as it applies to end-time events. One of these topics is the mark of the beast.

The Mark of the Beast

Probably the most profound significance of the number 666 emerges from those passages of Scripture which concern the mark of the beast. The Greek word for *mark* is χαραγμα, and it means "to engrave, mark, or stamp" something. Revelation, chapter 13, tells how those that worship the image of the beast will receive a mark on their right hand or forehead. For centuries people wondered what the real significance of this was. Since the invention of the computer, it is very easy to see how every person in the world could be marked and cata-logued with a number, which in turn would be programmed into a computer. Revelation 13:17 tells us that no one would be able to buy or sell, except those who have the mark, the name of the beast, or the number of its name.

With the coming of the computer, this idea would be very feasible. In fact, right now in certain parts of the world, banks and retail outlets are experimenting with the idea of a cashless society. Test programs have already been set up where people in certain communities who desire to purchase something go into a store or place of business and can conduct their complete transaction without money. Here's how it works: Let's say that Mrs. Jones goes grocery shopping one morning. Upon going through the checkout stand, the purchase price is added up and fed into a computer terminal sitting next to the cash register. The terminal is connected to Mrs. Jones's bank and to her checking account, which has been assigned a number. Mrs. Jones carries a card, which is then placed in the computer, and the transaction is recorded.

The computer simply deducts the money from her account, and there is no cash handled at all. Many bankers think that this system is inevitable within the next decade. In fact, many supermarkets around the country are already being set up for this. You may have noticed that the grocery items you presently buy have computer keys printed on the label. These are rows of lines, with a series of numbers written beneath them. This computer key on the packages of food items is just part of the overall system now being developed.

The advantages mentioned to promote this idea sound very good at first glance. If there was no cash present, how could there be robberies? Also, cheating on income taxes could be eliminated. The government would know where every penny was, which would provide for a more stable economy.

On the surface, this all sounds very good—but watch out! This would be only the first step toward the mark of the beast, because the system must have one more change before it could be truly successful. What if somebody stole Mrs. Jones's identification card and went on a spending spree? To solve this problem the number would simply be placed on her forehead or hand. The number would be invisible to the naked eye, but when placed under a certain kind of light, it would be clearly visible. This way every person in the world would be branded and identified by his own personal number. It is presumed that crime could be controlled better. If the number were tattooed into a person's flesh, false identification would be virtually impossible.

There is little question in our minds that the mark of the beast may in some way involve a worldwide computer network. Christians who refuse to take the mark would be unable to buy or sell anything. The fact that this idea is seriously in the development stages makes us only aware of the fact that the end is upon us. Taking the mark, however, will involve much more than simply being able to buy or sell. There is something horrendous and blasphemous about this mark that we don't know about yet. When the time comes, it will be quite obvious as to what this is.

There are seven references in the book of Revelation to the mark of the beast. All of these, without exception, are structured on multiples of 666. Let's begin by examining three features from Revelation 13:16–17. These two verses explain perfectly how the antichrist will cause all unbelievers to receive his mark. Here is verse 16:

It causes all, the small and the great, and the rich and   666 × 40
the poor, and the free men and the slaves, to be given a
mark on their right hand or forehead
Rev 13:16 ποιει παντας τους μικρους και τους μεγαλους και τους
πλουσιους και τους πτωχους και τους ελευθερους και τους
δουλους ινα δωσιν αυτοις χαραγμα τα επι της χειρος αυτων
της δεξιας η επι των μετωπων αυτων"

Verse 17, which follows, continues to tell the story of how "no one should be able to buy or sell, except the one who has the mark or the name of the beast or the number of its name." Two features are found in this verse, the first of which comprises the complete verse. The second feature is the more distinct portion.

And it provides that no one should be able to buy   666 × 16
or sell, except the one who has the mark, or the name
of the beast, or the number of its name
Rev 13:17 και ινα μη τις δυνηται αγορασαι η πωλησαι ει μη ο εχων το
χαραγμα η το ονομα του θηριου η αριθμον του ονοματος
αυτου

The one who has the mark, or the name of the beast,   666 × 11
or the number of its name
Rev 13:17 ο εχων χαραγμα η ονομα του θηριου η τον αριθμον του
ονοματος αυτου'

Revelation 16:2 states that:

Foul and evil sores came upon the men who bore the mark   666 × 19
of the beast and worshiped its image
Rev 16:2 εγενετο ελκος κακον και πονηρον επι τους ανθρωπους τους
εχοντας το χαραγμα θηριου και τους προσκυνουντας τη εικονι
αυτου'

But let's now take the most distinct portion from the above and watch what happens.

The men who bore the mark   666 × 9
Rev 16:2 τους ανθρωπους τους εχοντας το χαραγμα"

The next two features contain outstanding significance. Revelation 19:20 says that "the beast was seized, and with him the false prophet who performed the signs in his presence, by which he deceived those who had received the mark of the beast and those who worshiped its image."

Nothing could be more outstanding than the following:

Those who had received the mark of the beast   666 × 3
Rev 19:20 λαβοντας χαραγμα θηριου'

The design of 666 is also found in the verses that speak of those who worship the image of the beast. Revelation 13:13–14 tells how the beast causes those who dwell on the earth to make an image to the first beast: "It works great signs, even making fire come down from heaven in the sight of men; and by the signs which it is allowed to work in the presence of the beast, telling those who dwell on the earth to make an image to the beast, who was wounded by the sword and yet lived."

Telling those who dwell on the earth to make   666 × 9
an image to the beast
Rev 13:14 λεγων τοις κατοικουσιν επι της γης ποιησαι εικονα τω θηριω'

Here are the words from Revelation 14:11: "And the smoke of their torment goes up for ever and ever; and they have no rest, day or night, those who worship the beast and its image and whoever receives the mark of its name."

The next two features from the above passage will absolutely and completely amaze you!

Those who worship the beast and its image   666 × 6
Rev 14:11 οι προσκυνουντας το θηριον και εικονα αυτου

Whoever receives the mark of its name   666 × 6
Rev 14:11 λαμβανει το χαραγμα του ονοματος αυτου'

The probability against just the above two features working out the way they have is overwhelming. In fact, you might say that these two features by themselves could almost prove the existence of the theomatic design in the Word of God. But what about all of the other references to the mark of the beast that have theomatic values of 666? Take these into consideration, and your statistical probability would be staggering!

To conclude this theme, one last feature will be shown from Revelation, chapter 20. Here John describes how he "saw the souls of those who had been beheaded for their testimony of Jesus and for the Word of God, and who did not worship the beast or its image and did not receive its mark on their foreheads or their hands." The following feature is a multiple of 666, because it is emphasizing the fact that these saints did not worship the beast or receive its mark.

Did not worship the beast or its image, and did not receive   666 × 14
its mark on their foreheads or their hands
Rev 20:4 ου προσεκυνησαν θηριον ουδε εικονα αυτου και ουκ ελαβον
χαραγμα επι μετωπον και επι την χειρα αυτων'

Now we shall focus our attention on a different design that exists is these passages related to the mark of the beast. Do you remember the number 276 from the last chapter? This number, of course, bespeaks all that is satanic and diabolical—which the mark of the beast is. Flowing through all of these passages on the mark of the beast are many multiples of 276. Because of the limits of time and space, we have neglected to show them. For example, "the man of sin, the son of perdition" not only is a multiple of 666, but also of 276. So it is throughout this design. Wherever 666 can be found, 276 is also present. The next five features will prove this fact.

The mark of the beast is the satanic mark! The name of the beast is the satanic name! The number of its name is the satanic number! That is why 276, the number for Satan and his kingdom, is so closely related to 666. Let us now quote the last half of Revelation 13:17, which has already been shown to be a multiple of 666: "The one who has the mark, or the name of the beast, or the number of its name."

Name of the beast   276 × 3
Rev 13:17 ονομα θηριου

The number of its name   276 × 15
Rev 15:2 του αριθμου του ονοματος αυτου"

Here now is a verse that contains three multiples of 276: "Foul and evil sores came upon the men who bore the mark of the beast and worshiped its image." We have already seen how this complete phrase was 666 × 19, and "the men who bore the mark" was 666 × 9. Look at what happens now!

The men who bore the mark of the beast and   276 × 31
worshiped its image

Rev 16:2 ανθρωπους τους εχοντας χαραγμα θηριου και προσκυνουντας εικονι αυτου'

Bore the mark 276 × 12
Rev 16:2 τους εχοντας το χαραγμα

The mark of the beast 276 × 9
Rev 16:2 το χαραγμα του θηριου'

The Kingdoms of the World

The number 666 is an unusual number for many reasons. It is found in many different facets of Scripture, and all of these facets interrelate to each other. So far we have seen only a portion of what is symbolized by 666. This number pops up whenever it refers to the antichrist and to the mark of the beast. But there is another side to this number. The number 666 also concerns the world system and the kingdoms of the world. It is here that the true import of the number is found, for the mark of the beast is a symbol of that corrupt system which lies beneath the surface. The one world system of Satan and the beast is the root of all that which is to take place in the last day. Here is where the true meaning of 666 may be found.

To begin, let's examine the Greek word for world, κοσμος. This word has a number value of 600, which is extremely significant. The number six being amplified by two zeros demonstrates that six is the number of the world and the world system.

World 600
Jn 1:10 κοσμος

Along with the word *world*, the word *earth* holds the same significance.

Earth 60
Rev 19:2 γην'

But the real significance is found in the next feature. In John 1:9 Jesus is described as the true light coming into the world. The Greek word εις means "into" or "in." Thus, the two words *in* and *world* have the meaning "in the world." These words equal 666, which along with *world* being 600, produce tremendous significance.

In the world 666
Jn 1:9 εις κοσμον'

Galatians 4:3 talks about "the elements of the world." The Greek word for *elements* is very interesting in that it carries several connotations. It could apply to the material world, which is, of course, composed of chemical elements, or the term could refer to the systematic elements such as the religious, political, or satanic world system. The term is extremely relevant to the number 666.

Elements of the world 666 × 3
Gal 4:3 στοιχεια κοσμου"

And now comes the significant aspect of this truth. Do you remember the feature from Chapter 5 on light, darkness, and power, where Satan offered Jesus all his power: "And the devil said to Him, 'I will give You all this power and its glory; for to me it has been delivered, and I give it to whomever I will. If You, then, will worship me, it shall all be yours." If you recall, the last segment of this passage had a theomatic value of 10,000, which indicated the tremendous power delegated to Satan. Back in verse 5 of this story, there is still another feature, which ties in perfectly with the design of the world system: "And he led Him up and showed Him all the kingdoms of the world in a moment of time."

The kingdoms of the world 666 × 2
Lk 4:5 βασιλειας οικουμενης

In the last chapter on 276 we showed that in the New Testament there were three references to the "ruler of this world." All were divisible by 276.

The ruler of this world is coming 276 × 15

Concerning judgment, because the ruler of this world has been judged 276 × 23

Now is the ruler of this world cast out 276 × 24

While you were reading these features, the question may have entered your mind, What about just "ruler of this world"? Here's your answer:

Ruler of this world 666 × 7
Jn 12:31 αρχων του κοσμου τουτου'

Since Satan is the ruler of this world, he is also in charge of the kingdoms of the world. Throughout the book of Revelation, "the kings of the earth" are referred to. These kings are under the control of Satan, of course, and they play a vital part in end-time events. The world system of the beast is administered and run by the kings of the earth. Revelation 16:14 refers to the "kings of the whole world." In the Greek, the word *whole* follows the word *world*, so it reads "kings of the world whole." The Greek word οικουμενης is translated as "world," but it really has the meaning of "inhabited earth." The above feature ("the kingdoms of the world") also uses the same Greek word, and it could have been translated "kingdoms of the inhabited earth." Connect this now with the following from Revelation:

Kings of the inhabited earth   666 × 2
Rev 16:14 βασιλεις οικουμενης'

Another highly significant aspect of the world system involves the commercial world—business, trade, commerce, and so forth. Revelation speaks a great deal about the commercial aspect of antichrist. In 2 Peter there is a very interesting Greek word, εμπορευσονται. It is defined as "to travel for business's sake; traffic, for trade, commerce, merchandise."

Merchandise   666 × 2
2 Pet 2:3 εμπορευσονται'

But Revelation 18:3 talks of Babylon the great: "The kings of the earth have committed fornication with her, and the merchants of the earth have grown rich with the wealth of her wantonness." We have already seen how "kings of the earth" was 666. Now connect the word *merchandise* with the "merchants of the earth":

Merchants of the earth   666
Rev 18:3 οι εμποροι γης

In Revelation, Babylon the great is shown not only to be a city, but also a symbol of the political and commercial world system. This political and commercial world system is the system of Satan, and for this reason everything works out to multiples of 276. Listed below are five complete phrases concerning Babylon the great:

Fallen, fallen is Babylon the great, she who has made   276 × 26
all the nations drink of the wine of the passion
of her immorality

Rev 14:8 επεσεν επεσεν Βαβυλων μεγαλη η εκ του οινου του θυμου
πορνειας αυτης πεποτικεν παντα τα εθνη

Babylon the great came in remembrance before God,   276 × 34
to give unto her the cup of the wine of the fierceness
of His wrath
Rev 16:19 Βαβυλων μεγαλη εμνησθη ενωπιον του Θεου δουναι αυτη το
ποτηριον οινου θυμου οργης αυτου

And upon her forehead a name was written, a mystery,   276 × 40
BABYLON THE GREAT, THE MOTHER
OF HARLOTS AND OF THE
ABOMINATIONS OF THE EARTH
Rev 17:5 και επι το μετωπον αυτης ονομα γεγραμμενον μυστηριον
ΒΑΒΥΛΩΝ ΜΕΓΑΛΗ ΜΗΤΗΡ ΠΟΡΝΩΝ ΚΑΙ ΤΩΝ ΒΔΕΛΥ-
ΓΜΑΤΩΝ ΤΗΣ ΓΗΣ

Fallen, fallen is Babylon the great! and has become   276 × 30
a dwelling place of demons and a prison of every
unclean spirit
Rev 18:2 επεσεν επεσεν Βαβυλων η μεγαλη και εγενετο
κατοικητηριον δαιμονιων και φυλακη παντος πνευματος
ακαθαρτου

So shall Babylon the great city be thrown down with   276 × 22
violence, and shall be found no more
Rev 18:21 ουτως ορμηματι βληθησεται Βαβυλων η μεγαλη πολις και ου
μη ευρεθη ετι

All of these long phrases have been building up toward one thing
—the most specific words possible:

Babylon the great   276 × 5
Rev 17:5 Βαβυλων η μεγαλη

Now we shall see something remarkable. A few features ago, we
showed that the words "kings of the inhabited earth" had a theomatic
value of 666 × 2. You may have asked yourself the question: What
about just the words "the inhabited earth"? Since Babylon the great
bespeaks the world system, the following will have the same theomatic
value of 276 × 5:

The inhabited earth   276 × 5
Rev 16:14 της οικουμενης'

Chapter 17 of Revelation is especially significant, because here is where the text talks about the harlot and the beast which carries her. In verse 7 the angel is found speaking to John: "But the angel said to me, 'Why marvel? I will tell you the mystery of the woman, and of the beast which carries her, having seven heads and ten horns.' "

Mystery of the woman   276 × 7
Rev 17:7 μυστηριον γυναικος

The beast which carries her   666 × 5
Rev 17:7 θηριου του βασταζοντος αυτην'''

Having seven heads and ten horns   666 × 5
Rev 17:7 εχοντος τας ζ κεφαλας και τα ι κερατα'

In verse 15 the angel continues to describe this woman: "And he said to me, 'The waters that you saw, where the harlot sits, are people and multitudes and nations and tongues.' "

Where the harlot sits   666
Rev 17:15 η πορην καθηται'

Let's now quote verse 17, and then show a feature of outstanding significance: "For God has put it into their [the ten kings'] hearts to carry out His purpose by being of one mind and giving over the kingdom of them to the beast."

The kingdom   666
Rev 17:17 την βασιλειαν'

To conclude this topic, two features will be shown from the last verse in chapter 17, which tells of the woman who is that city which has authority over the kings of the earth:

And the woman that you saw is the great city having   666 × 8
a kingdom over the kings of the earth
Rev 17:18 και η γυνη ην ειδες εστιν πολις μεγαλη η εχουσα βασιλειαν
          επι βασιλεων της γης'

The great city having a kingdom over the kings   666 × 6
of the earth

Rev 17:18 η πολις η μεγαλη η εχουσα βασιλεαιν επι βασιλεων της γης"

Miscellaneous Features

So far in this chapter we have established several facts concerning the number 666. First of all, it bespeaks the spirit of antichrist and the man of sin, the son of perdition. Second, it is emphatically tied to the mark of the beast and all those who receive that mark. And last, 666 refers to the kingdoms of the world and the world system that is to prevail in the last day.

Jesus refers to the last days in Matthew 24:19, when He says: "And woe unto them that are with child, and to them that give suck in those days!"

Those days   666
Mt 24:19 εκειναις ημεραις'

It's heartwarming how the theomatic design in the Bible weaves its way together, because three verses later Jesus said: "And unless those days had been cut short, no flesh would have been saved."

Those days   276
Mt 24:22 αι ημεραι εκειναι

The above two features are a perfect example of how the complete theomatic design fits together. In one passage "those days" is 666, and in another it is 276. Each passage is spelled out with different Greek words, and for this reason God is able to bring forth two truths with the same words.

Jesus again spoke concerning the last days when He said that "the harvest is the completion of the age."

The harvest is the completion of the age   666 × 5
Mt 13:39 θερισμος συντελεια αιωνος εστιν'

Let's continue this theme through the next few features. Matthew 24:30 states that "then the sign of the Son of Man will appear in heaven, and then all the tribes of the earth will mourn." These words are again spoken in Revelation 1:7: "Behold, He is coming with clouds, and every eye will see Him, even those who pierced Him; and all the tribes of the earth will mourn over Him."

All the tribes of the earth will mourn   666 × 4
Mt 24:30 κοψονται πασαι φυλαι γης'

In His message to the churches in Revelation, Jesus said to the church in Philadelphia: "I also will keep thee from the hour of temptation, which shall come upon all the world, to try those that dwell upon the earth."

To try those that dwell upon the earth   666 × 4
Rev 3:10 πειρασαι κατοικουντας επι της γης'

Revelation 11:18 tells how Christ is coming to reward His saints, "and to destroy the ones destroying the earth."

And to destroy the ones destroying the earth   666 × 5
Rev 11:18 και διαφθειραι τους διαφθειροντας την γην

Probably the most outstanding feature in reference to those dwelling on the earth is found in Revelation, chapter 13. Here it says:

The whole world wandered after the beast   666 × 5
Rev 13:3 εθαυμασθη ολη η γη οπισω του θηριου'''

To conclude the miscellaneous features, we will look at five features, all of which bring forth an outstanding little design. Revelation 16:13 states that three unclean spirits like frogs came out of the mouth of the dragon, beast, and false prophet.

Mouth of the dragon   666 × 3
Rev 16:13 στοματος δρακοντος"

Earlier in this chapter we saw how the dragon was the one who gave the beast its power and its throne and its great authority. Connect this next feature now with the mouth of the dragon: "And the beast was given a mouth uttering haughty and blasphemous words, and it was allowed to exercise authority for forty-two months; And it opened its mouth in blasphemy against God, to blaspheme His name, and His tabernacle, and them that dwell in heaven."

Blasphemy against God   666 × 3
Rev 13:6 βλασφημιας προς τον Θεον"

A perfect feature which ties the last two together is found in Revelation 12:12: "Woe to the earth and the sea; because the devil has come down to you, having great wrath, knowing that he has only a short time."

Great wrath 666
Rev 12:12 θυμον μεγαν"

Now we are going to see a precious spiritual truth. In the Greek language of the New Testament there existed two words for *love*. One was ερως, pronounced *eros*, which meant a physical or sensual love. The other word was φιλια, pronounced *philea*, which referred more to a tender love, or a brotherly love. But how could God's love be expressed by either of these two words? So what the writers of the New Testament did was to use a new word, αγαπη, pronounced *agape*, which expressed the love of God. The number seven is, of course, God's perfect number, therefore "love of God" produces the following:

Love of God 777
Rom 8:39 αγαπες Θεου

And guess what the theomatic value of "wrath of God" is?

Wrath of God 666
Col 3:6 οργε Θεου'

Heaven and Earth

In the final stages of research for this book, we discovered something astounding. A verse in chapter 21 of Revelation opened up a completely new design with the number 666. As this design began to unfold itself, another design based on the number 11 became apparent. Everything to do with heaven and earth was structured on the number 666 or the number 11.

We still do not understand everything concerning what you are about to see. All we can do is simply present the features as the Lord has placed them in His Word. Further research should unlock the significance of this design. Here now are some of the more outstanding features from our files dealing with the subject of heaven and earth.

Toward the end of the book of Revelation, John describes how he saw a new heaven and a new earth, after the old heaven and earth had passed away. We will now quote the complete verse of Revelation 21:1:

And I saw a new heaven and a new earth;   666 × 11
for the first heaven and first earth had passed away,
and there was no longer any sea
Rev 21:1 και ειδον ουρανον καινον και γην καινην ο γαρ πρωτος
        ουρανος και η πρωτη γη απηλθαν και η θαλασσα ουκ εστιν ετι

Now this verse is talking about heaven and earth passing away, and it is a multiple of 666. When we turned to The Acts 17:24, the following feature appeared:

Heaven and earth   666 × 2
Acts 17:24 ουρανου και γης'

Perhaps the most famous reference in the Bible to heaven and earth passing away is found in the following:

Heaven and earth shall pass away,   666 × 7
but My words shall not pass away
Mt 24:35 ουρανος και η γη παρελευσεται οι δε λογοι μου ου μη παρ-
        ελθωσιν'

Now comes the interesting part of this design. While working with the above feature in Revelation 21:1, it was noticed that the complete verse had a theomatic value of 666 × 11, but something else presented itself, too. The little word *earth* by itself had a theomatic value of only 11, and the complete verse was 666 × 11.

Earth   11
Rev 21:1 γη

At first, this fact did not register until further research revealed a verse in 1 John 2:17: "And the world is passing away, and also its lusts."

World is passing away   1,100
1 Jn 2:17 κοσμος παραγεται'

These three features of eleven were exciting, but somehow the meaning was rather unclear until the next two features appeared from Ephesians: "That in the dispensation of the fullness of times, he might gather together in one all things in Christ, things in heaven and on earth."

In heaven and on earth   666 × 2
Eph 1:10 επι ουρανοις και επι γης'

Woven inside this verse was the key we were looking for. The word *heaven* along with the word *earth* produce the following:

Heaven and earth 1,100
Eph 1:10 τοις ουρανοις της γης

So in one passage of Scripture "heaven and earth" is 666, and in another it is 1,100. As we did more research, a picture started to unfold itself. As a general rule the number 666 was always the predominant number when the text referred to the heavens alone; 1,100 was always predominant when it referred to just the earth. However, both 666 and 1,100 could be found when the text spoke of both heaven and earth, and sometimes 666 was present in many passages that spoke of just the earth.

Now there is a very important fact, which we would like to explain to the reader. When many Christians think of heaven, they think of the place where God lives, in other words, a single locality somewhere in the universe. However, this is not the heaven that is spoken of in this design. When Genesis 1:1 states that God created the heaven and the earth, *heaven* is referring to the "universe," that is, the stars and the galaxies, not the heaven or paradise where God dwells. As we said earlier, we still do not understand everything about this design. The reason we are showing it is that we want the reader to understand that there is much in God's Word that is a mystery, and that all of the intricate truths of Christianity are wrapped up in the theomatic design of the Bible.

Now we shall examine just a few of the features in our files that are multiples of 1,100 and speak of only the earth. 2 Peter 3:13 states the following: "But new heavens and a new earth according to His promise we await." In this verse, only the last portion fits the design. Here it is.

A new earth according to His promise we await 1,100 × 3
2 Pet 3:13 γην καινην κατα επαγγελμα αυτου προσδοκωμεν

Here are the words from The Acts 1:8: "But ye shall receive power when the Holy Ghost is come upon you: and ye shall be witnesses unto Me both in Jerusalem, and in all Judea, and in Samaria, and unto the uttermost part of the earth."

Unto the uttermost part of the earth 1,100 × 3
Acts 1:8 εως εσχατου της γης

Jesus taught His disciples not to lay up for themselves "treasures upon earth."

Treasures upon earth   1,100 × 2
Mt 6:19 θησαυρους επι της γης"

Matthew 9:6 states that "the Son of Man has authority on earth to forgive sins."

Authority on earth   1,100
Mt 9:6 εξουσιαν επι γης"

In the well-known parable of the seeds and soil Jesus talks about the seed that fell "into good earth."

Into good earth   1,100
Mk 4:8 εις την γην την καλην'

Revelation 19:2 talks about the great harlot who "defiled the earth."

Defiled the earth   1,100
Rev 19:2 εφθειρεν την γην'''

From The Acts 2:19 come two features that tie together perfectly the numbers 1,100 and 666: "And I will show wonders in heaven above, and signs in the earth below; blood, and fire, and vapor of smoke."

Signs in the earth below   1,100 × 2
Acts 2:19 σημεια επι της γης κατω'

Earth below   666 × 2
Acts 2:19 γης κατω

Finally, we shall look at a few features on the heavens that will culminate in two features from the Old Testament. In Revelation 18:5, the following words are spoken concerning Babylon the great:

For her sins are piled up as high as heaven   666 × 6
Rev 18:5 οτι εκολληθησαν αυτης αι αμαρτιαι αχρι ουρανου

The next feature is one of the most significant in this entire chapter. Throughout the gospels, Jesus refers to the tribulation period in the last day, when the "powers of the heavens shall be shaken."

Powers of the heavens   666 × 5
Lk 21:26 δυναμεις των ουρανων'

There must be a tremendous connection between the mark of the beast and powers of the heavens. Why did Jesus say that in the last day the powers of the heavens would be shaken? The clue may be found in Revelation 12:4, which speaks of the dragon being cast to earth, his tail drawing a third part of the stars of heaven. Could this be what Jesus was referring to as the powers of the heavens?

And his tail drew the third part of the stars of heaven $666 \times 6 \times 2$
and cast them to the earth
Rev 12:4 κα ουρα αυτου συρει τριτον αστερων ουρανου και εβαλεν
αυτους εις την γην"

Revelation, chapter 10, talks about the angel who came down to earth and stood with one foot on the land and the other foot on the sea: "And he swore by Him Who lives for ever and ever, Who created heaven and the things therein."

Created heaven 666×2
Rev 10:6 εκτισεν ουρανου'

Let us now quote the complete verse: "And he swore by Him Who lives for ever and ever, Who created heaven and the things therein, and the earth and the things in it, and the sea and what is in it."

From this verse come the following Greek words:

Created heaven and the earth $1,100 \times 2$
Rev 10:6 εκτισεν τον ουρανον και την γην'

Which one verse in the whole Bible do people think of when they think of God creating? In the light of all that we have seen thus far, the chance against the next two features from Genesis 1:1 having the theomatic values that they do is absolutely astronomical. Here now is the first part of Genesis 1:1 from the Hebrew of the Old Testament:

In the beginning God created the heaven 666×3
Gen 1:1 בראשית ברא אלהים את השמים

This complete verse reads: "In the beginning God created the heaven and the earth." Here is the last portion:

Heaven and the earth $1,100$
Gen 1:1 השמים ואת הארץ

Making Clay to Open Blind Eyes

A few passages of Scripture mention clay. What is clay? Clay is earth, and proof of this can be found in a verse from Romans 9:21: "Hath not the potter power over the clay, of the same lump to make one vessel unto honor, and another unto dishonor?" The two words *lump* and *clay* produce the following feature:

Lump of clay $1,100 \times 2$
Rom 9:21 πηλου φυραματος

Of all the designs present in 666, the last five features will best portray the overpowering manner in which God has mathematically written His Word. These features will demonstrate that God has designed these numbers to bring forth the hidden meanings in Scripture.

The entire ninth chapter of John is devoted to the story of how Jesus opened the eyes of the blind man. In the first portion of the chapter it tells how He made clay from the spittle and then applied the clay to the blind man's eyes.

Let's now take verse 14 and see what happens: "Now it was a Sabbath on the day when Jesus made the clay, and opened his eyes."

Day when Jesus made the clay, and opened his eyes 666×10
Jn 9:14 ημερα τον πηλον εποιησεν ο Ιησους και ανεωξεν αυτου τους οφθαλμους'

Made clay   666
Jn 9:14 πηλον εποιησεν

Clay is earth, and 666 also bespeaks the earth. When Jesus placed the clay on this man's eyes, He told him to go wash in the pool of Siloam, and he would then see. When the man washed the earth out of his eyes, he could see.

In verse 10 the scribes and Pharisees were muttering amongst themselves, wondering how this blind man could now see: "Therefore they were saying to him, 'How then were opened your eyes?'" The first three Greek words in this phrase, "how then were opened," produce the same design. These words mean simply "how were they opened?"

How were they opened? 666×5
Jn 9:10 πως ουν ηνεωχθησαν'

They were opened because it was Jesus Who made the clay. That's why these features all work out to 666. Down in verse 26 the scribes and Pharisees were still talking among themselves: "They said therefore to him, 'What did He do to you? How did He open your eyes?'"

How did He open   666 × 2
Jn 9:26 πως ηνοιξεν'

The last feature comes from verse 32 of this chapter:

Open eyes of the blind   666 × 6
Jn 9:32 ηνεωξεν οφθαλμους τυφλου"

8
The 144 Thousands

"And I looked, and behold, the lamb stood on Mt. Zion, and with him 144 thousands having His name and the name of His Father written on their forehead."

The 144 thousands   144 × 7
Rev 14:1 ρμδ χειλιαδες'

Who are these 144 thousands who stand on Mt. Zion with the lamb? Speculation has prevailed as to what this might mean. A good example of this are the Jehovah witnesses, who base their entire religion on the idea that there will only be a 144,000 people in heaven. Even Christians have differed amongst themselves concerning the interpretation of this passage of Scripture.

In the last chapter we saw how Revelation 13:18 described the number of the beast, which is 666. But now the scene changes. Verse 1 of chapter 14, which immediately follows, tells how John looked, "and behold, the lamb stood on Mt. Zion, and with Him 144 thousands. . . ." Here the direct contrast is made from the scene of the world system of Satan and the antichrist to the 144 thousands. Again, who are these 144 thousands?

Earlier in this book it was shown that the numbers 666 and 144 appear in the earliest copy of the book of Revelation with the letters of the Greek alphabet standing for these numbers. If you will turn back to page 46 and look at the picture of the papyrus, you will see the letters for 144, ρμδ, followed by the word for *thousands* in Greek, χειλιαδες.

The number 144, as most people know, is 12 × 12, and 12 is

extremely significant throughout Scripture. It is emphatically the number of the chosen. In the Old Testament God called forth His chosen people, the Jews, and all Christians will readily agree that God calling forth a chosen people in the Old Testament symbolizes His calling forth His chosen people now, which is the body of Christ. We who have put our trust in Jesus are now God's chosen people. And how many tribes were there in the Old Testament? The answer is twelve.

In the New Testament Christ originally chose twelve men out of this world, which were His twelve disciples. Those twelve disciples symbolize all of us, who were chosen out of this world. Here again twelve is the number of the elect.

Let's now look at one more example involving the number twelve. In Matthew and John the text tells how the multitudes were fed, and afterwards twelve basketfulls of the fragments and the fishes were gathered up. Many Bible commentators have readily seen that these multitudes symbolize all mankind who hear the gospel, but that out of that mass of humanity twelve basketfuls were gathered up, which stand for those chosen out of the human race. Here, too, the number twelve typifies those who belong to Christ.

Now here is the key that unlocks the whole thing. In the original Greek of the papyrus and in all the other Greek texts of this passage, the number is not "144,000," as has been popularly supposed. Instead, it is the "144 thousands." The difference between these two is all the difference in the world. The Greek word for *thousands* (χειλιαδες) is not singular but plural. Translators have simply assumed that it was singular in meaning, because this was the only interpretation that made sense—at that time. But in the Greek of the New Testament the number is not 144,000, but rather the *144 thousands*.

Here is the difference between the two. Since the number 12 is the number of all the chosen, 144 is simply an amplification of that number, because 144 is 12 × 12. So 144 is even more emphatically the number of the chosen, and it is followed by the word *thousands*. Thousands of the what? Of the 144! And what is the 144? It is a symbolic number of all the redeemed, the elect, the bride of the lamb, the body of Christ the church—in short, all those who have put their trust in Jesus. And there are thousands upon thousands of them, standing on Mt. Zion with the lamb. Hallelujah!

This truth is further confirmed by the fact that the word *thousands* by itself has a theomatic value of 144 × 6. This definitely indicates that the thousands referred to here are thousands of the 144, which is the number of all the redeemed.

Thousands 144 × 6
Rev 14:1 χειλιαδες'

Twice in the book of Revelation this number of the redeemed is mentioned (Revelation 7:3–10 and Revelation 14:1–5). We will be examining both of these passages in detail. In verse 2 of chapter 14 John describes the sound of many waters in heaven along with the sound of harpers harping. In verse 3 he describes how these harpers sang a new song before the throne and before the four living creatures and before the elders. Here is the concluding portion of that verse:

And no one could learn the song except the   144 × 32
144 thousands, the ones purchased from the earth
Rev 14:3 και ουδεις εδυνατο μαθειν ωδην ει μη αι ρμδ χειλιαδες οι
ηγορασμενοι απο γης'

The 144 thousands, the ones purchased from the earth   144 × 17
Rev 14:3 αι ρμδ χειλιαδες ηγορασμενοι απο της γης'

And as we saw at the very beginning of this chapter, the most distinct feature possible is also a multiple of 144. Here it is again:

The 144 thousands   144 × 7
Rev 14:3 ρμδ χειλιαδες'

So right in the text of the Word of God it states that these 144 thousands are those who were purchased from the earth. This statement applies to all Christians, because we are the ones who have been purchased out of the satanic kingdoms of this world. For this reason we are able to sing a new song before the throne of God, and it is the song of the redeemed. And no one could learn it except the 144 thousands, the ones purchased from the earth.

The last portion of this passage on the 144 thousands from Revelation, Chapter 14, reads as follows:

These have been purchased from mankind as firstfruits to   144 × 98
God and the lamb, and in their mouth no lie was found,
for they are blameless
Rev 14:4–5 ουτοι ηγορασθησαν απο ανθρωπων απαρχη Θεω και αρνιω

και εν τω στοματι αυτων ουχ ευρεθη ψευδος αμωμοι γαρ εισιν'

This passage of Scripture states that the 144 thousands "have been purchased from mankind as firstfruits." Here are the leading two words from this verse:

Purchased firstfruits   144 × 10
Rev 14:4 *ηγορασθησαν απαρχη*

The second passage on the number 144 is found in Revelation, chapter 7. Here are described the four angels who are given power to harm the earth and the sea: "Then I saw another angel ascend from the rising of the sun, with the seal of the living God, and he called out with a loud voice to the four angels who had been given power to harm the earth and the sea, saying":

Do not harm the earth nor the sea nor the trees, until we   144 × 103
seal the servants of our God upon their foreheads
Rev 7:3 *μη αδικησητε την γην μητε την θαλασσαν μητε τα δενδρα αχρι*
   σφραγισωμεν τους δουλους του Θεου ημων επι των μετωπων
   αυτων'

Seal the servants of our God   144 × 31
Rev 7:3 *σφραγισωμεν δουλους Θεου ημων'*

In verse 4, which follows, John describes the number having been sealed as 144 thousands out of every tribe of the sons of Israel. Each of the tribes are then named, with twelve thousands being sealed from each one. Here again the Greek word for *thousands* is in the plural, and not the singular.

There is tremendous significance behind the names of the twelve tribes of Israel as they apply to all of the redeemed. We will be discussing this toward the end of this chapter. In verses 5–8 John lists and names these twelve tribes of Israel, but in verse 9, which follows, he describes this great multitude of 144 thousands, which has just been sealed: "After this I looked, and behold, the great multitude which to number it no one was able, from every nation, from all tribes and peoples and tongues, standing before the throne and before the lamb, clothed in white robes, with palm branches in their hands." This passage of Scripture is loaded with multiples of 144. For sake of illustration, here are two features which are the most distinct portions:

And behold, the great multitude which to number it 144 × 116
no one was able, from every nation, from all tribes
and peoples and tongues, standing before the throne and before the lamb
Rev 7:9 και ιδου οχλος πολυς ον αριθμησαι αυτον ουδεις εδυνατο εκ
παντος εθνους και φυλων και λαων και γλωσσων εστωτες
ενωπιον θρονου και ενωπιον αρνιου"

The great multitude which to number it no one 144 × 42
was able, from every nation
Rev 7:9 οχλος πολυς ον αριθμησαι αυτον ουδεις εδυνατο εκ παντος
εθνους'

At the beginning of this chapter, we made mention of the fact that the number 12 was symbolic of all the redeemed, and that 144 was simply an amplification of that number. Existing in the above phrase, there is another feature of prime importance, because it bears out the fact that this great multitude comprises all of the redeemed.

The Greek words "to number it" from the phrase "the great multitude which to number it no one was able" have a theomatic value of 1,200. These words actually are referring to the number of it, that is, the great multitude.

To number it 1,200
Rev 7:9 αριθμησαι αυτον

The Ones Coming out of the Great Tribulation

This account of all the redeemed continues to the end of chapter 7. Let us now pick up on verse 13: "And one of the elders answered saying to me, 'These, the ones who are clothed in white robes, who are they, and from where have they come?' "

The ones who are clothed in white robes 144 × 13
Rev 7:13 περιβεβλημενοι στολας λευκας"

"And I [John] said to him, 'My lord, you know.' And he said to me, 'These are the ones coming out of the great tribulation, and they have washed their robes and made them white in the blood of the lamb.' "

The ones coming out of the great tribulation   144 × 28
Rev 7:14 ερχομενοι εκ της θλιψεως της μεγαλης

Many are the references throughout the book of Revelation to those saints who victoriously come out of the great tribulation. The number 144 weaves its way through the most outstanding verses that speak of those who overcome and endure until the end.

Revelation 12:10 describes how Satan, who is the accuser of our brethren, was cast down to earth. Verse 11 says the following: "And they overcame him by the blood of the lamb and by the word of their testimony, and they loved not their lives unto death."

They overcame him by the blood of the lamb, and by   144 × 39
the word of their testimony
Rev 12:11 αυτοι ενικησαν αυτον δια αιμα αρνιου και δια λογον μαρτυριας αυτων

Here are the words from the second portion of this verse:

They loved not their lives unto death   144 × 42
Rev 12:11 ουκ ηγαπησαν την ψυχην αυτων αχρι θανατου"

John describes in chapter 19, verse 1, how he heard the sound of a great multitude from heaven saying: "Hallelujah! Salvation and glory and power belong to our God; because His judgments are true and righteous; for He has judged the great harlot who was corrupting the earth with her fornication, and He has avenged the blood of His servants on her."

He has avenged the blood of His servants   144 × 31
Rev 19:2 εξεδικησεν το αιμα των δουλων αυτου

Here are the words from Revelation 13:15: "And it was allowed to give breath to the image of the beast so that the image of the beast should both speak, and cause that as many as would not worship the image of the beast should be killed."

As many as would not worship the image of the beast   144 × 29
Rev 13:15 οσοι εαν μη προσκυνησωσιν εικονι του θηριου"

John then describes in chapter 15 the following vision: "And I saw, as it were, a sea of glass mixed with fire, and the ones overcoming the beast and its image and the number of its name, standing on the sea of glass holding harps of God."

The ones overcoming the beast and its image   144 × 36
Rev 15:2 τους νικωντας εκ θηριου και εκ της εικονος αυτου'

What makes the theomatic design in the Word of God so overpowering is that not only do the complete phrases work out, but also the most distinct portions within those phrases. The next feature from the passage above is a perfect example of this:

The ones overcoming the beast   144 × 21
Rev 15:2 τους νικωντας εκ θηριου'

Here now is the complete verse of Revelation 14:12:

Here is the endurance of the saints, who keep the   144 × 52
commandments of God and the faith in Jesus
Rev 14:12 Ωδε η υπομονη αγιων εστιν οι τηρουντες τας εντολας Θεου
και πιστιν Ιησου'

The most distinct portion from the above would be the following:

Endurance of the saints   144 × 11
Rev 14:11 υπομονη αγιων"

But this verse states that the saints:

Keep the commandments   144 × 18
Rev 14:12 τηρουντες τας εντολας"

The faith   144 × 7
Rev 14:12 την πιστιν

Jesus spoke the following concerning endurance in Revelation, chapter 3: "Because you have kept the word of My endurance, I also will keep you from the hour of temptation, which shall come upon all the world."

The word of my endurance   144 × 15
Rev 3:10 λογον της υπομονης μου'

Which verse can you think of that is undoubtedly the best known relating to the topic of endurance?

He that endureth until the end shall be saved   144 × 30
Mt 24:13 ο υπομεινας εις τελος ουτος σωθησεται'

Later on in the same chapter of Matthew 24, Jesus said the following:

On account of the elect the days shall be cut short   144 × 20
Mt 24:22 δια εκλεκτους κολοβωθησονται αι ημεραι

Tie this feature together with this next verse from Mark, chapter 13: "For false Christs and false prophets will arise, and show signs and wonders, to lead astray, if possible, the elect."

To lead astray, if possible, the elect   144 × 16
Mk 13:22 αποπλαναν ει δυνατον εκλεκτους'

There is one other verse that speaks of the elect, and it is found in Luke's gospel: "And will not God vindicate the elect of Him, who cry to Him day and night."

Will not God vindicate the elect   144 × 19
Lk 18:7 Θεος ου μη ποιηση εκδικησιν εκλεκτων'

To conclude this basic theme, we will present a verse containing two features. The following is most precious, as it relates to the end-time saints of God:

Blessed are those servants whom the Lord shall find   144 × 38
watching when He comes
Lk 12:37 μακαριοι δουλοι εκεινοι ους ελθων ο κυριος ευρησει
γρηγορουντας'

Blessed are those servants   144 × 7
Lk 12:37 μακαριοι δουλοι εκεινοι"

Features from Revelation

At this time we present those features found in the book of Revelation that have not been placed under other topical headings. The entire book of Revelation is saturated with multiples of 144 whenever it refers to all of the redeemed. Many of the longer phrases that contain multiples of 144 will not be shown, because in presenting this design we want to be as explicit as possible. For this reason only a portion of all the features present will be given.

In verse 3 of the first chapter of Revelation the following appears:

Blessed is the one who reads and those who hear the words   144 × 64
of the prophecy, and heed the things which are written in it

Rev 1:3 μακαριος ο αναγινωσκων και οι ακουοντες τους λογους προφητειας και τηρουντες εν αυτη γεγραμμενα'

Here is the most distinct portion of the above passage.

The one who reads and those who hear the words   144 × 37
of the prophecy
Rev 1:3 ο αναγινωσκων και οι ακουοντες λογους προφητειας'

Toward the end of Revelation, in chapter 20, the following is found:

Everyone who hears the words of the prophecy of this book   144 × 38
Rev 22:18 παντι ακουοντι λογους προφητειας βιβλιου τουτου'

In the first chapter of Revelation, the Lord Jesus tells John to send a message to the seven churches in Asia. In verse 12 of chapter 1 John describes how he turned and saw seven golden lampstands. In verse 20 of the same chapter Jesus tells John that these seven lampstands are the seven churches.

7 lampstands   144 × 9
Rev 1:12 ζ λυχνιας"

7 churches   144 × 8
Rev 1:20 ζ εκκλησιων"

In His address to the seven churches, Jesus referred seven times to the "one overcoming." As we showed in Chapter 5 on light, darkness, and power, the theomatic value of the "one overcoming" was 1,000. This was extremely significant, because overcoming and power go hand in hand.

The saints that overcome will be clothed in white: "And they shall walk with Me in white, for they are worthy." The theomatic value of all these words is 4,000, because they speak of overcoming. Let's take the most distinct portion of this phrase:

They shall walk in white   144 × 16
Rev 3:4 περιπατησουσιν εν λευκοις

Many of the phrases pertaining to the one overcoming contain multiples of 144. We will not take time to list all of them; however, one feature that is extremely significant is found in Revelation 2:17: "To the one overcoming will I give to eat of the hidden manna, and will give him a white stone, and a new name written on the stone which no one knows but he who receives it."

New name   144 × 3
Rev 2:17 ονομα καινον

Here are the words from Revelation 1:5–6: "To Him Who loves us and has freed us from our sins by His blood, and made us a kingdom of priests to God and Father of Him."

And made us a kingdom of priests to God   144 × 11
Rev 1:6 και εποιησεν ημας βασιλειαν ιερεις Θεω'

In Revelation 20:6, it reiterates that the saints shall reign as priests of God.

Priests of God   144 × 11
Rev 20:6 ιερεις του Θεου

And now we proudly present what has to be the most significant feature possible from the entire book of Revelation. Here is the word *saints* by itself:

Saints   144 × 6
Rev 8:3 αγιων

Here is Revelation 2:13: "And you hold fast the name of Me, and did not deny the faith of Me even in the days of Antipas the witness of Me, the faithful of Me."

Witness   144 × 8
Rev 12:11 μαρτυριας

The faithful of Me   144 × 10
Rev 2:13 ο πιστος μου

The faith   144 × 7
Rev 2:13 την πιστιν

An interesting feature occurs in Revelation 18:4, which talks about Babylon the great: "Then I heard another voice from heaven saying, 'Come out, my people, out of her, lest you take part in her sins, lest you share in her plagues.' "

Come out, My people   144 × 9
Rev 18:4 εξελθατε ο λαος μου

When we show theomatics to our friends, there is one feature that gets them more excited than any other and that is this one. Revelation 1:7 says: "Behold He is coming with clouds." Have you ever thought what this might mean? In Chapter 5 on light, darkness, and power, we showed how everything to do with clouds came out to multiples of 100, which bespoke power, but then in Revelation the word *clouds* has a theomatic value of 1,440, or 144 × 10. Why? Because He is coming with clouds of saints.

Clouds   144 × 10
Rev 1:7 νεφελων

Revelation 14:13 fits in beautifully with this entire design: "And I heard a voice from heaven saying, 'Write, blessed are the dead, the ones dying in the Lord from now on!' "

Ones dying in the Lord   144 × 17
Rev 14:13 εν κυριω αποθνησκοντες

One outstanding feature of tremendous significance occurs in chapter 15, verse 3. We have already seen a series of features from verse 2, where the great multitude stands on the sea of glass, the ones who overcame the beast and its image and the number of its name. Here's what happens next in verse 3:

And they sing the song of Moses, the servant of God,   144 × 70
and the song of the lamb
Rev 15:3 και αδουσιν την ωδην Μωυσεως του δουλου του Θεου και την
        ωδην του αρνιου'

Here is Revelation 22:17. "And the spirit and the bride say, 'Come.' And let the one who hears say, 'Come.' And let the one who is thirsty come; let him who desires take the water of life without cost." This complete verse is a multiple of 144; but here now are its two most distinct phrases.

And let the one who hears say, Come   144 × 26
Rev 22:17 και ακουων ειπατω ερχου'

And let the one who is thirsty come   144 × 23
Rev 22:17 και διψων ερχεσθω"

But let's tie these features together with the words of Jesus from Revelation 21:6. "I am the alpha and the omega, the beginning and the end. To the one thirsting, I will give of the water of life freely."

The one thirsting   144 × 13
Rev 21:6 διψωντι″

The New Jerusalem

Now is when we begin to present some really exciting theomatics. As the reader probably knows, everything to do with the New Jerusalem is structured on the number 12. The holy city has 12 gates, and at the 12 gates there are 12 angels, and the names of the 12 tribes of the sons of Israel are inscribed thereupon. The city also has 12 foundations on which are written the 12 names of the apostles of the lamb; and the wall of the city is 144 cubits.

So everything to do with the New Jerusalem is structured around the numbers 12 and 144. There is a powerful connection between the holy city, or New Jerusalem, and all of the redeemed. This will become quite apparent as you progress reading.

In Revelation, chapter 3, there exists a verse which shows forth an outstanding design. Here is the last portion of that verse. "And I will write on him the name of My God, and the name of the city of My God, the New Jerusalem which comes down from My God out of heaven."

The city of My God   144 × 24
Rev 3:12 της πολεως του Θεου μου′

Jerusalem   144 × 6
Rev 3:12 Ιερουσαλημ

New Jerusalem   144 × 8
Rev 3:12 καινης Ιερουσαλημ′

But here now is the complete thing:

And I will write on him the name of My God,   144 × 74
and the name of the city of My God, the New Jerusalem
Rev 3:12 και γραψω επ αυτον το ονομα του Θεου μου και το ονομα της
        πολεως του Θεου μου της καινης Ιερουσαλημ

Probably the most famous reference to the New Jerusalem is the term "holy city." The theomatic value of the holy city is 1,400, or 700 × 2. The number 700, as you will recall, speaks of perfection and holiness.

The holy city 700 × 2
Rev 22:19 πολεως αγιας

In Revelation 21:2 John describes how he saw:

The holy city, New Jerusalem coming down out of heaven 144 × 27
Rev 21:2 πολιν την αγιαν Ιερουσαλημ καινην καταβαινουσαν εκ ουρανου

One of the most fascinating aspects of theomatics, in which we are currently involved, is what we have termed "sacred geometry." This is the study of the dimensions of the New Jerusalem as given in chapter 21 of Revelation. Inside of the theomatic values which comprise the words descriptive of the New Jerusalem are the actual dimensions of the city. In fact, a complete model of the New Jerusalem can be built from the number values of the words. This study has not been completed yet, but when it is, the results will be astounding.

The Bride of the Lamb

The New Jerusalem is described in chapter 21 of Revelation as being the "bride, the wife of the lamb," which we as saints are also. The complete design of the holy city is structured around all of the redeemed, which make up the bride of the lamb. This is why the names of the twelve tribes of the sons of Israel are inscribed on the New Jerusalem. The numbers 12 and 144 bespeak the kingdom of God and kingdom of heaven, because the saints are to reign forever with Christ. The New Jerusalem along with the saints forms that kingdom.

Now here is a marvelous truth. As we mentioned earlier in Chapter 2, the words in Greek often have different spellings. We also mentioned that each of these spellings produces a different aspect of God's truth. For this reason, Jerusalem spelled one way is 144, and spelled another way it comes out 888, the same as the theomatic value of Jesus. This demonstrates that the city, which represents the redeemed, and Jesus are unified as one.

Jerusalem 144 × 6
Rev 3:12 Ιερουσαλημ

Jerusalem 888 × 2
Mt 4:25 Ιεροσολυμων'

And now we come to seven features. These seven features may be by far the most outstanding in this entire book. We will not take the time to introduce each one singularly, because they are very easy to understand. Please read them carefully and slowly, for nothing could be more revealing than the following:

For the marriage of the lamb has come, 144 × 32
and His bride has made herself ready
Rev 19:7 οτι ηλθεν ο γαμος αρνιου και γυνη αυτου ητοιμασεν εαυτην

The marriage of the lamb and His bride 144 × 24
Rev 19:7 ο γαμος του αρνιου και η γυνη αυτου

The bride, the wife of the lamb 144 × 20
Rev 21:9 την νυμφην την γυναικα αρνιου

Bride of the lamb 144 × 17
Rev 21:9 νυμφην του αρνιου'

The bride 144 × 7
Rev 22:17 η νυμφη"

The ones having been invited to the marriage 144 × 19
supper of the lamb
Rev 19:9 οι εις δειπνον του γαμου αρνιου κεκλημενοι'

The marriage supper 144 × 8
Rev 19:9 το δειπνον γαμου'

One verse in the book of Ephesians best describes this glorious bride which is to be presented to Christ:

Church not having spot or wrinkle or any such thing, 144 × 54
that it may be holy and unblemished
Eph 5:27 εκκλησιαν μη εχουσαν σπιλον η ρυτιδα η τι των τοιουτων αλλ
    ινα η αγια και αμωμος

The marriage supper which takes place in the book of Revelation is depicted in a beautiful manner in the gospels. Matthew and Luke both tell the story of the man who gave a wedding feast for his son and invited many. The man who gave the feast, of course, stands for God the Father and the son for Jesus. Let's begin by examining Matthew's account of this story: "And again Jesus spoke to them in parables, saying, 'The kingdom of heaven may be compared to a king who gave a marriage feast for the son of him.' "

We have already seen how "the marriage supper" in Revelation has a theomatic value of 144. Here Jesus says: "The kingdom of heaven is likened unto a man who gave a marriage feast for the son of him."

Marriage feast for the son   144 × 21
Mt 22:2 γαμους τω υιω

This parable then goes on to tell how the servants went forth and invited many, but they refused to come. Finally the king told his servants to go into the highways and invite as many as they could find to the marriage feast. "And those servants went out into the streets, and gathered together all whom they found, both evil and good; and the wedding hall was filled with guests." They assembled all "whom they found."

Whom they found   144 × 9
Mt 22:10 ους ευρον'

The last portion of the verse states:

And the wedding hall was filled with guests   144 × 23
Mt 22:10 και επλησθη ο νυμφων ανακειμενων'

The second account of the marriage supper occurs in Luke. Here are the words of Jesus to Luke from verse 16: "But He said to him, 'A man once made a great supper, and invited many.' "

Made a great supper   144 × 7
Lk 14:16 τις εποιει δειπνον μεγα

This story then proceeds in the same manner as the Matthew account. The lord sent forth his servant, and those invited still refused to come in. "And the servant said, 'Lord, what you have commanded has been done, and there is still room.' And the master said to the servant, 'Go out to the highways and hedges, and compel them to come in, that my house may be filled.' "

Compel them to come in   144 × 5
Lk 14:23 αναγκασον εισελθειν

So in the parables of the wedding feast Jesus is speaking about that final marriage supper which is to take place in heaven. When we compiled this design, we could find no instance where a reference to any of those invited worked out to a multiple of 144. The only time 144 showed up was when the text referred directly to those who actually came into the feast.

We will shortly be showing the reader some more features from the gospels which speak of the marriage supper. Before we do, however, there is one other aspect of this design that is quite meaningful.

In the last feature we looked at, we saw how the words "compel them to come in" had a theomatic value of 144 × 5. The word *compel* is defined as "to bring together by force; to overpower and drive together, such as a flock of sheep; to drag together by force." In this parable of the marriage supper, it is those who are chosen that the Holy Spirit compels to come in. Let's now examine two features that bear this truth out.

Do you remember the story of the 153 fishes from Chapter 4. In that chapter we showed how there was a design of 153 running through the many different references to fishes and fishing. John 21:11 states: "Simon Peter went up, and drew the net to land, full of large fish, a hundred and fifty-three." Now the Greek word for *drew*, ειλκυσεν, means emphatically "to drag by force," and guess what its theomatic value is. It's exactly the same as that of "compel them to come in," or 144 × 5.

Drag   144 × 5
Jn 21:11 ειλκυσεν

But what was it that Simon Peter drew to land? The answer is *fishes*, and in this story of the 153 fishes, the fishes are symbolic of all the redeemed. This is why the word *fishes* from the fish story of John 21 has a theomatic value of 144. How beautifully God has woven together the mathematical design of His Word!

Fishes   144 × 20
Jn 21:10 των οψαριων'

As we mentioned earlier, the Greek language has been structured by God so that each word has several possible combinations of spellings.

Each spelling has been designed by God to bring forth a different aspect of spiritual truth. So if the word *fishes* is spelled one way, it has a theomatic value of 153; and it specifically states that they caught 153 fishes. But if the word for *fishes* is spelled another way, it has a value of 144, which speaks of all the redeemed.

Another outstanding reference to the fishes being symbolic of all the redeemed is found in the following parable from Matthew. "Again, the kingdom of heaven is like unto a net, that was cast into the sea, and gathered of every kind: Which, when, they drew to shore, and sat down, and collected the good into vessels, but cast the bad away."

Collected the good   144 × 8
Mt 13:48 συνελεξαν τα καλα"

The most significant reference to this theme is found in three of the gospels, where Jesus feeds the multitudes, and afterwards twelve basketfuls of the fragments and fishes are gathered up.

12 baskets full of the fragments and the fishes   144 × 52
Mk 6:43 κλασματα δωδεκα κοφινων πληρωματα και απο των ιχθυων

Twelve is of course the number of the chosen. How could anything possibly be as outstanding as the above feature? In John, Jesus had the following to say:

Gather up the left-over fragments that not anything is lost   144 × 28
Jn 6:12 συναγαγετε περισσευσαντα κλασματα ινα μη τι αποληται

The left-over fragments   144 × 17
Jn 6:12 τα περισσευσαντα κλασματα"

But in the Matthew account, the word *fragments* is spelled a little differently in Greek.

The fragments   144 × 18
Mt 14:20 των κλασματων

The second reference to that final wedding supper which is to take place in heaven is found in the story of the last supper, which Christ had with His twelve disciples before going to the cross. This story of the last supper has been improperly named, for it should have been called the first supper, and here's why.

The original twelve disciples are typical of all the redeemed. When Christ sat down with His chosen, before going to the cross, that supper was symbolic of the final wedding feast which is to take place in heaven. The first supper, or the feast of the Passover, is a perfect model of that which is to take place in the kingdom of heaven.

Here are the words of Jesus to His disciples in Matthew, chapter 26. "Go into the city to such a one, and say to him, 'The teacher says, My time is at hand; I will keep at your house the Passover with My disciples.' "

The Passover with My disciples   144 × 31
Mt 26:18 το πασχα μετα των μαθητων μου"

From Luke come the following words: "And He [Jesus] sent Peter and John, saying, 'Go and prepare the Passover for us, that we may eat it.' "

Go and prepare the Passover for us, that we may eat it   144 × 32
Lk 22:8 πορευθεντες ετοιμασατε ημιν πασχα ινα φαγωμεν"

Here are the words of Jesus from verse 15: "And He said to them [his disciples], 'Earnestly, I have desired to eat this Passover with you before I suffer.' "

I have desired to eat this Passover with you before I suffer   144 × 41
Lk 22:15 επεθυμησα τουτο πασχα φαγειν μεθ υμων προ του με παθειν'

To eat this Passover   144 × 18
Lk 22:15 τουτο πασχα φαγειν'

From John 18:28 come these simple words:

Eat the Passover   144 × 17
Jn 18:28 φαγωσιν πασχα"

Now we shall turn and focus our attention on a somewhat different aspect of the feast of the Passover. From Luke 22:1 come the following words:

The feast of the unleavened bread which is called   144 × 28
the Passover
Lk 22:1 εορτη των αζυμων η λεγομενη πασχα

The unleavened bread   144 × 17
Lk 22:1 των αζυμων

When the above features were found, it was a little surprising to see that "the unleavened bread" worked out to a multiple of 144. This led to further investigation. The word *leaven* is a term used in the Bible to describe a substance such as yeast, used to produce fermentation in bread dough before baking. If bread was unleavened, this meant that it was unfermented. Could it be that the unleavened bread was a symbol of all the redeemed? Upon looking up a verse in 1 Corinthians, we found the answer.

"Purge out therefore the old leaven, that ye may be a new lump, as ye are unleavened. For even Christ our Passover was sacrificed for us." Here the apostle Paul is telling the Christians that they are a new lump without leaven. So the feast of the unleavened bread, which is called the Passover, is the marriage feast, because we are the unleavened bread that has been cleansed by the blood of Christ and is without leaven or fermentation. Theomatic design bears this out, because the following words from the above verse are also a multiple of 144:

Ye may be a new lump, as ye are unleavened   144 × 25
1 Cor 5:7 ητε νεον φυραμα καθως εστε αζυμοι"

Let's now take the complete thought, and see what happens:

That ye may be a new lump, as ye are unleavened.   144 × 54
For even Christ our Passover was sacrificed for us.
1 Cor 5:7 ινα ητε νεον φυραμα καθως εστε αζυμοι και γαρ πασχα ημων ετυθη Χριστος

The words of Jesus from Luke 14:15 fit in beautifully with this design: "Blessed is he who shall eat bread in the kingdom of God."

Eat bread in the kingdom of God   144 × 17
Lk 14:15 φαγεται αρτον εν τη βασιλεια Θεου'

The next feature is in our estimation the most precious of all in this entire chapter. In John 6:54 Jesus said: "The one eating My flesh and drinking My blood has eternal life, and I will raise him up in the last day." The complete verse is a multiple of 144, but here is the outstanding portion:

The one eating My flesh and drinking My blood   144 × 34
Jn 6:54 ο τρωγων μου την σαρκα και πινων μου αιμα

And now to conclude this theme, three features will be shown which climax in a beautiful way the design for that great day in heaven when all the saints of God will dine at the feast of the wedding supper prepared for the lamb and his bride. Here are the words of Jesus from Luke, chapter 22:

And I appoint you as My Father appointed Me   144 × 54
a kingdom that you may eat and drink at My table
in My kingdom
Lk 22:29–30 καγω διατιθεμαι υμιν καθως διεθετο μοι πατηρ μου
βασιλειαν ινα εσθητε και πινητε επι τραπεζης μου εν
βασιλεια μου'

And here are the words of Jesus from Matthew, chapter 8:

For many will come from the east and west   144 × 60
and sit at table with Abraham, Isaac, and Jacob
in the kingdom of heaven
Mt 8:11 οτι πολλοι απο ανατολων και δυσμων ηξουσιν και ανακλι-
θνσονται μετα Αβρααμ και Ισαακ και Ιακωβ εν βασιλεια
ουρανων

In the final address to His disciples before going to the cross, Jesus spoke the following words: "But I say to you, I will not drink of this fruit of the vine from now on until that day when I drink it new with you in the kingdom of My Father."

That day when I drink it new with you   144 × 41
in the kingdom of My Father
Mt 26:29 ημερας εκεινης οταν αυτο πινω μεθ υμων καινον εν βασιλεια
πατρος μου

Kingdom of God and Kingdom of Heaven

The first two features need no introduction.

Kingdom of God   144 × 8
Mt 21:31 την βασιλειαν Θεου'

Kingdom of heaven   144 × 20
Mt 3:2 βασιλεια των ουρανων

The Bible teaches that the saints are to reign with Christ. This is why "kingdom of God" and "kingdom of heaven" work out to multiples of 144. We who have put our trust in Jesus comprise that kingdom, which will be revealed in the last day.

One of the best-known references to the kingdom of God is the following words spoken by Jesus, as He began His ministry on earth: "The time is fulfilled, and the kingdom of God is at hand; repent and believe in the gospel."

The time is fulfilled and the kingdom of God is at hand   144 × 24
Mk 1:14 πεπληρωται καιρος και ηγγικεν βασιλεια του Θεου"

In proclaiming that the kingdom of God was at hand, Jesus also said: "Repent and believe the gospel." Christians have always believed that the gospel was a proclamation of the kingdom of God. Theomatics seems to confirm this. In Galatians 2:2 Paul refers to "the gospel which I proclaim amongst the nations." Both the words *gospel* and *proclaim* are multiples of 144.

Gospel   144 × 4
Gal 2:2 ευαγγελιον'

Proclaim   144 × 12
Gal 2:2 κηρυσσω

One of the most famous verses in the Bible is the following:

Allow the little children to come unto Me,   144 × 56
and forbid them not: For of such is the kingdom of God
Mk 10:14 αφετε παιδια ερχεσθαι προς με μη κωλυετε αυτα γαρ τοιουτων
  εστιν βασιλεια Θεου

Of such is the kingdom of God   144 × 31
Mk 10:14 των τοιουτων εστιν η βασιλεια Θεου"

Many are the references to the kingdom of God and kingdom of heaven which work out to multiples of 144. For the sake of illustration, only a few will be shown which speak directly of the redeemed.

At the very conclusion of His parable on the wheat and the tares, Jesus describes how the sinners will be cast into the furnace of fire. The verse that immediately follows says this:

Then the righteous will shine forth in the kingdom   144 × 52
of the Father of them

Mt 13:43 τοτε οι δικαιοι εκλαμψουσιν ως ο ληιος εν τη βασιλεια του πατρος αυτων

Kingdom of the Father   144 × 7
Mt 13:43 βασιλεια πατρος"

Here is an outstanding feature from Colossians:

He transferred us into the kingdom of His dear Son   144 × 39
Col 1:13 μετεστησεν εις την βασιλειαν του υιου της αγαπης αυτου'

In Matthew, chapter 20, a woman comes to Jesus and asks if her two sons could sit one on His left and the other on His right, when He came into His kingdom. Jesus replied by saying:

This is not Mine to give, but it is for those   144 × 29
for whom it has been prepared
Mt 20:23 ουκ εστιν εμον τουτο δουναι αλλ οις ητοιμασται

This feature is a multiple of 144 because it is demonstrating that to sit on the right and on the left of Jesus is for all of the redeemed.

In 1 Corinthians, Paul speaks of that final day, when the kingdom is delivered up to God: "Then the end, when He delivers up the kingdom to God the Father, when He has abolished all rule and all authority and power."

The end, when He delivers up the kingdom to God   144 × 27
1 Cor 15:24 τελος οταν παραδιδοι την βασιλειαν τω Θεω'

Now let's connect this next feature with the one we just looked at. In Revelation 11:15 we find the following words: "Then the seventh angel blew his trumpet, and there were loud voices in heaven, saying, 'The kingdom of the world has become the kingdom of our Lord and of His Christ.' " We have already seen how "kingdoms of this world" had a theomatic value of 666. Here now is "the kingdom of our Lord and of His Christ":

The kingdom of our Lord and of His Christ   144 × 35
Rev 11:15 βασιλεια κυριου ημων και Χριστου αυτου'

Many features can be shown for the number 144 that relate to final inheritance and kingdom waiting for us in the heavenlies. To climax this theme, we will simply list five features that best speak for themselves:

The inheritance among all the ones having been sanctified 144 × 10
Acts 20:32 κληρονομιαν εν ηγιασμενοις πασιν"

The eternal inheritance 144 × 17
Heb 9:15 της αιωνιου κληρονομιας

The heavenly gift 144 × 23
Heb 6:4 της δωρεας της επουρανιου

The heavenly calling 144 × 17
Heb 3:1 κλησεως επουρανιου'

The calling of our God 144 × 21
2 Thess 1:11 της κλησεως ο Θεος ημων'

The Lamb's Book of Life

Perhaps no references to all the redeemed could be more significant than those which concern the names written in the lamb's book of life. In Revelation 21:27 the following words are found pertaining to the New Jerusalem: "And nothing unclean and no one who practices abomination and lying shall ever come into it, but only those who are written in the lamb's book of life."

Those who are written in the lamb's book of life 144 × 33
Rev 21:27 γεγραμμενοι εν τω βιβλιω ζωης του αρνιου

The lamb's book of life 144 × 25
Rev 21:27 τω βιβλιω ζωης αρνιου

In Revelation 20:12 it says the following: "And I saw the dead, the great and the small standing before the throne, and books were opened. And another book was opened, which is the book of life."

Which is the book of life 144 × 15
Rev 20:12 ο εστιν της ζωης"

Here are the words from Revelation 17:8: "The beast that thou sawest was, and is not; and shall ascend out of the bottomless pit, and go into perdition: and they that dwell on the earth shall wonder, whose names have not been written in the book of life from the foundation of the world." Now here is something interesting. If the two words "have not" are removed from the above verse, the following features would be found:

Names written in the book of life   144 × 14
Rev 17:8 γεγραπται ονομα επι βιβλιον ζωης"

Names written in the book of life from   144 × 25
the foundation of the world
Rev 17:8 γεγραπται ονομα επι βιβλιον ζωης απο καταβολης κοσμου'

There is only one reference to the book of life outside of Revelation. It occurs in Philippians, wherein Paul addresses Clement: "And the rest of my fellow workers, whose names are in the book of life."

Names in the book of life   144 × 17
Phil 4:3 ονοματα εν βιβλω ζωης"

In describing the New Jerusalem, John says the following in chapter 21, verse 12: "It had a great, high wall, with twelve gates, and at the gates twelve angels, and the names which are inscribed are of the twelve tribes of the sons of Israel."

The names which are inscribed   144 × 10
Rev 21:12 ονοματα επιγεγραμμενα α εστιν'

And now we present two features that have great significance. In speaking to His twelve disciples, who symbolize all of us, Jesus said the following: "Rejoice not, because the spirits are subject unto you; but rather rejoice, because your names are written in heaven." We saw in the last design how "kingdom of heaven" had a theomatic value of 144 × 20. Here now from the above verse are the words:

Names written in heaven   144 × 20
Lk 10:20 τα ονοματα εγγεγραπται εν τοις ουρανοις

And from Matthew:

Kingdom of heaven   144 × 20
Mt 3:2 βασιλεια των ουρανων

Another feature that relates to the fact that our names are written in heaven is found in Philippians: "For of us the citizenship is in heaven, from which also we eagerly wait for a Savior, the Lord Jesus Christ."

The citizenship is in heaven   144 × 24
Phil 3:20 το πολιτευμα εν ουρανοις υπαρχει"

Connect the next feature with the one we just looked at: "For this reason I bow my knees before the Father, from whom every family in heaven and on earth is named."

Every family in heaven   144 × 12
Eph 3:15 πασα πατρια εν ουρανοις"

One particular reference to our heavenly inheritance is found in Luke, chapter 6, where Jesus told His disciples to: "Love your enemies, and do good, and lend, hoping for nothing again; and your reward will be great, and ye will be sons of the most high."

And ye will be sons of the most high   144 × 21
Lk 6:35 και εσεσθε υιοι υψιστου'

One of our favorite features is the following: "And Jesus said to them, 'The sons of this age marry and are given in marriage, but those that are considered worthy to attain unto that age and the resurrection of the dead, neither marry, or are given in marriage."

Those that are considered worthy to obtain unto that age   144 × 34
Lk 20:35 οι καταξιωθεντες αιωνος εκεινου τυχειν'

The Elect

Perhaps no other term in Scripture is more applicable to all of the redeemed than the word *elect.* The Greek word for *elect* refers to those who are chosen by God for salvation. Romans 11:7 offers a perfect example of how the word is used: "What then? That which Israel is seeking for, it has not obtained, but the elect obtained it, and the rest were hardened." Look at the number value of this feature!

The elect   144
Rom 11:7 η εκλογη

The best feature is found in Romans 9:11, which concerns the birth of Esau and Jacob: "For though the twins were not yet born, and had not done any good or evil, that the elect purpose of God might stand, not of works, but of Him that calleth." When the Greek words for "elect of God" are taken from this verse, their theomatic value is the following:

Elect of God 144 × 10
Rom 9:11 εκλογην του Θεου

In his closing salutation to the Roman church, Paul said this: "Greet Rufus, the elect in the Lord, also His mother and mine."

Elect in the Lord 144 × 16
Rom 16:13 τον εκλεκτον εν κυριω'

The same basic theme of election is also found in those verses which speak of those whom the Father has given to His Son. In Hebrews 2:13 we find the words: "And again, 'I will put my trust in Him.' And again, 'Here I am, and the children whom God has given Me.'"

And the children whom God has given Me 144 × 12
Heb 2:13 και τα παιδια α μοι εδωκεν Θεος'

John, chapter 17, is undoubtedly one of the great classics of all Scripture, for in this chapter, Jesus makes known His requests concerning all those whom the Father has given Him. The next feature is theomatically the most important in this entire chapter, because it demonstrates that the "144 thousands" mentioned in the book of Revelation symbolize all the redeemed. In order to get the full impact of this next feature, let's begin with verse 1: "These words spake Jesus, and lifted up His eyes to heaven, and said, 'Father, the hour is come; glorify Thy Son, that Thy Son also may glorify Thee: As Thou hast given Him power over all flesh, that to all which Thou hast given Him, He may give eternal life.'"

All which Thou hast given Him 144 × 19
Jn 17:2 παν ο δεδωκας αυτω

The next feature in John, chapter 17, is found in verse 6: "I have manifested Thy name to the men whom Thou gavest to Me out of the world."

The men whom Thou gavest 144 × 25
Jn 17:6 τοις ανθρωποις ους εδωκας

Down in verse 24, toward the end of the chapter, Jesus says the following: "Father, I desire that those whom Thou hast given Me may be with Me where I am, to behold My glory which Thou hast given Me."

Those whom Thou hast given Me   144 × 8
Jn 17:24 δεδωκας μοι"

A perfect cross reference to these features is found in John, chapter 10, where Jesus says: "My Father, Who has given them to Me, is greater than all."

Given them to Me   144 × 7
Jn 10:29 δεδωκεν μοι

John, chapter 17, contains many references, some of which are quite general, that work out to multiples of 144. One of these is of extreme significance, and for this reason it will be shown. In verse 12 Jesus said the following: "While I was with them I kept them in Thy name, which thou hast given Me."

Kept them   144 × 16
Jn 17:12 ετηρουν αυτους

The Ones Believing

Here is a question. What one factor is it that makes up the difference between those who are saved and those who are not? The answer is very simple. Those who are saved believe in the gospel, and those who are not saved do not believe. In other words, there are two and only two classes of people on the earth—believers and unbelievers.

Here now are the words pertaining to believers from 1 Timothy 4:12: "Let no man despise thy youth; but be thou an example of the believers."

Believers   144 × 10
1 Tim 4:12 πιστων

In 1 Corinthians Paul speaks further concerning the ones believing: "But prophecy is for a sign, not to unbelievers, but to the ones believing."

The ones believing   144 × 16
1 Cor 14:22 τοις πιστευουσιν'

Now here is an amazing spiritual truth. When a person believes, he also has faith. Believing and faith are inseparable. We have already seen from earlier in this chapter that the word *faith* is a multiple of 144. Here now is the word *believe* along with the word *faith*:

Believe   144 × 15
Rom 15:13 τω πιστευειν

Faith   144 × 7
Rev 2:13 την πιστιν

John 3:16 without question is the most famous verse in the entire Bible. The central theme of this verse is that God gave His only begotten Son, and that by believing in Him, one has everlasting life. Here now is that complete verse:

For God so loved the world that He gave His   144 × 95
only begotten Son, that whosoever believeth in Him should
not perish but have everlasting life
Jn 3:16 ουτως γαρ ηγαπησεν ο Θεος τον κοσμον ωστε τον υιον τον
         μονογενη εδωκεν ινα πας ο πιστευων εις αυτον μη αποληται αλλ
         εχη ζωην αιωνιον'

In verse 18 of the same chapter, the text says: "The one believing in Him is not condemned."

The one believing in Him   144 × 20
Jn 3:18 πιστευων εις αυτον'

Now look at these words from John 6:47!

The one believing has eternal life   144 × 30
Jn 6:47 πιστευων εχει ζωην αιωνιον'

To conclude this topic, four features will be given that best speak for themselves:

The one believing in Him will not be put to shame   144 × 39
1 Pet 2:6 ο πιστευων επ αυτω ου μη καταισχυνθη"

The one believing in the Son   144 × 18
Jn 3:36 πιστευων εις υιον"

Everyone believing is justified   144 × 21
Acts 13:39 πας ο πιστευων δικαιουται"

That ye may believe that Jesus is the Christ   144 × 33
Jn 20:31 ινα πιστευητε οτι Ιησους εστιν ο Χριστος

The Seed in the Good Soil

One of the best-known parables that Christ told concerns the sowing of the seed. Jesus begins this parable by telling how: "A sower went out to sow his seed: and as he sowed, some fell by the wayside; and it was trodden down, and the fowls of the air devoured it. And some seed fell on rocky soil; and as soon as it was sprung up, it withered away, because it lacked moisture. And other seed fell among the thorns; and the thorns sprang up with it, and choked it. And other seed fell into the soil, and sprang up and bare fruit an hundredfold."

And other seed fell into the soil, and sprang up   144 × 29
and bore fruit an hundredfold
Lk 8:8 και ετερον επεσεν εις γην αγαθην και φυεν εποιησεν καρπον
εκατονταπλασιονα"

Seven verses later, Jesus explains the meaning of this parable: "And the seed in the good soil, these are the ones who have heard the word in an honest and good heart, and hold it fast, and bear fruit with perseverance."

The seed in the good soil   144 × 3
Lk 8:15 εν τη καλη γη'

Now this parable is also related in Mark's gospel. The first feature we will be looking at has the same theomatic value of 144 as its parallel passage in Luke, even though the words are completely different in Greek.

Other seeds fell into the good soil   144 × 8
Mk 4:8 αλλα επεσεν εις γην την καλην"

Down in verse 20 of Mark, chapter 4, Jesus again explains the meaning of this parable: "But these are the ones sown upon the good soil, who hear the word and accept it and bear fruit."

These are the ones sown upon the good soil   144 × 17
Mk 4:20 εκεινοι εισιν οι επι την γην την καλην σπαρεντες'

The type of consistency found in the features above is overwhelming and could never happen by chance. For proof of this fact refer to the last chapter, dealing with the science of statistics and probability.

Another parable that evinces the same design is that of the wheat and the tares. In these familiar words of our Lord Jesus describes how an enemy came and sowed tares in the field of a man who had sown good seed. Upon finding this out, the servants came to their master and said: " 'Wilt thou then that we go and gather them up?' But he said, 'Nay; lest while ye gather up the tares, ye root up also the wheat with them. Let both grow together until the harvest: and in the time of the harvest I will say to the reapers, gather ye together first the tares, and bind them in bundles to burn them; but gather the wheat into my barn.' "

Gather the wheat 144×14
Mt 13:30 τον σιτον συναγαγετε"

In Luke, chapter 3, Jesus gives another parable very similar to the one in Matthew: "And his winnowing fork is in his hand to clean out his threshing-floor, and to gather the wheat into the barn of him; but he will burn up the chaff with unquenchable fire."

Gather the wheat into the barn 144×18
Lk 3:17 συναγαγειν τον σιτον εις την αποθηκην

Body of Christ

Perhaps no other term is as popular among Christians today as the expression "body of Christ." This book has been dedicated to that body, and as you might expect, there is a theomatic design present in the many different references to the body of Christ. Most of the features that concern the body of Christ are found in 1 Corinthians, chapter 12, so for this reason all but one of our features will be from this chapter.

The leading verse in this chapter is verse 12, which is a multiple of 144.

For just as the body is one and has many members, 144×79
and all the members of the body, though many,
are one body, so it is with Christ
1 Cor 12:12 καθαπερ γαρ το σωμα εν εστιν και μελη πολλα εχει παντα

δε τα μελη σωματος πολλα οντα εν εστιν σωμα ουτως και
ο Χριστος

The last words in this verse, "body, so it is with Christ," carry the meaning of "body of Christ." The living Bible translates this verse in the following manner: "Our bodies have many parts, but the many parts make up only one body when they are all put together. So it is with the body of Christ." Here now are the Greek words for "body of Christ":

Body of Christ   144 × 18
1 Cor 12:12 σωμα ο Χριστος'

Two verses later, in verse 14, the apostle Paul states:

For the body is not one member, but many   144 × 22
1 Cor 12:14 και το σωμα ουκ εστιν εν μελος αλλα πολλα"

Is not one member, but many   144 × 12
1 Cor 12:14 ουκ εστιν εν μελος αλλα πολλα

Down in verses 18 and 19 the same design continues. Here is verse 18:

God has placed the members, each one of them   144 × 40
in the body, as it hath pleased Him
1 Cor 12:18 Θεος εθετο μελη εν εκαστον αυτων εν σωματι καθως
ηθελησεν'

The next feature is found in verse 24 of the same chapter: "For God has so composed the body, giving more abundant honor to that member which lacked." The words "composed the body" mean that God fitted the body together, of which we are members.

Composed the body   144 × 17
1 Cor 12:24 συνεκερασεν το σωμα'

The last feature from 1 Corinthians 12 is found in verse 27: "Now ye are the body of Christ, and members in part."

Ye are the body of Christ   144 × 27
1 Cor 12:27 υμεις εστε σωμα Χριστου"

There is one particular reference to the body of Christ from Colossians, which ties in perfectly with this design: "And let the peace of Christ rule in your hearts, to which also ye were called in one body."

To which also ye were called in one body   144 × 15
Col 3:15 εις ην και εκληθητε εν ενι σωματι

Miscellaneous Features

Under this heading of miscellaneous features, we will be presenting only a few of the better-known Scripture passages that contain multiples of 144. Let the reader understand that these are merely a sampling of those that can be found.

The last portion of Matthew, chapter 25, tells how the Son of Man will sit on His glorious throne and separate the sheep from the goats: "Then shall the king say to unto them on His right hand, 'Come, ye blessed of the Father of Me, inherit the kingdom prepared for you from the foundation of the world.' " This complete verse as it has just been quoted is a multiple of 144, but here is the most distinct portion:

Ye blessed of the Father   144 × 10
Mt 25:34 ευλογημενοι πατρος"

This passage of Scripture concerns Christ's sheep, who are on His right. One of the most famous verses in the entire Bible concerning sheep is the following:

He calls His own sheep by name, and leads them out   144 × 23
Jn 10:3 ιδια προβατα φωνει κατ ονομα και εξαγει αυτα'

In 1 Peter 5:2 the apostle Peter gives the following advice to the elders: "Shepherd the flock of God that is among you."

The flock of God   144 × 6
1 Pet 5:2 ποιμνιον Θεου

In Acts 20:28 the text states: "Take heed to yourselves and to all the flock, in which the Holy Spirit has made you overseers, to shepherd the church of God."

The flock   144 × 15
Acts 20:28 τω ποιμνιω

Shepherd the church of God   144 × 8
Acts 20:28 ποιμαινειν εκκλησιαν Θεου"

One of the most significant terms in relation to all of the redeemed is the word *church*. The Greek word for *church* means "an assembly, or gathering of believers."

In going through the New Testament, we found very few features in reference to the church that worked out to multiples of 144. This puzzled us at first, but then we discovered the reason why. Everything to do with the church was structured on the number seven, which bespeaks perfection.

The church 700
Mt 16:18 την εκκλησιαν"

The real significance of this, however, was discovered in the book of Revelation. The entire message of the Apocalypse is structured around John writing to the seven churches in Asia. The reason there were seven churches is that the church has been made perfect through the blood of Christ.

7 churches in Asia 777
Rev 1:4 ζ εκκλησιαις εν Ασια'

The church of God is also portrayed throughout Scripture as the tabernacle, or building, of God. Here now are three features that tie together perfectly:

Church of God 777
1 Tim 3:15 εκκλησια Θεου'

Tabernacle of God 777
Rev 21:3 η σκηνη Θεου'

Building of God 777
1 Cor 3:9 Θεου οικοδομη'

Probably the one verse in the Bible that best portrays the perfection of the church is found in Ephesians 5:27. We have already seen how this passage was a multiple of 144. Let us now examine it again.

Church not having spot or wrinkle or any such thing, 7,777
that it may be holy and unblemished
Eph 5:27 εκκλησιαν μη εχουσαν σπιλον η ρυτιδα η τι των τοιουτων αλλ
ινα η αγια και αμωμος'

Now that we understand the significance of the church being perfect, let us return to the design having to do with the number 144. The Acts 12:1 says: "Herod the king laid violent hands upon some of those who belong to the church."

Those who belong to the church   144 × 16
Acts 12:1 των απο της εκκλησιας'

And in Galatians 5:24 we find these words: "And those who belong to Christ Jesus have crucified the flesh with its passions and lusts."

Those who belong to Christ Jesus   144 × 17
Gal 5:24 οι Χριστου Ιησου

Here are the words of Jesus from Luke 12:8: "Also I say unto you, 'Whosoever shall confess Me before men, also the Son of Man will confess him before the angels of God.' " This complete verse, as usual, is a multiple of 144. Here now are its most explicit words.

The Son of Man will confess him   144 × 30
Lk 12:8 ο υιος ανθρωπου ομολογησει εν αυτω"

When we turn to the book of Revelation, we find these words:

And I will confess his name before My Father and   144 × 57
before His angels
Rev 3:5 και ομολογησω ονομα αυτου ενωπιον πατρος μου και ενωπιον
αγγελων αυτου'

2 Thessalonians 2:10 states that Christ is coming:

To be glorified in His saints and to be marveled at   144 × 40
in all who have believed
2 Thess 1:10 ενδοξασθηναι εν τοις αγιοις αυτου και θαυμασθηναι εν
πασιν τοις πιστευσασιν

Look at these next three features, all from one verse! "So that He may establish your hearts unblamable in holiness before our God and Father, at the coming of our Lord Jesus Christ with all His saints."

At the coming of the Lord Jesus Christ with all His saints   144 × 59
1 Thess 3:13 εν τη παρουσια του κυριου Ιησου μετα παντων των αγιων
αυτου'

All His saints   144 × 31
1 Thess 3:13 παντων των αγιων αυτου"

Saints   144 × 6
1 Thess 3:13 αγιων

Here are three features that need no special introduction:

He who is of God hears the words of God   144 × 22
Jn 8:47 ο ων εκ Θεου τα ρηματα Θεου ακουει"

Everyone hearing and learning from the Father   144 × 37
comes to Me
Jn 6:45 πας ακουσας παρα του πατρος και μαθων ερχεται προς εμε

The one doing the truth comes to the light   144 × 29
Jn 3:21 ο δε ποιων αληθειαν ερχεται προς φως"

One day while doing research in the book of The Acts, we noticed that the word *temple* had a theomatic value of 144.

The temple   144 × 14
Acts 26:21 τω ιερω'

When this feature was found, not too much thought was given to it at the time, but another day, while we were researching a verse in 1 Corinthians, chapter 3, the following presented itself:

For ye are the temple of God, and the   144 × 24
Holy Spirit dwells within you
1 Cor 3:16 οτι ναος Θεου εστε και πνευμα Θεου εν υμιν οικει

Of course! The reason that the word *temple* is 144 is that we are the temple of the Holy Spirit. This fact was even further confirmed by the verse which immediately follows, 1 Corinthians 3:16: "If anyone destroys God's temple, God will destroy him. For the temple of God is holy, which you are."

The temple of God which you are   144 × 24
1 Cor 3:17 ο ναος του Θεου οιτινες εστε υμεις'

Here are the words from Romans 9:23:

In order to make known the riches of His glory   144 × 49
on vessels of mercy which He prepared beforehand for glory
Rom 9:23 και ινα γνωριση πλουτον της δοξης αυτου επι σκευη ελεους α
          προητοιμασεν εις δοξαν'

On vessels of mercy   144 × 10
Rom 9:23 επι σκευη ελεους"

Romans 6:3 says: "All who have been baptized into Christ Jesus were baptized into His death."

All who have been baptized   144 × 10
Rom 6:3 οτι οσοι εβαπτισθημεν

This next one is one of our favorites. We think you'll agree. "For whom the Lord loves He chastens."

Whom the Lord loves   144 × 7
Heb 12:6 ον αγαπα κυριος"

Matthew 7:14 says: "Strait is the gate, and narrow is the way, which leadeth unto life, and few are the ones finding it."

The ones finding   144 × 10
Mt 7:14 οι ευρισκοντες

From the parable of the talents come the following words: "His master said to him, 'Well done, good and faithful servant; you have been faithful over a little, I will set you over much.'"

Good and faithful servant   144 × 8
Mt 25:23 δουλε αγαθε και πιστε"

Peter in his second epistle wrote the following: "Once you were no people, but now you are God's people."

But now you are God's people   144 × 9
1 Pet 2:10 νυν δε λαος Θεου"

Here are some more words of Jesus: "But He said to them, 'My mother and my brothers are those who hear the Word of God and do it.'"

Those who hear the word of God and do it   144 × 27
Lk 8:21 οι λογον του Θεου ακουοντες και ποιουντες'

Here are some well-known words of Jesus from Luke: "If any one comes to Me and does not hate his own father and mother and wife and children and brothers and sisters, yes, and even his own life, he cannot be My disciple."

Be My disciple   144 × 8
Lk 14:26 ειναι μου μαθητης

While putting together the features for this chapter, we noticed something rather cute. The Acts 6:7 says that "the number of the disciples multiplied." And The Acts 2:47 says that the Lord "added the ones being saved." So right in the text it talks about multiplication and addition!

The number of disciples multiplied   144 × 26
Acts 6:7 επληθυνετο αριθμος των μαθητων'

Added the ones being saved   144 × 25
Acts 2:47 προσετιθει τους σωζομενους'

Mark 10:45 states that Christ came:

To give His life as a ransom for many   144 × 43
Mk 10:45 δουναι την ψυχην αυτου λυτρον αντι πολλων'

In order to demonstrate how the hidden truths of Scripture are interwoven into these numbers, we will show several examples that bring forth outstanding spiritual truths. When Jesus raised Lazarus from the dead and called him out of the tomb, he was a symbol of all of us who will be resurrected in the last day. For this reason *Lazarus* has a theomatic value of 144.

Lazarus   144
Jn 11:43 Λαζαρε

Another example of how the hidden truths of Scripture are interwoven into these numbers is found in the story of Lot in the Old Testament. When God saved righteous Lot out of Sodom and Gomorrah, he was a type of the elect who will be redeemed from this wicked world.

Righteous Lot   144 × 9
2 Pet 2:7 δικαιον Λωτ'

In the time of Noah, the whole world was just as wicked as Sodom and Gomorrah. This is why God told Noah to "build an ark for the salvation of the household of him." Now if we were to take the number value of this complete phrase, it would not be a multiple of 144, and the reason is very simple. The complete phrase refers to the ark, and it has a theomatic value that is the number of Jesus, because Jesus is our ark of safety. But if we take the distinct portion that concerns the household that was saved, we find that there is present a design of 144.

For the salvation of the household   144 × 21
Heb 11:7 εις σωτηριαν του οικου

Thus, from one verse of Scripture God is able to bring forth two spiritual truths: the ark, which is a symbol of Christ; and the redeemed household, who are in that ark of safety.

1 Peter 4:17 also talks about the "household of God."

Household of God   144 × 18
1 Pet 4:17 του οικου του Θεου"

We could go on and on showing the reader features—pages and pages of them. But all good things must come to an end. So under this, the next to the last heading, we will show one last feature. Do you remember the story of the 276 souls who were saved in Paul's shipwreck? Who were those 276 souls in that ship who were saved out of the sea? Let's find out.

We were in all, two hundred and seventy-six persons   144 × 36
in the ship
Acts 27:37 ημεθα αι πασαι ψυχαι εν τω πλοιω διακοσιαι εβδομηκοντα
εξ'

The True Israel

One of the great spiritual truths of Scripture lies in the fact that God calling forth a chosen people in the Old Testament symbolizes us who are now the chosen people of God. The original blessings of Israel are now our blessings; for we who have put our trust in Jesus are the true inheritors of the blessing of Abraham.

Many times in Scripture, when it refers to Israel, it is speaking of the true Israel, which is the corporate body of believers. When the Jews rejected their Messiah, the promises of the Abrahamic blessing then became obtainable by faith. This is why the 144 thousands are those who have been sealed from the twelve tribes of the sons of Israel.

Revelation, chapter 7, lists and names these twelve tribes of Israel. A careful examination will reveal that the names of the twelve tribes listed in Revelation are completely different from those listed in the Old Testament. There are several tribes named in Revelation that never existed in Old Testament days; and in Revelation several tribes that existed in the Old Testament are deleted. This indicates that there is something spiritual involved here with the 144 thousands rather than natural physical Jews. These twelve tribes are symbolic of all the redeemed, who constitute the true Israel. The features to be presented in the remaining portion of this chapter will bear out this truth.

Throughout the New Testament, whenever the text refers to the true Israel, the design of 144 can be found. In this book, only a sampling of these features will be shown, since this one topic is so vast that it demands serious study over an extended period of time.

Let's begin now by examining Hebrews 8:10: "For this is the covenant that I will make with the house of Israel after those days, says the Lord: I will put My laws into their minds, and I will write them upon their hearts. And I will be their God, and they shall be My people." Now this verse tells us that in the covenant that God makes with the house of Israel, the laws will be written upon the heart. The Old Testament Jews had their laws written on stone tablets! So what covenant is this, which the Lord makes with the house of Israel, and who is this house of Israel? Let's find out what theomatics has to say about it.

Covenant which I will covenant with the house of Israel   144 × 12
Heb 8:10 η διαθηκη ην διαθησομαι οικω Ισραελ

House of Israel   144 × 5
Acts 2:36 οικος Ισραελ'

Matthew 10:5, 6 tells how Jesus sent forth the twelve disciples and told them to "go to the lost sheep of the house of Israel."

The lost sheep of the house of Israel   144 × 24
Mt 10:6 τα προβατα τα απολωλοτα οικου Ισραηλ'

When the wise men came looking for Jesus, they inquired of Herod where the Christ was to be born. Herod then assembled the chief priests and scribes and inquired where He was to be born. They told him, "In Bethlehem of Judea; for so it is written by the prophet: 'And you, O Bethlehem, in the land of Judah, are by no means least among the rulers of Judah; for out of thee shall come forth a Governor who will shepherd my people Israel.' "

My people Israel 144 × 7
Mt 2:6 λαον μου Ισραελ"

When John the baptist was born, his father Zechariah was filled with the Holy Spirit, and prophesied, saying, "Blessed be the Lord God of Israel, for He has visited and redeemed His people."

Redeemed His people 144 × 30
Lk 1:68 εποιησεν λυτρωσιν λαω αυτου

Matthew's account says this concerning the virgin Mary: "She will bear a Son and you shall call His name Jesus, for He will save His people from their sins."

For He will save His people 144 × 23
Mt 1:21 αυτος γαρ σωσει τον λαον αυτου

In The Acts 5:31 it is stated that "God exalted Him [Christ] at His right hand as leader and savior, to give repentance to Israel and forgiveness of sins."

To give repentance to Israel and forgiveness of sins 144 × 32
Acts 5:31 δουναι μετανοιαν τω Ισραηλ και αφεσιν αμαρτιων"

The Acts 13:24 refers to the:

Baptism of repentance to all the people of Israel 144 × 28
Acts 13:24 βαπτισμα μετανοιας παντι τω λαω Ισραηλ

In speaking to His disciples, Jesus told them the following: "And Jesus said to them, 'Truly I say to you, in the generation when the Son of Man sits on His glorious throne, you also will sit upon twelve thrones, judging the twelve tribes of Israel.' "

You also will sit upon twelve thrones, judging 144 × 52
the twelve tribes of Israel
Mt 19:28 καθησεσθε και αυτοι επι δωδεκα θρονους κρινοντες τας
δωδεκα φυλας του Ισραελ'

Judging the twelve tribes of Israel 144 × 27
Mt 19:28 κρινοντες δωδεκα φυλας του Ισραελ'

Here are words on this topic from Romans 2:28: "For he is not a Jew who is one outwardly; neither is circumcision that which is outward in the flesh; but he is a Jew who is one inwardly; and real circumcision is of the heart, by the spirit, not by the letter."

He is a Jew who is one inwardly   144 × 18
Rom 2:28 ο εν κρυπτω Ιουδαιος"

When Jesus was speaking to the chief priests and Pharisees, He told them the following: "Therefore I say to you, the kingdom of God will be taken away from you, and given to a nation producing the fruit of it." And what nation is that? That nation is we who have put our trust in Jesus—by faith.

The kingdom of God will be taken away from you   144 × 61
and given to a nation producing the fruits of it
Mt 21:43 οτι αρθησεται αφ υμων η βασιλεια του Θεου και δοθησεται
εθνει ποιουντι τους καρπους αυτης'

Given to a nation producing the fruits of it   144 × 24
Mt 21:43 δοθησεται εθνει ποιουντι καρπους αυτης

Probably the most profound Scripture, which ties this whole design together, is found in Romans 11:17. In this passage Paul speaks of his fellow Jews and how he wanted to save some of them. In this epistle Paul was writing to the Gentile believers in Rome, and here is what he said in verse 17: "But if some of the branches were broken off, and you, being a wild olive, were grafted in their place to share the richness of the olive tree. . . ." Now in this passage the branches that were broken off stand for natural Israel after the flesh. This Scripture states that the Gentile believers were grafted in their place, and that is why the kingdom of God was taken away from the Jews who rejected their Messiah and given to the true Israel. For this reason all believers in Jesus, whether they be Jew or Gentile, have been grafted in their place.

And you, being a wild olive, were grafted in their place   144 × 27
Rom 11:17 συ δε αγριελαιος ων ενεκεντρισθης εν αυτοις'

Earlier in this chapter, Paul spoke of his trying to save some of his fellow Jews: "Now I am speaking to you Gentiles. Inasmuch then as I am an apostle to the Gentiles, I magnify my ministry in order to make my fellow Jews jealous, and thus save some of them."

Save some of them   144 × 29
Rom 11:14 σωσω τινας εξ αυτων᾽

In Romans, chapter 9, Paul says the following: "In order to make known the riches of His glory on the vessels of mercy, which He has prepared beforehand for glory, even us whom He has called, not only of the Jews, but also of the Gentiles."

Not only of the Jews   144 × 14
Rom 9:24 ου μονον εξ Ιουδαιων

Also of the Gentiles   144 × 7
Rom 9:24 και εξ εθνων᾽᾽

The design of 144, which flows through the many references to the true Israel, is vast. One of the designs that we have uncovered, which was not shown in this book, is the design connected with Abraham's seed. There are several key numbers that tie together all of the topics pertaining to Abraham's seed, both his natural seed and his spiritual seed.

Here now are several examples of features that refer to Abraham's spiritual seed: "For not all who are descended from Israel belong to Israel, neither are they all children because they are Abraham's descendants, but: 'In Isaac shall thy seed be called.' "

In Isaac shall thy seed be called   144 × 11
Rom 9:7 εν Ισαακ κληθησεται σοι σπερμα

Probably the most significant feature is this one: "And if ye belong to Christ, then ye are Abraham's seed, and heirs according to promise."

Then ye are Abraham's seed, and heirs   144 × 15
according to promise
Gal 3:29 αρα Αβρααμ σπερμα εστε κατ επαγγελιαν κληρονομοι

Here are words on the same topic from Galatians 3:14: "That in Christ Jesus the blessing of Abraham might come to the Gentiles, so that we might receive the promise of the spirit through faith."

The blessing of Abraham   144 × 10
Gal 3:14 η ευλογια του Αβρααμ᾽᾽

Abraham   144
Gal 3:14 Αβρααμ᾽

Faith   144 × 7
Rev 14:12 την πιστιν

It was by faith that Abraham went forth to the promised land. Whenever Abraham is mentioned in the Bible, there is always one message being brought forth. Faith!

For the last feature of this book, we have selected one best describing the one factor that unites all of God's people—their common faith in Jesus. And for that reason we are the seed of Abraham, which is the seed of faith, the true Israel.

"For the law worketh wrath, but where there is no law, neither is there transgression. That is why it depends upon faith, that it might be by grace; in order that the promise might be sure to all the seed; not only to that seed which is of the law, but also to that which is the seed of the faith of Abraham, who is the father of us all."

The seed of the faith   144 × 24
Rom 4:16 τω σπερματι εκ πιστεως

9

Let's Tie It All
Together

What you have seen in this book could be compared to a single grain of sand on the beach. Better yet, to a mere drop of water in the ocean. In other words, the subject is inexhaustible. Perhaps the depths of theomatics will not become fully known until we get to heaven. The theomatic design in the Word of God is as vast, as intricate, and as complex as all creation, for it is eternal. In heaven we will be able to sit down with our calculators and gain new spiritual insight which we never had before. The Bible will become a treasure and a reminder of our redemption here on earth.

Only a few months have transpired from the time the truth of theomatics was discovered to the writing of this book. There are many things concerning the theomatic structure which we do not fully understand. As we mentioned earlier, this subject is so vast that in order to do it justice years of research by many people would be required. Theomatics is a whole new science, and at this time we must honestly admit that we do not have all of the answers to all of the questions it poses.

The purpose of this next to the last chapter is to tie together the whole concept of theomatics. There are several very important questions and objections which some people have repeatedly brought to our attention. These will be dealt with at this time. Also, we will discuss our future plans for theomatics in the way of research and development.

Let's Not Make Anything More of It Than What It Is

In his Foreword, Jerry mentioned something that both of us would like to elaborate on at this time. Our one hope and prayer is that nobody will make anything more or less of theomatics than what it is. Our worst fears do not come from those who might seek to make less of it, but rather from those who will seek to make more of it than what it is. When we have presented theomatics to people, they invariably start asking: What does this mean? What does that mean? Would you look up this verse or that verse and tell us what it means?

Some persons may take the attitude that theomatics is some sort of "instant cure-all" for every doctrinal ailment. Many people will say: "Oh boy, all I have to do now is just look up the numbers and I can find out anything that I want to know." Nothing could be further from the truth! God is not going to allow anyone to find out anything more than that which he is supposed to know. God's security systems are impregnable, for no one finds out anything about the divine other than what God chooses to reveal.

Needless to say, these attitudes on the part of some people scare both of us. God holds us responsible not to go and tell people that something means such and such if we do not know for a fact that it does. At this point in our research, we have only established one thing. If you take the words and phrases which have related spiritual meaning, they will be found to be divisible by a common multiple. At this point this is all we claim to know. Future research will no doubt reveal more intricate aspects of theomatics.

One of the major objections that some people raise toward theomatics is that it may lend itself to those who will take the numbers and come up with strange and absurd interpretations of Scripture; that theomatics may hold an attraction for those bent on the spectacular and unusual; that it may become a drawing card for sensationalists; and that people will try and use theomatics for the express purpose of proving their own doctrines. That these are distinct possibilities we will readily concede, but that does not change the fact that theomatics exists! To throw out theomatics because some may seek to pervert it would be throwing out the baby with the bath water.

For years, we as Christians have accepted and believed the written word to be the inspired Word of God. But what has happened? Along come the false cults, and what do they do? They pervert the written

Word of God which we as Christians hold dear and sacred. Now, does this mean that we are going to throw out the written Word, just because somebody comes along and perverts it. No! We accept what is true, and reject what is false. To try and throw out theomatics just because some may try and pervert it would make as much sense as trying to throw out the written word, just because someone perverts it also.

Now at this point we would like to give some advice to the reader. Just because someone may come along and say, "Look! These numbers prove such and such, and this means such and such," don't always believe it! As it was shown in Chapter 2, there is an almost unlimited number of potential combinations, when a person starts matching the different spellings for the words or playing with totals. This is why the Golden Rule of theomatics is so important: *All of the features must be taken right out of the text exactly as God put them there.* When this rule is heeded, it eliminates much of the flexibility that a person would need in trying to invent his own features.

In spite of all the difficulties, we can rest assured in one thing. God is in complete control of the situation. If God has kept theomatics secret for thousands of years, then He certainly could have kept the lid on it a few more years until Christ returned. If God has chosen to reveal it at this time, then He is certainly capable of protecting it. Theomatics does not belong to man. It belongs to God. Our only responsibility lies in treating it with respect and maturity. Let's not make anything less of it than what it is, and nothing more of it than what it is.

Does Everything Work Out?

The theomatic design in the Bible can be compared to a giant jig-saw puzzle. At this time we have only a few of the larger pieces put in place. Many times after looking over a design, people will ask us a question, Does everything work out to multiples of the same number? In other words, does every single reference to Jesus in the Bible fit the design of 37 or 111? Or does every single reference to Satan work out to multiples of 276? Before this question can be adequately answered it must be clarified. When a person asks, Does everything work out? is he referring to everything that he thinks should work out, or is he referring to everything that God says should work out? In reply to this:

Yes, everything that God says should work out does work out. This does not mean, however, that every single reference to a particular topic in the Bible has to be a multiple of the same number. If it is found that a particular feature does not work out to our expectations, it is always for one of two reasons: (1) *It is not supposed to work out;* or (2) *we have got the wrong text.*

Let's examine the first reason. Many times in theomatics there are several different designs or key numbers related to a particular topic. A perfect example of this is found in the following three features.

Jn 14:30 The ruler of this world is coming   276 × 15

Jn 16:11 Concerning judgment, because the ruler of this world has been judged   276 × 22

Jn 12:31 Now is the ruler of this world cast out   276 × 24

As you can see, it's quite remarkable that all three of these phrases work out to multiples of 276. But a person who is hypercritical will look at these features and say, Wait a minute! Why do you have to take these complete phrases? Why not just take the most distinct portion, which would be simply "ruler of this world" by itself? The answer is simple. "Ruler of this world" by itself is 666.

Jn 12:31 Ruler of this world   666 × 7

So, as you can see, God is bringing forth two truths with these two numbers. The complete phrases work out to being multiples of 276, and the most distinct portion is 666.

Let's say that we didn't know anything about the number 666. Upon examining these phrases then, we would think "ruler of this world" by itself had completely missed. But fortunately we happen to know about the number 666. Therefore, it was revealed that in this verse, there were two designs present.

By this time, you can begin to see the picture. If something doesn't always work out to our expectations, the reason is simple. There is another key number or design present which we have not discovered yet. When it is found, then everything will fit together perfectly.

Here is an example of what we mean when we say there are other key numbers present.

1 Pet 5:8 Your adversary the devil goes about as a roaring lion
276 × 24

1 Pet 5:8 Your adversary the devil goes about as a roaring lion,
  seeking whom he may devour   276 × 31

But what about just the word *adversary*?

Adversary   666
1 Pet 5:8 αντιδικος΄

In Chapter 5 we saw the marvelous design on light, darkness, and power. Here it was shown that everything related to power was structured on multiples of 100. The consistency was almost total. But in Luke 21:26 a strange thing happened. Here the text concerned the "powers of the heavens." These words were not a multiple of 100. Why? Later on it was shown where there was a complete design of 666 related to the heavens and God's creation of it. For this reason, "powers of the heavens" was not a multiple of 100, but rather of 666.

Lk 21:27 Powers of the heavens   666

Another feature which brings out this truth is found in The Acts 26:18: "To open their eyes, and turn them from darkness to light, and from the power of Satan to God." In going through the New Testament, we found that more than eighty percent of the references to Satan or the devil contained multiples of 276; but in this verse we find that there is no design of 276 present. Why? The reason is simple. "Power of Satan" has a theomatic value of 1,500, which is the number of power.

Acts 26:18 Power of Satan   1,500

For one last example we will present the following. In the last chapter on 144, we saw that the following features all contained multiples of 144:

Jn 17:2 All which thou hast given Him   144 × 19

Jn 17:6 The men whom Thou gavest   144 × 25

Jn 17:24 Those whom Thou hast given Me   144 × 8

Jn 10:29 Given them to Me   144 × 7

Heb 2:13 And the children whom God has given Me   144 × 12

Now we come to a verse in John 6:37: "All whom the Father has given Me shall come to Me." In light of what we have just seen in the above, and by all expectations, these words should also work out to 144. But guess what? They don't! Why?

In the beginning of the chapter on 144, we mentioned how the number twelve always referred to the redeemed: twelve tribes of Israel, twelve disciples, and twelve baskets full of the fragments and fishes. The number twelve is the root number which refers to all of the redeemed. Let us now take these words from John 6:37, and see what happens:

All whom the Father has given Me shall come to Me   1,200 × 2
Jn 6:37 παν διδωσιν μοι πατηρ προς εμε ηξει′

Whom the Father has given Me   1,200
Jn 6:37 διδωσιν μοι″

On the surface it would appear that this verse was a clear miss, and that there was no design present. But a closer examination revealed the exact opposite. There was a design present, and it had perfect meaning.

As we have stated, if something in theomatics does not work out, there is a reason for it. There are other designs and other key numbers present that we have not found yet. Once these are found, then all of the gaps will be filled.

Now the second reason why something may not work out to our expectations is that we have the wrong text. Those who are familiar with New Testament Greek will know exactly what we are talking about. In the section on 666, we pointed out that in the papyrus there were a few words spelled differently from the Nestle text, which we used exclusively for this book.[1] This is also true for the entire New Testament. The basic text of the Bible as we know it has been transmitted very accurately down through the years. However, throughout many of the early manuscripts, there are hundreds, even thousands, of little variations. For the most part, these variations are of little importance to meaning, but they are crucial to theomatics. If even one letter is different from the original text that God wrote, then there would be no design present. One misplaced letter would throw all of the theomatic values off.

There are many dozens of early manuscripts for the entire New Testament, particularly for the gospels. Some of these were made as

[1]Refer to p. 197 for textual information.

early as the third century; others as recently as the tenth century. These manuscripts are all copies made from other copies, which were made from the originals. When these early manuscripts were being copied, the process was sometimes by dictation. A group of scribes would be sitting at a table, and another scribe would dictate the original copy out loud. The other scribes would then copy it. During this process it would be very easy for someone to make a mistake, because many words in Greek that sound alike are not necessarily spelled alike. Thus, existing among all of the early manuscripts, there are hundreds of little variations.

What certain Bible scholars have done is compare all of these varying manuscripts. If it was found that there was one manuscript that had a reading which disagreed with all of the others, then it was assumed that the one manuscript was in error. That reading would then be cast out in favor of the majority. By this process of deduction, the scholars have been able to decipher which readings are most likely the original. One such scholar was Dr. D. Eberhard Nestle of Germany. He devoted his entire life to textual criticism, and his text is considered by many to be the most trustworthy in existence. For this reason it is the one that we use. In our research we have found it to be very accurate.

These difficulties with ascertaining which is the original text explain why many of the features do not work out—we may have the wrong text. In future theomatics research, all of the texts will be compared. For statistical reasons, we have limited ourselves in this book to the Nestle text. One of Del's goals in life is to use theomatics for the purpose of establishing a text, particularly for the book of Revelation. Although there is no way that theomatics can absolutely prove which readings are true and which are false, it can throw definite light on the subject, adding weight to one reading over another in cases where textual comparison alone is inconclusive.

In spite of all the textual variations, the theomatic design as found in Nestle's text is overwhelmingly consistent. Very few features failed to work out. Many of those that did not could have easily been attributed to a copyist error. The consistency of theomatics will be discussed more fully in the next chapter on statistics and probability.

Where Do We Go from Here?

Now that we know for a fact that God has written His entire Word mathematically, where do we go from here? What do we do?

While doing his research, Del constantly had a vision going through his mind. He could picture himself standing in a valley full of beautiful flowers. The flowers were so thick that he could hardly walk through them. They stretched toward the horizon in every direction as far as the eye could see. As Del was trying to pick these flowers, he would be weeping, because he was trying to pick so hard and so fast, and he had only two hands with which to pick.

This picture is a perfect analogy to the theomatic design in the Word of God. It is so vast that no matter where you turn, there are flowers waiting to be picked. One of our chief aims, now that that this book has been completed, is to organize an all-out research program. This research would involve not only ourselves, but also others who may become interested.

We are currently in the process of developing the tools necessary for research. The first item we hope to publish is the Greek-English New Testament. This tool is an absolute necessity for any type of research in theomatics. Another thing we hope to do in the future is use the computer for research. The entire Bible could be programmed onto a computer tape, and then the computer could help find theomatic designs and be used for other areas of research. The computer is extremely valuable for developing research tools and for cataloguing. Once the program is established, it can do in a few hours what would take thousands of hours to do manually.

Probably the one area of research that needs the most work is the Old Testament. At the time this book was completed, Del had not spent over thirty hours of research in the Hebrew. The main problem is that there is no existing Hebrew-English Old Testament, so for one to do research in Hebrew, he would have to be an authority in the language. The small amount of research which we have done has only proven that the same design present in the Greek is also found throughout the Old Testament. The Hebrew is a goldmine waiting to be uncovered, but before it can be, the necessary knowledge and tools will have to be developed.

As this book becomes widely known, there will develop a tremendous interest in the study of theomatics, and many people will want to do their own research. One of our goals in the future is to set up an international research exchange.

Let's say that John Smith, who lives in Kansas City, finds part of a design on his own, following all the rules of theomatics. Over in Germany someone else doing research finds a design that ties together with the design that John Smith found. Both of these people, as members of the exchange, would mail in their findings, and an office staff would coordinate them. When the two findings were put together, there would be an even further design. If we coordinated research efforts in this manner, great strides could be made in finding all the designs theomatics can offer. The international research exchange could put out a monthly publication that would list all of the news, developments, and theomatics designs, as they were being discovered.

The research exchange could be directed by a group of Christian and church leaders from all denominations. It would be nonsectarian in every respect. The only requisite for belonging would be a true born-again experience and a holding fast to the fundamental beliefs of Christianity. The guiding principle of the international research exchange would be to approach theomatics not with the idea of proving doctrine, but rather to let the theomatic design speak for itself.

The idea of a research exchange is only a dream at present, but as this book becomes well-known, the interest necessary to get it started will develop.

One thing that both Del and Jerry realize is that many readers will want to write to us and ask questions about theomatics. If enough readers were to do this, we would find ourselves flooded with mail. We would love to answer every letter personally, but because of the secretarial costs involved, it would be impossible for us to write to each person on an individual basis. However, if there are some readers interested in pursuing their own research, and who wish to contribute toward research—either with time or money—we would be happy to hear from you.

In order to reach everybody who is interested in theomatics, we have decided to publish a bimonthly newsletter. This newsletter will give all of the information concerning our research, plus any other news relevant to theomatics. We will also show some of the new theomatic designs as they are being developed.

In closing, there are so many things that we would like to say. Time will not permit. This book is only the beginning. This is why we have called it a John-the-baptist book. Three or four years from now, we will probably know ten times as much as we do now. Our one hope and prayer is that what has been written has blessed and comforted your heart and at the same time built up your faith. We only want to see the very best come about from the disclosure of this truth. Most important, and above all else, it must glorify the name of the Lord Jesus.

The next chapter is the chapter on statistics and probability. It scientifically proves that God wrote his entire Word mathematically by the number values of the Hebrew and Greek letters and has been included for those who wish to have scientific confirmation that these findings are correct. If you have read this book with an open mind, and your heart has been blessed, and the Holy Spirit has borne witness to you that what you have read is true, then it will not be necessary for you to keep on reading. But if you still have doubts, or if you are just plain skeptical and wish to have it proven scientifically, then the next chapter is for you. No person—believer or nonbeliever—will be able to say, "There is nothing to theomatics," after reading the next chapter.

10
Statistics and Probability

In order to prove the existence of the theomatic design in the Word of God, we are going to hinge our entire case on one scientific statement of fact. This statement of fact is the most important statement that we will ever make in this entire book, because on it rests our entire case, as to whether or not theomatics exists. Here it is:

Numbers must occur at random, unless there is a design. If there is no theomatic design present in the Bible, then all of the number values for the words would simply be one great big conglomeration of random numbers.

What does this mean? It means that if there is nothing to theomatics, then any one number would have as good a chance of occurring as any other number; in other words, they will occur on a random basis. The dictionary definition of the word *random* applies to all that occurs by accident, or is done without careful aim, plan, design.

If the number values in the Bible have no special design, it would be a very simple matter for someone to disprove theomatics. All he would have to do is simply demonstrate that other theomatic designs equal to ours could be built from number values randomly assigned to the letters of the Greek alphabet. If this should happen, the entire subject of theomatics would be completely discredited. But if it can be proven that the number values in the Bible are not random numbers, the question must be raised: How did these nonrandom numbers get into the text of the Word of God? This question demands an answer, because science declares that numbers must occur at random unless there is a design. Therefore, if it can be proven that these are not random numbers, then there would be a design present. This would settle the issue once and for all.

Furthermore, we are going to demonstrate and prove, that *no* number values *other* than those that God put in the papyrus will produce any kind of consistent design. When other number-letter equivalencies are used, there will be nothing present but random numbers. More on that later.

What Is Statistics and Probability?

Statistics, as defined by Webster's dictionary, means "facts or data of a numerical kind, assembled, classified, and tabulated so as to present significant information about a given subject." The definition of *probability* reads "the likelihood, chance, or possibility of something happening." When we hear the words "statistics and probability" as they relate to theomatics, it means the compiling of a certain classification of theomatic features, and then computing the odds, chance, and likelihood of those features occurring.

For the purpose of this study, we are going to present three methods of computing probability. Each of these will unequivocally establish design, particularly the latter. These three methods will be called Method 1, Method 2, and Method 3.

METHOD 1

Method 1[1] can establish the actual probability of something occurring. We will use the basic formula of probability: if the chance of one event happening is *1* in *x,* and the probability of another and independent invent happening is *1* in *y,* then the probability of both events happening is *1* in $x \times y$.

To illustrate this, suppose we were to take a box of random numbers from 1 to 10,000, with each number written on a card. If you or I were to reach into the box blindfolded, and pull out a number that was a

[1]The methodology in this chapter was set up and the calculations done by Arjan Bhatia. Mr. Bhatia has just finished the requirements for his doctorate, and has studied statistics and probability extensively at the University of Washington. He is currently employed in the computer department of Boeing Aircraft Company, Seattle, Washington.

direct multiple of 10, the probability of this happening would be 1 chance in 10, *i.e.*, 0.1, or 10 percent.

Probability is always figured by percentage. In the above example, the probability of drawing a card that was a direct multiple of 10 was only 1 chance in 10, or 10 percent probability. This means that the person drawing the card had a 10 percent probability of drawing a multiple of 10. Since for every 10 numbers in the box, 9 numbers are not multiples of 10, the chance of *not* drawing a multiple of 10 is 9 chances in 10, *i.e.*, 0.9, or 90 percent probability.

Let's say that the person who reached in and drew out the multiple of 10 reached in again, and pulled out another multiple of 10. The chance of this happening twice in a row would be 1 chance in 10 × 10, or 100, *i.e.*, 0.01, or 1 percent probability. The chance of it happening three times in a row would be 1 chance in 10 × 10 × 10, or 1,000, *i.e.*, 0.001, or 0.1 percent probability.

Proving Theomatics by Method 1

For the purpose of proving theomatics by Method 1, we are going to use a very short and explicit example. John 21:11 states that the disciples caught 153 fishes. Earlier it was shown that the following five references worked out to multiples of 153:

Lk 9:13 Fishes   153 × 8 ±0
Jn 21:11 The net   153 × 8 ±0
Mt 4:18 Casting a net into the sea   153 × 20 ±0
Lk 5:6 Multitude of fishes   153 × 16 ±1
Mk 1:17 Fishers of men   153 × 14 ±1

When these features were shown, it was also pointed out that the chance of all five working out to multiples of 153 was only 1 chance in 254,646. Let's now see how we arrived at that number.

In Chapter 2, which defined the theomatic structure, it was shown that many times in Greek a word will have several possible spellings. These spellings are called *cases*. In the New Testament, the word for *fishes* is spelled in two different forms, of which there are five combinations. Furthermore, three of these combinations appear with the Greek article. This then gives us a total of eight possibilities in the New Testament for the word *fishes*.

Mt 15:36 τους ιχθυας ιχθυας
Lk 9:13 ιχθυες   153 × 8 ±0
Jn 21:6 των ιχθυων ιχθυων
Jn 6:9 οψαρια
Jn 21:10 των οψαριων οψαριων

Now here is something very important. In figuring probability, one must always take into consideration every single possibility that he could have used for a theomatic feature. In the above example, there are eight possible combinations for the word *fishes* in the New Testament. One of them turned out to be a multiple of 153. But what if another one of these spellings had been 153 instead? We could have used it, couldn't we? Therefore, every combination possible must be taken into consideration when figuring probability. This also holds true for the phrases. If a phrase has articles or conjunctions in it, then every combination possible must be taken into consideration. If there are other points at which that phrase could have been cut off, then these must also be considered. Anything that could have been used must be taken into consideration when figuring probability calculations.

The next feature is the word *net*. It is spelled in only two forms, once with the article. This then gives us three possibilities. In the fish story of John 21:11, the word *net* appears in the singular. In Matthew 4:21, the word *net* appears in the plural as *nets*. Some people may argue that we could have used the word in the plural instead of the singular. For this reason, we will take into consideration every combination possible in the New Testament, singular or plural.

Jn 21:11 το δικτυον δικτυον 153 × 8 ±0
Mt 13:47 σαγηνη
Mt 4:21 τα δικτυα δικτυα

For the third reference, there are six combinations. Three times in the New Testament the text refers to "casting a net into the sea." All three phrases contain one article. Therefore, each phrase could be shown with the article or without the article.

Mt 4:18 βαλλοντας αμφιβληστρον εις την θαλασσαν   153 × 20 ± 0
         βαλλοντας αμφιβληστρον εις θαλασσαν
Mk 1:16 αμφιβαλλοντας εν τη θαλασση
         αμφιβαλλοντας εν θαλασση

Mt 13:47 σαγηνη βληθειση εις την θαλασσαν

σαγηνη βληθειση εις θαλασσαν

References to a "multitude of fishes" occur twice in the New Testament. Here are all of the combinations:

Lk 5:6 πληθος ιχθυων πολυ

πληθος ιχθυων

ιχθυων πολυ   153 × 16 ±1

Jn 21:6 του πληθους των ιχθυων

πληθους   ιχθυων

του πληθους   ιχθυων

πληθους των ιχθυων

And the last feature, "fishers of men," is spelled with only one combination.

Mk 1:17 αλεεις ανθρωπων   153 × 14 ±1

We have now tabulated all of the combinations in the New Testament for these five references. All five of these fall within the cluster of ±1 of the multiples of 153. We will now calculate the chance, or probability, of these five features occurring within these references.

For our first calculation, we will find the probability of at least one of the eight spellings for the word *fishes* falling within the cluster of ±1 of the multiples of 153. Since there is one number on each side of the multiple of 153 that forms the cluster (a total of three numbers: 152, 153, 154), we would then subtract 3 from 153, which would give us 150. Next, we would divide 150 by 153, and multiply it to the eighth power, because there are eight combinations possible.

$$150/153 \times 150/153 \times 150/153 \times 150/153 \times 150/153 \times 150/153$$
$$\times 150/153 \times 150/153 = 0.85349037$$

An easier way to express this would be: $(150/153)^8 = 0.85349037$

This number, 0.85349037, gives us the probability of none of the combinations having a feature within ±1 of the multiples of 153. Therefore, to figure the probability of at least one of the combinations being within ±1 of 153, we simply subtract 0.85349037 from the number 1, which gives us 0.14650963.

As we stated earlier, all probability is figured by percentage. To arrive at the percentage represented by 0.14650963, we would simply multiply by 100, or move the decimal point over two places to the right, 14.650963. Therefore, the chance of at least one of the features being a multiple within ± 1 of 153 is 14.650963 percent. Subsequently, the chance of a complete miss is 85.349037 percent.

Here now are the calculations for all five of the features:

Fishes $(150/153)^8 = 0.85349037$, or 0.14650963, i.e., 14.650963%
The net $(150/153)^5 = 0.90573081$, or 0.09426919, i.e., 9.426919%
Casting a net into the sea $(150/153)^6 = 0.88797138$, or 0.11202862, i.e., 11.202862%
Multitude of fishes $(150/153)^7 = 0.87056018$, or 0.12943982, i.e., 12.943982%
Fishers of men $(150/153)^1 = 0.98039216$, or 0.01960784, i.e., 1.960784%

To calculate our final probability, we will use the basic formula for Method 1. If the chance of one event happening is 1 in x, and the probability of another and independent event happening is 1 in y, then the probability of both events happening is simply 1 in $x \times y$. This means that we would take all of the probabilities for these five references, and multiply them by themselves:

$$0.14650963 \times 0.09426919 \times 0.11202862 \times 0.12943982 \times 0.01960784 = 0.000003927$$

And to calculate the final probability, we simply divide 0.000003927 by the number 1:

$$0.000003927/1 = 254{,}646$$

Therefore, the chance of all five of these features being within ± 1 of the multiple of 153 is 1 chance in 254,646.

Throughout this book, all of the features have fallen within the cluster of ± 2 of the multiples.[2] In making a quick survey of all these features, we discovered that approximately twenty percent were ± 2, and the rest (eighty percent) were either exact multiples or within ± 1. If our features had been randomly selected, then the cluster distribution would have been forty percent, forty percent, twenty percent. This is because for the five numbers in the cluster two out of five,

[2]With the exception of five features in the book, which were ± 3. For statistical purposes, these will be thrown out and counted as misses.

or forty percent, are ± 2; two out of five, or forty percent, are ± 1; and one out of five, or twenty percent, are ± 0. The fact that approximately twenty percent are ± 2 (instead of forty percent) proves that the number values are all clustering around the multiples, with the greatest percentage being in the center of the cluster.

If we wanted to, we could calculate all of the probabilities on this ratio of twenty percent ± 2 and eighty percent ± 1 or ± 0. This would give us a definite advantage. However, to be conservative, we will not do this. Since we do show features that are within ± 2 of the direct multiples, we will then calculate all of our probabilities as: What is the chance that the theomatic values could all fall within the cluster of ± 2? This would give us results that are less impressive, but this is the most conservative way of figuring the probabilities.

Now in the design of the 153 fishes, we calculated everything as being within ± 1, because all of the features fell within this cluster. But what if "fishers of men" had been ± 2 instead of the observed result of ± 1? We would have still shown it, wouldn't we? Therefore, let us now recalculate the same five references to find out what the probability is of all the features falling within the cluster of ± 2.

In the cluster of ± 2, there are five numbers (151, 152, 153, 154, 155) as opposed to only three numbers in the cluster of ± 1. For this reason, we would then subtract 5 from 153, which would give us 148. Next, we would divide 148 by 153, and multiply it to the appropriate power. Here are the calculations for all five of the references:

Fishes $(148/153)^8 = 0.76658846$, or 0.23341154, *i.e.*, 23.341154%

The net $(148/153)^5 = 0.84693762$, or 0.15306238, *i.e.*, 15.306238%

Casting a net into the sea $(148/153)^6 = 0.81925992$, or 0.18074008, *i.e.*, 18.074008%

Multitude of fishes $(148/153)^7 = 0.79248672$, or 0.20751328, *i.e.*, 20.751328%

Fishers of men $(148/153)^1 = 0.96732026$, or 0.03267974, *i.e.*, 3.267974%

$0.23341154 \times 0.15306238 \times 0.18074008 \times 0.20751328 \times 0.03267974 = 0.0000437895$

$$0.0000437895/1 = 22,837$$

Therefore, the chance that all five of these references would fall within ± 2 of the multiples of 153 is 1 chance in 22,837.

The Birth and Coming of Christ

Next, we will show an example of thirty-two references which will be much more complicated. In Chapter 3, on the design of Jesus, it was shown that the many difference references to Christ all worked out to multiples of 37. However, the vast majority of the features were also multiples of 111. What we are going to do now is show a complete design on those references to the birth and coming of Christ and the child Jesus. All of these references are multiples of 111, and they will be calculated as falling within the cluster of $+2$ of the multiples of 111.

As we mentioned earlier in this chapter, whenever one figures the probability of a feature, he must always take into consideration every possible combination that he could have used from that reference. If a phrase has articles in it, then every combination possible, with all of the articles or conjunctions, must be taken into consideration. If there are other points at which the phrase could have been cut off, then these also must be considered. Any combination that has intelligible meaning and could have been used for a feature must be taken into consideration.

Reference 1. Our first reference comes from Matthew 1:20. Here it says: "But while he thought on these things, behold, the angel of the Lord appeared unto him in a dream, saying, 'Joseph, thou son of David, fear not to take unto thee Mary thy wife: for the one, her begotten of the spirit, is holy.' "

Now this complete phrase has one article and one conjuction ($\gamma\alpha\rho$). This then gives us three combinations for the complete phrase.

For the one, her begotten of the spirit, is holy

1-1	το γαρ εν αυτη γεννηθεν εκ πνευματος εστιν αγιον
1-2	το εν αυτη γεννηθεν εκ πνευματος εστιν αγιον
1-3	εν αυτη γεννηθεν εκ πνευματος εστιν αγιον

This phrase could also have read:
The one, her begotten of the spirit

1-4	το εν αυτη γεννηθεν εκ πνευματος
1-5	εν αυτη γεννηθεν εκ πνευμαγος

Or it could have read:
The one, her begotten

1–6 το εν αυτη γεννηθεν

1–7 εν αυτη γεννηθεν

The purpose of the numerical notations at the left is to organize the combinations. The first figure refers to the scriptural reference, and the second figure refers to the combination for that reference.

Now the little word for *one* in Greek is εν. It precedes the Greek word for *her*, αυτη. By eliminating it, the phrase would still carry the same essential meaning. It would now run:

Her begotten of spirit is holy

1–8 αυτη γεννηθεν εκ πνευματος εστιν αγιου $111 \times 28 \pm 1$

Her begotten of spirit

1–9 αυτη γεννηθεν εκ πνευματος

Her begotten

1–10 αυτη γεννηθεν $111 \times 8 \pm 1$

As we can now see, this phrase contains ten distinct possibilities that could have been used for theomatic features. Two of these possibilities worked out to multiples of 111.

Now we will proceed to list the remaining 31 references, with all of their combinations:

Reference 2. "And she will bear a Son, and thou shall call the name
Mt 1:21   of Him Jesus: for He will save His people from their sins." (12 combinations—1 hit.)

And she will bear a Son, and thou shall call the name of Him Jesus

2–1 τεξεται δε υιον και καλεσεις το ονομα αυτου Ιησουν

2–2   –   –

2–3   δε   –

2–4   –   το

And she will bear a Son

2–5 τεξεται δε υιον $111 \times 11 \pm 1$

2–6   –

And thou shall call the name of Him Jesus

2–7 και καλεσεις το ονομα αυτου Ιησουν

2–8 –   –

2–9 και   –

2–10 –   το

The name of Him Jesus

2–11 το ονομα αυτου Ιησουν

2–12 –

Reference 3. "Behold, a virgin shall conceive and bear a Son, and
Mt 1:23   they will call the name of Him Emmanuel, which is
             being interpreted, with us God." (51 combinations—3
             hits.)

*Behold, a virgin shall conceive and bear a Son, and they will call
the name of Him Emmanuel, which is being interpreted, with
us God.*

ιδου η παρθενος εν γαστρι εξει και τεξεται υιον και καλεσουσιν το ονομα
αυτου Εμμανουηλ ο εστιν μεθερμηνευομενον μεθ ημων ο Θεος

(ALL COMBINATIONS PRESENT IN THIS PHRASE.)

3–1	ιδου	η	το	ο
3–2	ιδου	—	—	—
3–3	ιδου	η	—	—
3–4	ιδου	—	το	—
3–5	ιδου	—	—	ο
3–6	ιδου	η	το	—
3–7	ιδου	—	το	ο
3–8	ιδου	η	—	ο
3–9	—	η	το	ο
3–10	—	—	—	—
3–11	—	η	—	—
3–12	—	—	το	—
3–13	—	—	—	ο
3–14	—	η	το	—
3–15	—	—	το	ο
3–16	—	η	—	ο

$111 \times 80 \pm 1$

*Behold, a virgin shall conceive and bear a Son, and they will call
the name of Him Emmanuel*

3–17 ιδου η παρθενος εν γαστρι εξει και τεξεται υιον και καλεσουσιν το ονομα
      αυτου Εμμανουηλ

3–18 ιδου –   –

3–19 ιδου η   –

3–20 ιδου –   το

3–21   -   η̲   το̲
3–22   -   -   -
3–23   -   η̲   -
3–24   -   -   το̲

Behold, a virgin shall conceive and bear a Son

3–25   ιδου η παρθενος εν γαστρι εξει και τεξεται υιον $111 \times 27 \pm 1$
3–26   ιδου -
3–27   -   η̲
3–28   -   -

And bear a Son

3–29   και τεξεται υιον
3–30   -

And they will call the name of Him Emmanuel, which is being interpreted, with us God

3–31   και καλεσουσιν το ονομα αυτου Εμμανουηλ ο εστιν μεθερμηνευομενον
       μεθ ημων ο Θεος
3–32   και̲   -̲   - $111 \times 53 \pm 2$
3–33   και̲   -   ο̲
3–34   και̲   το̲   -
3–35   -   το̲   ο̲
3–36   -   -   -
3–37   -   -   ο̲
3–38   -   το̲   -

And they will call the name of Him Emmanuel

3–39   και καλεσουσιν το ονομα αυτου Εμμανουηλ
3–40   -̲   -̲
3–41   και̲   -
3–42   -̲   το̲

The name of Him Emmanuel, which is being interpreted, with us God

3–43   το ονομα αυτου Εμμανουηλ ο εστιν μεθερμηνεουομενον μεθ ημων ο̲ Θεος
3–44   -̲   -
3–45   -   ο̲
3–46   το̲   -

The name of Him Emmanuel

3-47 το ονομα αυτου Εμμανουηλ

3-48 —

Emmanuel

3-49 Εμμανουηλ

Emmanuel, which is being interpreted, with us God

3-50 Εμμανουηλ ο εστιν μεθερμηνεουομενον μεθ ημων ο Θεος

3-51 —

Reference 4. "But He [Joseph] knew her not until she bore a Son; and
Mt 1:25 called the name of Him Jesus." (9 combinations—1
hit.)

She bore a Son; and called the name of Him Jesus

4-1 ετεκεν υιον και εκαλεσεν το ονομα αυτου Ιησουν $111 \times 34 \pm 2$

4-2 —

She bore a Son

4-3 ετεκεν υιον

And called the name of Him Jesus

4-4 και εκαλεσεν το ονομα αυτου Ιησουν

4-5 — —

4-6 και —

4-7 — το

The name of Him Jesus

4-8 το ονομα αυτου Ιησουν

4-9 —

Reference 5. "And the angel said unto her, 'Fear not, Mary: for thou
Lk 1:31 hast found favor with God. And behold, you shall conceive in thy womb, and bring forth a Son, and you shall
call the name of Him Jesus.'" (16 combinations—1
hit.)

*And behold, you shall conceive in thy womb and bear a Son, and
you shall call the name of Him Jesus*

5-1 και ιδου συλλημψη εν γαστρι και τεξη υιον και καλεσεις το ονομα αυτου
Ιησουν

5-2 — —

5–3 καὶ   –
5–4 –   το

You shall conceive in thy womb and bear a Son, and you shall
call the name of Him Jesus

5–5 συλλημψη εν γαστρι και τεξη υιον και καλεσεις το ονομα αυτου Ιησουν
5–6   – 111 × 51 ±0

And behold, you shall conceive in thy womb and bear a Son

5–7 και ιδου συλλημψη εν γαστρι και τεξη υιον
5–8 –

You shall conceive in thy womb and bear a Son

5–9 συλλημψη εν γαστρι και τεξη υιον

Bear a Son

5–10 τεξη υιον

And you shall call the name of Him Jesus

5–11 και καλεσεις το ονομα αυτου Ιησουν
5–12 –   –
5–13 καὶ   –
5–14 –   το

The name of Him Jesus

5–15 το ονομα αυτου Ιησουν
5–16 –

Reference 6.   "And the angel answered and said unto her, 'The Holy
Lk 1:35   Spirit will come upon thee, and the power of the most
               high will overshadow thee: therefore also the holy off-
               spring shall be called the Son of God.' " (14 combina-
               tions—1 hit.)

The Holy Spirit will come upon thee, and the power of the most
high will overshadow thee: therefore also the holy offspring shall
be called the Son of God

6–1 πνευμα αγιον επελευσεται επι σε και δυναμις υψιστου επισκιασει σοι
     διο και το γεννωμενον αγιον κληθησεται υιος Θεου

6–2

                    –

And the power of the most high will overshadow thee: therefore
also the holy offspring shall be called the Son of God

6–3 και δυναμις υψιστου επισκιασει σοι διο και το γεννωμενον αγιον
κληθησεται υιος Θεου

6–4 -   -

6–5 και   -

6–6 -   το 111 × 64 ±1

Therefore also the holy offspring shall be called the Son of God

6–7 διο και το γεννωμενον αγιον κληθησεται υιος Θεου

6–8 -   -

6–9 διο και -

6–10 -   και το

6–11 - - το

6–12 - - -

The holy offspring

6–13 το γεννωμενον αγιον

6–14 -

Reference 7. "And when eight days were completed to circumcise
Lk 2:21   Him; and was called the name of Him Jesus, the name
            given by the angel before He was conceived in the
            womb." (72 combinations—6 hits.)

*And was called the name of Him Jesus, the name given by the
angel before He was conceived in the womb*

και εκληθη το ονομα αυτου Ιησους το κληθεν υπο του αγγελου προ του
συλλημφθηναι αυτον εν τη κοιλια

(ALL COMBINATIONS PRESENT IN THIS PHRASE.)

7–1	και	το	το	του	του	τη
7–2	και	—	—	—	—	—
7–3	και	το	—	—	—	—
7–4	και	—	—	του	—	—
7–5	και	—	—	—	—	τη
7–6	και	το	το	—	—	—
7–7	και	—	—	του	του	—
7–8	και	το	—	του	—	—
7–9	και	το	—	του	του	—
7–10	και	το	—	του	—	τη
7–11	και	το	—	του	του	τη
7–12	και	το	—	—	—	τη
7–13	και	το	το	του	—	—

7–14	και	το	το	του	του	—
7–15	και	το	το	του	—	τη
7–16	και	το	το	—	—	τη
7–17	και	—	—	του	του	—
7–18	και	—	—	του	—	τη	111 × 65 ±1
7–19	και	—	—	του	του	τη
7–20	—	το	το	του	του	τη
7–21	—	—	—	—	—	—	111 × 55 ±2
7–22	—	το	—	—	—	—
7–23	—	—	—	του	—	—
7–24	—	—	—	—	—	τη
7–25	—	το	το	—	—	—
7–26	—	—	—	του	του	—
7–27	—	το	—	του	—	—
7–28	—	το	—	του	του	—
7–29	—	το	—	του	—	τη
7–30	—	το	—	του	του	τη	111 × 75 ±0
7–31	—	το	—	—	—	τη
7–32	—	το	το	του	—	—
7–33	—	το	το	του	του	—
7–34	—	το	το	του	—	τη
7–35	—	το	το	—	—	τη
7–36	—	—	—	του	του	—
7–37	—	—	—	του	—	τη
7–38	—	—	—	του	του	τη

And was called the name of Him Jesus

7–39 και εκληθη το ονομα αυτου Ιησους

7–40 –   ⸺

7–41 και   -

7–42 -   το

The name of Him Jesus

7–43 το ονομα αυτου Ιησους

7–44 ‾

And was called the name of Him Jesus, the name given by the angel

7–45 και εκληθη το ονομα αυτου Ιησους το κληθεν υπο του αγγελου

7–46 και   ‾   ‾   ‾

7-47	και	το	-	-
7-48	και	-	-	του
7-49	και	το	το	-
7-50	και	το	-	του
7-51	-	το	το	του
7-52	-	-	-	- $111 \times 32 \pm 2$
7-53	-	το	-	-
7-54	-	-	-	του
7-55	-	το	το	-
7-56	-	το	-	του

Jesus, the name given by the angel before He was conceived in the womb

7-57 Ιησους το κληθεν υπο του αγγελου προ του συλλημφθηναι αυτον εν τη κοιλια

7-58	-	-	-	-
7-59	το	-	-	-

$$111 \times 45 \pm 0$$

7-60	-	του	-	-
7-61	-	-	-	τη
7-62	-	του	του	-
7-63	το	του	-	-
7-64	το	του	του	-
7-65	το	-	-	τη
7-66	το	του	-	τη
7-67	-	του	-	τη
7-68	-	του	του	τη

Jesus, the name given by the angel

7-69 Ιησους το κληθεν υπο του αγγελου

7-70	-	-	
7-71	το	- $111 \times 22 \pm 0$	
7-72	-	του	

Reference 8. "And when they saw it they made known the saying
Lk 2:17   spoken to them concerning the child this." (12 combinations—1 hit.)

The saying spoken to them concerning the child this

8-1 του ρηματος του λαληθεντος αυτοις περι του παιδιου τουτου
8-2 - - -

8–3   του   –   –

8–4   του   του   –

The saying spoken concerning the child this

8–5   του ρηματος του λαληθεντος περι του παιδιου τουτου

8–6   –   –   –

8–7   του   –   –

8–8   του   του   –

The child this

8–9   του παιδιου τουτου $111 \times 26 \pm 1$

8–10 –

The child

8–11   του παιδιου

8–12 –

Reference 9.   "And inspired by the Spirit he came into the temple;
Lk 2:27   and in brought the parents the child Jesus, to carry out
           for Him the custom of the law." (20 combinations—2
           hits.)

And in brought the parents the child Jesus

9–1   και εν τω εισαγαγειν τους γονεις το παιδιον Ιησουν

9–2   και   –   –   –

9–3   και   τω   –   – $111 \times 25 \pm 0$

9–4   και   –   τους   –

9–5   και   –   –   το

9–6   και   τω   τους   –

9–7   και   –   τους   το

9–8   και   τω   –   το

9–9   –   τω   τους   το

9–10 –   –   –   –

9–11 –   τω   –   –

9–12 –   –   τους   –

9–13 –   –   –   το

9–14 –   τω   τους   –

9–15 –   –   τους   το

9–16 –   τω   –   το

The child Jesus

9–17   το παιδιον Ιησουν $111 \times 12 \pm 1$

9–18 –

The Child
9–19   το παιδιον
9–20   -

Reference 10. "While Thou stretchest out Thy hand to heal, and signs
Acts 4:30   and wonders are performed through the name of the
holy child of Thee Jesus." (14 combinations—1 hit.)

Name of the holy child of Thee Jesus
10–1   του ονοματος του αγιου παιδος σου Ιησου
10–2   -   -
10–3   του   -

Name of the holy child Jesus
10–4   του ονοματος του αγιου παιδος Ιησου
10–5   -   -
10–6   του   -   111 × 28 ±0

The holy child of Thee Jesus
10–7   του αγιου παιδος σου Ιησου
10–8   -

The holy child of Thee
10–9   του αγιου παιδος σου
10–10 -

The holy child Jesus
10–11 του αγιου παιδος Ιησου
10–12 -

The holy child
10–13 του αγιου παιδος
10–14 -

Reference 11. "And she exclaimed with a loud cry, 'Blessed are you
Lk 1:42   among women, and blessed is the fruit of the womb of
thee.'" (24 combinations—1 hit.)

And blessed is the fruit of the womb of thee
11–1   και ευλογημενος ο καρπος της κοιλιας σου
11–2   -   -   -
11–3   και   -   -
11–4   -   ο   -
11–5   -   -   της

11–6	<u>και</u>	<u>o</u>	–
11–7	–	<u>o</u>	της
11–8	<u>και</u>	–	της

And blessed is the fruit of the womb

11–9	και ευλογημενος ο καρπος της κοιλιας
11–10	<u>–</u> <u>–</u> <u>–</u>
11–11	<u>και</u> – –
11–12	<u>–</u> <u>o</u> –
11–13	– – της
11–14	<u>και</u> <u>o</u> –
11–15	– <u>o</u> της
11–16	<u>και</u> – της

The fruit of the womb of thee

11–17	ο καρπος <u>της</u> κοιλιας σου	
11–18	<u>–</u> <u>–</u>	
11–19	<u>o</u> –	$111 \times 14 \pm 2$
11–20	– της	

The fruit of the womb

11–21	ο καρπος <u>της</u> κοιλιας
11–22	<u>–</u> <u>–</u>
11–23	<u>o</u> –
11–24	– της

Reference 12.   "A certain woman of the company lifted up her voice,
Lk 11:27   and said unto Him, Blessed is the womb that bare Thee
and the paps which Thou has sucked." (8 combinations
—2 hits.)

Blessed is the womb that bare Thee

12–1	μακαρια η κοιλια η βαστασασα σε	$111 \times 13 \pm 2$
12–2	<u>–</u> <u>–</u>	
12–3	<u>η</u> –	

The womb that bare Thee

12–4	η κοιλια η βαστασασα σε
12–5	<u>–</u> <u>–</u>
12–6	<u>η</u> –

Bare Thee

12–7	<u>η</u> βαστασασα σε	
12–8	–	$111 \times 10 \pm 1$

Reference 13. "And it came to pass that while they were there, the
Lk 2:6   days were accomplished that she should be delivered."
(28 combinations—7 hits.)

And it came to pass that while they were there, the days were
accomplished that she should be delivered

13–1	εγενετο δε εν τω ειναι αυτους εκει επλησθησαν αι ημεραι του τεκειν αυτην			
	111 $\overline{\times}$ 5$\overline{2}$ ±2			
13–2	δε –	–		–
13–3	δε τω	–		–
	111 $\overline{\times}$ 4$\overline{5}$ ±2			
13–4	δε –		αι	–
13–5	δε –		–	του
	111 $\overline{\times}$ 42 ±1			
13–6	δε τω		αι	–
13–7	δε –		αι	του
13–8	δε τω		–	του
13–9	– τω		αι	του
13–10	– –		–	–
	111 × 35 ±1			
13–11	– τω		–	–
13–12	– –		αι	–
13–13	– –		–	του
13–14	– τω		αι	–
	111 × 4$\overline{5}$ ±0			
13–15	– –		αι	του
13–16	– τω		–	του

While they were there, the days were accomplished that she
should be delivered

13–17	εν τω ειναι αυτους εκει επλησθησαν αι ημεραι του τεκειν αυτην			
	$\overline{111}$ × 48 ±1			
13–18	–		–	–
13–19	τω		–	–
13–20	–		αι	–
13–21	–		–	του
	111 × 38 ±2			
13–22	τω		αι	–
13–23	–		αι	του
13–24	τω		–	του

The days were accomplished that she should be delivered

13–25 επλησθησαν αι ημεραι του τεκειν αυτην

13–26   -   -

13–27   <u>αι</u>   -

13–28   -   <u>του</u>

Reference 14. "And she bore the son of her the firstborn, and wrapped
Lk 2:7   Him in swaddling clothes, and laid Him in a manger."
(24 combinations—2 hits.)

*And she bore the son of her the firstborn, and wrapped Him in
swaddling clothes, and laid Him in a manger*

14–1   και ετεκεν τον υιον αυτης <u>τον</u> πρωτοτοκον και εσπαργανωσεν αυτον και

ανεκλινεν αυτον εν φατνη

14–2 -   -   -

14–3 <u>και</u>   -   -

14–4 <u>-</u>   <u>του</u>   - $111 \times 76 \pm 2$

14–5 -   <u>του</u>   <u>του</u>

14–6 και   <u>του</u>   -

And she bore the son of her the firstborn

14–7   και ετεκεν τον υιον αυτης τον πρωτοτοκον

14–8 <u>-</u>   <u>-</u>   -

14–9 και   -   -

14–10 <u>-</u>   <u>του</u>   -

14–11 -   <u>του</u>   <u>του</u>

14–12 και   <u>-</u>   <u>του</u>

And she bore the son the firstborn

14–13   και ετεκεν τον υιον τον πρωτοτοκον

14–14 <u>-</u>   <u>-</u>   - $111 \times 25 \pm 0$

14–15 και   -   -

14–16 <u>-</u>   <u>του</u>   -

14–17 -   <u>του</u>   <u>του</u>

14–18 και   <u>-</u>   <u>του</u>

The son of her the firstborn

14–19 τον υιον αυτης <u>τον</u> πρωτοτοκον

14–20 <u>-</u>   <u>-</u>

14–21 <u>του</u>   -

The son the firstborn

14–22 τον υιον τον πρωτοτοκον

14–23 –   –

14–24 τον   –

Reference 15. "And this will be a sign for you: You will find the babe

Lk 2:12   wrapped in swaddling clothes and lying in a manger."
           (5 combinations—2 hits.)

*You will find the babe wrapped in swaddling clothes and lying
in a manger*

15–1 ευρησετε βρεφος εσπαργανωμενον και κειμενον εν φατνη

111 × 41 ±1

The babe wrapped in swaddling clothes and lying in a manger

15–2 βρεφος εσπαργανωμενον και κειμενον εν φατνη

You will find the babe wrapped in swaddling clothes

15–3 ευρησετε βρεφος εσπαργανωμενον

The babe wrapped in swaddling clothes

15–4 βρεφος εσπαργανωμενον   111 × 21 ±1

The babe

15–5 βρεφος

Reference 16. "The shepherds said to one another, 'Let us now go

Lk 2:15   even unto Bethlehem, and see This Thing which is
           come to pass, which the Lord has made known unto
           us.' " (36 combinations—2 hits.)

*Let us now go even unto Bethlehem, and see This Thing which
is come to pass, which the Lord has made known unto us*

16–1 διελθωμεν δη εως βηθλεεμ και ιδωμεν το ρημα τουτο το γεγονς ο ο κυριος
εγνωρισεν ημιν

16–2   –   –   –

16–3   το   –   –

16–4   το   το   –

16–5   –   –   ο

16–6   το   –   ο

*Let us now go even unto Bethlehem, and see This Thing which
is come to pass*

278 / THEOMATICS

16–7 διελθωμεν δη εως βηθλεεμ και ιδωμεν το ρημα τουτο το γεγονος
111 × 49 ±0

16–8   –   –
16–9   το   –

And see This Thing which is come to pass

16–10 και ιδωμεν το ρημα τουτο το γεγονος
16–11 –   –   –
16–12 και   –   –
16–13 –   το   –
16–14 –   το   το
16–15 και   το   –

This Thing which is come to pass

16–16 το ρημα τουτο το γεγονος
16–17 –   –
16–18 το   –

*And see This Thing which is come to pass, which the Lord has
made known unto us*

16–19 και ιδωμεν το ρημα τουτο το γεγονος ο ο κυριος εγνωρισεν ημιν
16–20 και   –   –   –
16–21 και   το   –   –
16–22 και   το   το   –
16–23 και   το   –   ο
16–24 και   –   –   ο
16–25 –   το   το   ο
16–26 –   –   –   –
16–27 –   το   –   –
16–28 –   το   το   –
16–29 –   το   –   ο
16–30 –   –   –   ο

*This Thing which is come to pass, which the Lord has made
known unto us*

16–31 το ρημα τουτο το γεγονος ο ο κυριος εγνωρισεν ημιν
111 × 29 ±2

16–32 –   –   –
16–33 το   –   –
16–34 το   το   –
16–35 –   το   ο
16–36 –   –   ο

Reference 17. "And they went with haste, and found Mary and Jo-
Lk 2:16   seph, and the babe lying in the manger." (10 combina-
            tions—1 hit.)

And the babe lying in the manger

17–1   και το βρεφος κειμενον εν τη φατνη
17–2   - -   -
17–3   και -   -
17–4   - το   -
17–5   - -   τη
17–6   και το   -   111 × 22 ±0
17–7   - το   τη
17–8   και -   τη

The babe

17–9   το βρεφος
17–10 -

Reference 18. "Now when Jesus was born in Bethlehem of Judea in
Mt 2:1   the days of Herod the king, behold, there came wise
            men from the east to Jerusalem." (12 combinations—
            1 hit.)

*Jesus was born in Bethlehem of Judea in the days of Herod the
king*

18–1   του Ιησου γεννηθεντος εν Βηθλεεμ της Ιουδαιας εν ημεραις Ηρωδου του
       βασιλεως
18–2   -   -   -
18–3   του   -   -
            111 × 55 ±2
18–4   -   της
18–5   του   της   -
18–6   του   -   του

Jesus was born in Bethlehem of Judea

18–7   του Ιησου γεννηθεντος εν βηθλεεμ της Ιουδαιας
18–8   -   -
18–9   του
18–10 -   της

Jesus was born in Bethlehem

18–11 του Ιησου γεννηθεντος εν βηθλεεμ
18–12 -

Reference 19. "And thou, O Bethlehem, in the land of Judah, are by
Mt 2:6   no means least among all the rulers of Judah; for out of
thee shall come forth a governor, who will shepherd the
people of Me Israel." (12 combinations—1 hit.)

*For out of thee shall come forth a governor, who will shepherd
the people of Me Israel*

19–1	εκ σου γαρ εξελευσεται ηγουμενος οστις ποιμανει τον λαον μου τον
	Ισραηλ

19–2	–		–	–
19–3	γαρ		–	–
19–4	–		τον	–
19–5	–		τον	τον
19–6	γαρ		–	τον

For out of thee shall come forth a governor

19–7	εκ σου γαρ εξελευσεται ηγουμενος $111 \times 24 \pm 2$
19–8	–

Governor who will shepherd the people of Me Israel

19–9	ηγουμενος οστις ποιμανει τον λαον μου τον Ισραηλ
19–10	–	–
19–11	–	τον

Governor

19–12 ηγουμενος

Reference 20. "Where is the one born king of the Jews? For we have
Mt 2:2   seen His star in the east, and have come to worship
Him." (11 combinations—1 hit.) (The first portion of
this verse will be counted as a missed feature.)

*For we have seen His star in the east and have come to worship
Him*

20–1	ειδομεν γαρ αυτου τον αστερα εν τη ανατολη και ηλθομεν προσκυνησαι
	αυτω

20–2	–	–	–
20–3	γαρ	–	–
20–4	–	τον	–
20–5	–	–	τη
20–6	γαρ	τον	–

20–7   –   <u>τον</u>

20–8   γαρ   <u>–</u>   <u>τη</u>   111 × 52 ±0
                        τη

And have come to worship Him

20–9   και ηλθομεν προσκυνησαι αυτω

20–10 <u>–</u>

Worship Him

20–11   προσκυνησαι αυτω

Reference 21. "And, lo, the star which they had seen in the east went
Mt 2:9   before them, until it came and stood over where the
         child lay." (8 combinations—1 hit.)

Until it came and stood over where the child lay

21–1   εως ελθων εσταθη επανω ου ην το παιδιον

21–2   <u>–</u>

It came and stood over where the child lay

21–3   ελθων εσταθη επανω ου ην το παιδιον

21–4   <u>–</u>   111 × 28 ±0

Stood over where the child lay

21–5   εσταθη επανω ου ην το παιδιον

21–6   <u>–</u>

The child

21–7   το παιδιον

21–8 <u>–</u>

Reference 22. "And he sent them to Bethlehem, and said, 'Go and
Mt 2:8   search diligently for the child.'" (6 combinations—2
         hits.)

Go and search diligently for the child

22–1   πορευθεντες εξετασατε ακριβως περι του παιδιου   111 × 43 ±1

22–2   <u>–</u>

Search diligently for the child

22–3   εξετασατε ακριβως περι του παιδιου   111 × 32 ±2

22–4   <u>–</u>

The child

22–5   του παιδιου

22–6 <u>–</u>

Reference 23. "The angel of the Lord appeared to Joseph in a dream,
Mt 2:13   saying, 'Arise, take thou the child and His mother, and
flee into Egypt.' " (6 combinations—1 hit.)

Arise, take thou the child

23–1   εγερθεις παραλαβε το παιδιον

23–2   –

Take thou the child

23–3   παραλαβε το παιδιον

23–4   –   111 × 4 ±1

The child

23–5   το παιδιον

23–6   –

Reference 24. "And remain there until I bring thee word: For Herod
Mt 2:13   will seek the child to destroy Him." (16 combinations
—1 hit.)

For Herod will seek the child to destroy Him

24–1   μελλει γαρ Ηρωδης ζητειν το παιδιον του απολεσαι αυτο

24–2   –   –   –

24–3   γαρ   –   –

24–4   –   το   –

24–5   –   –   του

24–6   γαρ   το   –

24–7   –   το   του

24–8   γαρ   –   του   111 × 35 ±2

For Herod will seek the child

24–9   μελλει γαρ Ηρωδης ζητειν το παιδιον

24–10   –   –

24–11 γαρ   –

24–12   –   το

Seek the child

24–13 ζητειν το παιδιον

24–14   –

The child

24–15 το παιδιον

24–16 –

Reference 25. "For have died the ones seeking the life of the child."
Mt 2:20   (10 combinations—1 hit.)

Seeking the life of the child

25–1   ζητουντες την ψυχην του παιδιου
25–2   –   –
25–3   την   –
25–4   –   του

The life of the child

25–5   την ψυχην του παιδιου
25–6   –   – $111 \times 21 \pm 2$
25–7   την   –
25–8   –   του

The child

25–9   του παιδιου
25–10 –

Reference 26. "They returned to their own city Nazareth, and the
Lk 2:40   child grew and became strong, filled with wisdom; and
                 the grace of God was upon Him." (16 combinations—
                 1 hit.)

*And the child grew and became strong, filled with wisdom; and
the grace of God was upon Him*

26–1   το δε παιδιον ηυξανεν και εκραταιουτο πληρουμενον σοφια και χαρις
       Θεου ην επ αυτο
26–2   – –
26–3   το –

*And the child grew and became strong, filled with wis-
dom*

26–4   το δε παιδιον ηυξανεν και εκραταιουτο πληρουμενον σοφια
26–5   – –
26–6   το –

And the child grew and became strong

26–7   το δε παιδιον ηυξανεν και εκραταιουτο
26–8   – – $111 \times 19 \pm 2$
26–9   το –

And the child grew

26–10 το δε παιδιον ηυξανεν

26–11 – –

26–12 το –

The child

26–13 το παιδιον

26–14 –

And the grace of God was upon Him

26–15 και χαρις Θεου ην επ αυτο

26–16 –

Reference 27. "And Simeon blessed them and said to Mary His
Lk 2:34   mother, 'Behold, this child is set for the fall and rising
again of many in Israel, and for a sign spoken against.' "
(8 combinations—1 hit.)

*Behold, this child is set for the fall and rising again of many in
Israel, and for a sign spoken against*

27–1 ιδου ουτος κειται εις πτωσιν και αναστασιν πολλων εν τω Ισραηλ και εις
σημειον αντιλεγομενον

27–2 –   –

$$111 \times 60 \pm 2$$

27–3 ιδου   –

27–4 –   τω

*Behold, this child is set for the fall and rising again of many in
Israel*

27–5 ιδου ουτος κειται εις πτωσιν και αναστασιν πολλων εν τω Ισραηλ

27–6 –   –

27–7 ιδου   –

27–8 –   τω

Reference 28. "But when the time had fully come, God sent forth the
Gal 4:4   Son of Him, born of a woman, born under the law." (44
combinations—4 hits.)

*But when the time had fully come, God sent forth the Son of
Him, born of a woman*

οτε δε ηλθεν το πληρωμα του χρονου εξαπεστειλεν ο Θεος τον υιον αυτου
γενομενον εκ γυναικος

(ALL COMBINATIONS PRESENT IN THIS PASSAGE.)

	δε	το	του	ο	του	
28–1	δε	το	του	ο	του	111 × 75 ±2
28–2	—	—	—	—	—	
28–3	δε	—	—	—	—	
28–4	—	το	—	—	—	
28–5	—	—	του	—	—	
28–6	—	—	—	ο	—	
28–7	—	—	—	—	του	111 × 64 ±0
28–8	δε	—	—	ο	του	
28–9	δε	—	—	ο	—	
28–10	δε	—	—	—	του	
28–11	δε	—	του	ο	του	
28–12	δε	—	του	—	—	
28–13	δε	—	του	ο	—	
28–14	δε	—	του	—	του	111 × 71 ±2
28–15	δε	το	—	ο	του	
28–16	δε	το	—	—	—	
28–17	δε	το	—	ο	—	
28–18	δε	το	—	—	του	
28–19	δε	το	του	—	—	
28–20	δε	το	του	ο	—	
28–21	δε	το	του	—	του	
28–22	—	το	—	ο	του	
28–23	—	το	—	ο	—	
28–24	—	το	—	—	του	
28–25	—	το	του	ο	του	
28–26	—	το	του	—	—	
28–27	—	το	του	ο	—	
28–28	—	το	του	—	του	
28–29	—	—	του	ο	του	
28–30	—	—	του	ο	—	
28–31	—	—	του	—	του	
28–32	—	—	—	ο	του	

God sent forth the Son of Him, born of a woman

28–33	εξαπεστειλεν ο Θεος τον υιον αυτου γενομενον εκ γυναικος
28–34	‒ ‒
28–35	ο ‒
28–36	‒ τον

God sent forth the Son, born of a woman

28–37 εξαπεστειλεν ο Θεος τον υιον γενομενον εκ γυναικος
28–38 ‾ ‾
28–39 o̲ -
28–40 - τον̲   111 × 28 ±1

The Son of Him, born of a woman

28–41 τον υιον αυτου γενομενον εκ γυναικος
28–42 ‾

The Son, born of a woman

28–43 τον υιον γενομενον εκ γυναικος
28–44 ‾

Reference 29. "And she was with child and she cried out in her birth
Rev 12:2   pangs, in anguish for delivery." (4 combinations—1
              hit.)

*And she was with child and she cried out in her birth pangs, in
anguish for delivery*

29–1 και εν γαστρι εχουσα και κραζει ωδινουσα και βασανιζομενη τεκειν
      ‾111 × 41 ±1
29–2 -

And she was with child

29–3 και εν γαστρι εχουσα
29–4 ‾

Reference 30. "And the dragon stood before the woman who was
Rev 12:4   about to bear, that whenever she bears, the child of her
              he might devour." (12 combinations—1 hit.)

That whenever she bears, the child of her he might devour

30–1 ινα οταν τεκη το τεκνον αυτης καταφαγη
30–2 -   -
30–3 ινα̲   -
30–4 -   το̲

The child of her he might devour

30–5 το τεκνον αυτης καταφαγη
30–6 ‾ -

The child he might devour
30–7 το τεκνον καταφαγη
30–8 -

The child of her
30–9 το τεκνον αυτης 111 × 16 ±2
30–10 -

The child
30–11 το τεκνον
30–12 -

Reference 31. "And she brought forth the man child Who is about to
Rev 12:5   shepherd all nations with a rod of iron." (9 combina-
         tions—3 hits.)

And she brought forth the man child Who is about to shepherd
all nations with a rod of iron
31–1 και ετεκεν υιον αρσεν ος μελλει ποιμαινειν παντα τα εθνη εν ραβδω
      σιδηρα 111 × 37 ±1
31–2 -   -
               111 × 34 ±2
31–3 και   -
31–4 -   τα

And she brought forth the man child
31–5 και ετεκεν υιον αρσεν
31–6 -

The man child
31–7 υιον αρσεν 111 × 8 ±2

The man child Who is about to shepherd all nations with a rod
of iron
31–8 υιον αρσεν ος μελλει ποιμαινειν παντα τα εθνη εν παβδω σιδηρα
31–9   -

Reference 32. "And was caught up the child of her to God, and to the
Rev 12:5   throne of Him." (32 combinations—3 hits.)

And was caught up the child of her to God, and to the throne
of Him
32–1 και ηρπασθη το τεκνον αυτης προς τον Θεον και προς τον θρονον αυτου

32–2	και	–	–	–
32–3	και	το	–	–
32–4	και	–	τον	–
32–5	και	το	τον	–

$$111 \times 47 \pm 1$$

32–6	και	–	τον	τον
32–7	–	το	τον	τον
32–8	–	–	–	–
32–9	–	το	–	–
32–10	–	–	τον	–
32–11	–	το	τον	–
32–12	–	–	τον	τον

And was caught up the child of her to God

32–13	και ηρπασθη το τεκνον αυτης προς τον Θεον
32–14	– – –
32–15	και – –
32–16	– το –
32–17	– – τον
32–18	και το –
32–19	– το τον
32–20	και – τον

And was caught up the child to God

32–21	και ηρπασθη το τεκνον προς τον Θεον
32–22	– – –
32–23	και – –
32–24	– το –
32–25	– – τον
32–26	και το –
32–27	– το τον
32–28	και – τον

$$111 \times 17 \pm 1$$

The child of her

32–29	το τεκνον αυτης
32–30	–

$$111 \times 16 \pm 2$$

The child

32–31	το τεκνον
32–32	–

What Is the Chance?

We have now examined thirty-two references related to the birth and coming of Christ and the child Jesus. All of these contained features that were multiples of 111. In compiling these features, we took into consideration every single combination possible within those phrases that had intelligible meaning. Some of the features were not overly impressive, because only one combination produced a multiple of 111. But the one factor that clinches it is that the shorter key phrases (which have very few combinations) work out: "this child" (two combinations), "the child Jesus" (two combinations), "the child of her" (two combinations), "the man child" (one combination). These are the foundation features, and they have a very low probability of occurring by chance. Without these working out, the rest would be meaningless.

We are now going to calculate the probability of these thirty-two references occurring by chance. In performing these calculations, we sought two things: (1) What is the probability of at least one of the combinations from each reference falling within the cluster of ± 2 of the multiples of 111? (2) What is the actual probability of this occurring?

				COLUMN 1 The Chance of at Least One	COLUMN 2 The Actual Probability
Reference 1	10 comb.—2 hits	$1-(106/111)^{10}$	=	0.36929124	0.06314946
Reference 2	12 comb.—1 hit	$1-(106/111)^{12}$	=	0.42483210	0.42483210
Reference 3	51 comb.—3 hits	$1-(106/111)^{51}$	=	0.90469247	0.20830737
Reference 4	9 comb.—1 hit	$1-(106/111)^{9}$	=	0.33954082	0.33954082
Reference 5	16 comb.—1 hit	$1-(106/111)^{16}$	=	0.52167158	0.52167158
Reference 6	14 comb.—1 hit	$1-(106/111)^{14}$	=	0.47548198	0.47548198
Reference 7	72 comb.—6 hits	$1-(106/111)^{72}$	=	0.96379506	0.06230772
Reference 8	12 comb.—1 hit	$1-(106/111)^{12}$	=	0.42483210	0.42483210
Reference 9	20 comb.—2 hits	$1-(106/111)^{20}$	=	0.60220646	0.16816655
Reference 10	14 comb.—1 hit	$1-(106/111)^{14}$	=	0.47548198	0.47548198
Reference 11	24 comb.—1 hit	$1-(106/111)^{24}$	=	0.66918189	0.66918189
Reference 12	8 comb.—2 hits	$1-(106/111)^{8}$	=	0.30838709	0.04308731
Reference 13	28 comb.—7 hits	$1-(106/111)^{28}$	=	0.72488085	0.00016925
Reference 14	24 comb.—2 hits	$1-(106/111)^{24}$	=	0.66918189	0.20315459
Reference 15	5 comb.—2 hits	$1-(106/111)^{5}$	=	0.20582825	0.01767025

Reference 16	36 comb.—2 hits	$1-(106/111)^{36}$	=	0.80972404	0.26671825
Reference 17	10 comb.—1 hit	$1-(106/111)^{10}$	=	0.36929124	0.36929124
Reference 18	12 comb.—1 hit	$1-(106/111)^{12}$	=	0.42483210	0.42483210
Reference 19	12 comb.—1 hit	$1-(106/111)^{12}$	=	0.42483210	0.42483210
Reference 20	11 comb.—1 hit	$1-(106/111)^{11}$	=	0.39770154	0.39770154
Reference 21	8 comb.—1 hit	$1-(106/111)^{8}$	=	0.30838709	0.30838709
Reference 22	6 comb.—2 hits	$1-(106/111)^{6}$	=	0.24160176	0.02531144
Reference 23	6 comb.—1 hit	$1-(106/111)^{6}$	=	0.24160176	0.24160176
Reference 24	16 comb.—1 hit	$1-(106/111)^{16}$	=	0.52167158	0.52167158
Reference 25	10 comb.—1 hit	$1-(106/111)^{10}$	=	0.36929124	0.36929124
Reference 26	16 comb.—1 hit	$1-(106/111)^{16}$	=	0.52167158	0.52167158
Reference 27	8 comb.—1 hit	$1-(106/111)^{8}$	=	0.30838709	0.30838709
Reference 28	44 comb.—4 hits	$1-(106/111)^{44}$	=	0.86840269	0.08843957
Reference 29	4 comb.—1 hit	$1-(106/111)^{4}$	=	0.16836732	0.16836732
Reference 30	12 comb.—1 hit	$1-(106/111)^{12}$	=	0.42483210	0.42483210
Reference 31	9 comb.—3 hits	$1-(106/111)^{9}$	=	0.33954082	0.00582261
Reference 32	32 comb.—3 hits	$1-(106/111)^{32}$	=	0.77120192	0.11910403

The first thing that we are going to do is calculate the probability of at least one of the combinations from each reference containing a multiple within $+2$ of 111. To arrive at this, we simply multiply the numbers in Column 1 by themselves.

$0.36929124 \times 0.42483210 \times 0.90469247 \times 0.33954082 \times$
$0.52167158 \times 0.47548198 \times 0.96379506 \times 0.42483210 \times$
$0.60220646 \times 0.47548198 \times 0.66918189 \times 0.30838709 \times$
$0.7248808 \quad \times 0.66918189 \times 0.20582825 \times 0.80972404 \times$
$0.36929124 \times 0.42483210 \times 0.42483210 \times 0.39770154 \times$
$0.30838709 \times 0.24160176 \times 0.24160176 \times 0.52167158 \times$
$0.36929124 \times 0.52167158 \times 0.30838709 \times 0.86840269 \times$
$0.16836732 \times 0.42483210 \times 0.33954082 \times 0.77120192 =$
$$5.624170166 \times 10^{-12}$$

Next, we divide the answer by the number 1.

$$5.624170166 \times 10^{-12}/1 = 177,804,008,500$$

Therefore, the chance that all thirty-two of these references could contain at least one multiple within $+2$ of 111 is 1 chance in 177,-804,008,500. That's one-hundred and seventy-seven billion, eight hundred and four million, eight thousand five hundred. But this probability of 1 chance in 177,804,008,500 is really not true. The actual probability is much less likely than this. In thirteen of these thirty-two references, more than one of the combinations produced a multiple within ± 2 of 111. *Feature 7* ("His name was called Jesus, the name given by the angel before He was conceived in the womb") contained seventy-two combinations. Six of these fit into the design. The chance that this feature would contain at least one multiple within ± 2 of 111 was 96.38 percent probability, almost a certainty, but the chance of obtaining six out of seventy-two would be much much less. Let us now calculate the probability of obtaining six out of seventy-two combinations for *Feature 7*. The formula for calculating this would be the following:

$$\left(\frac{n}{r\,(n-r)}\right) \qquad \left(\frac{x}{y}\right)^r \qquad \left(\frac{y-x}{y}\right)^{n-r}$$

The calculations for our specific problem would look like this.

$$\frac{72 \times 71 \times 70 \times 69 \times 68 \times 67 \times 66}{6 \times 5 \times 4 \times 3 \times 2 \times 1 \quad 66} = 156{,}238{,}908$$

$$(5/111)^6 = 0.0000000084$$

$$(106/111)^{66} = 0.0477386911$$

To obtain our final answer, we would simply multiply the results from these three groups, by each other:

$$156{,}238{,}908 \times 0.0000000084 \times 0.0477386911 = 0.06230772$$

Therefore, the chance of obtaining six out of the seventy-two combinations is 6.27 percent probability as opposed to 96.38 percent probability. These results are substantially better than obtaining at least one of the combinations. Let us now recalculate all 32 of these references, in order to find out what the actual probability is:

$0.06314946 \times 0.42483210 \times 0.20830737 \times 0.33954082 \times$
$0.52167158 \times 0.47548198 \times 0.06230772 \times 0.42483210 \times$
$0.16816655 \times 0.47548198 \times 0.66918189 \times 0.04308731 \times$
$0.00016925 \times 0.20315459 \times 0.01767025 \times 0.26671825 \times$
$0.36929124 \times 0.42483210 \times 0.42483210 \times 0.39770154 \times$
$0.30838709 \times 0.02531144 \times 0.24160176 \times 0.52167158 \times$
$0.36929124 \times 0.52167158 \times 0.30838709 \times 0.08843957 \times$
$0.16836732 \times 0.42483210 \times 0.00582261 \times 0.11910403 =$
$3.163672477 \times 10^{-26}$

$3.163672477 \times 10^{-26}/1 = 31{,}608{,}834{,}580{,}000{,}000{,}000{,}000{,}000$

This is 1 chance in 31,608,834,580,000,000,000,000,000. That's thirty-one septillion, six hundred and eight sextillion, eight hundred and thirty-four quintillion, five hundred and eighty quadrillion.

The methodology presented here in Method 1 can be applied to any theomatic design in the Bible. In Method 1, we have limited ourselves to those passages of Scripture that spoke specifically of the birth of Christ and the child Jesus. If we had calculated the probability for all of the designs related to the topic of Jesus, the final probability would be unthinkable. Furthermore, the number 111 is relatively small in comparison with some of the other key numbers presented in this book. What about the number 144, or the number 276, or the number 666? The chance of these features occurring by chance would be much smaller.

Even though Method 1 is a very impressive way of proving the existence of theomatics, the methodology is still not complete without Method 2.

METHOD 2

It has been shown by Method 1 that the chance of obtaining at least one multiple within ± 2 of 111 for each of these thirty-two scriptural references was only 1 chance in 117,804,008,500. This is the probability of just these thirty-two references occurring.

As impressive as this may seem, it still does not prove the existence of the theomatic design in the Bible, and the reason is simple. What if these thirty-two references were carefully selected or chosen? In other words, what if there are many other references to the birth of Christ and the child Jesus that *do not* contain features falling within the cluster of the multiples of 111? What if there are many other references related to this topic which we inadvertently or deliberately failed to consider in proving the theomatic design concept? *If a sufficient number of such references could be found and shown not to have any combination that clusters around the multiples of 111, then one may easily conclude that the occurrence of these thirty-two happened merely by chance.*

A perfect way to illustrate this would be to suppose that we had a box containing all of the numbers from one to a hundred, with each numeral written on a card. Now let's say that someone reached into the box and carefully selected all of the cards bearing direct multiples of ten (10, 20, 30, 40, 50, 60, 70, 80, 90, and 100). To the untrained observer, these ten multiples of ten would make an outstanding selection of theomatic features. However, a closer examination would reveal nothing of the kind. There is nothing at all special about these ten features. Why? Because they were carefully selected. Within this series of one hundred numbers, there are ninety other numbers that are not direct multiples of ten. It is only to be expected that out of one hundred numbers, ten would be found to be multiples of ten.

The same principle applies to the features we have shown throughout this book. If there is nothing special or nonrandom about our features, and if they were carefully selected and chosen, then we can readily assume that there exists within the New Testament an equal number (proportionate to the probability of our features) that do not contain any multiples that fall within the cluster of ± 2 of the multiples.

Now in order to demonstrate how Method 2 proves the existence of theomatics, we will again show the simple design related to the 153 fishes:

Fishes   153 × 8   23.34% probability
The net   153 × 8   15.31% probability
Casting a net into the sea   153 × 20   18.07% probability
Multitude of fishes   153 × 16   20.75% probability
Fishers of men   153 × 14   3.27% probability

The chance of all five of these references containing multiples within ± 2 of 153 was only 1 chance in 22,837. Here again, what if these five references were carefully selected or chosen? What if there are many other references, just as outstanding, that do not work out to multiples of 153? If enough of these can be found, then we may easily conclude that these five features merely occurred by chance. We can roughly determine how many words or phrases one would have to find in order to nullify these five references and prove that they happened by chance.

For these five references, with one to eight combinations each, the probability of a word or phrase having a theomatic feature that falls within the cluster of ± 2 ranges approximately from 3.26 percent (for "fishers of men," which has one combination) to 23.34 percent (for "fishes," which has eight combinations). Now what we must do is add up all of the probabilities for these five references, and then figure out the average percentage for each reference:

$$23.34\% + 15.31\% + 18.07\% + 20.75\% + 3.27\% = 80.74\%$$

To obtain the average, we simply divide this figure by 5, which gives us a 16.15 percent probability. Therefore, the average probability for each of these five references is 16.15 percent.

And in order to find out how many references are needed that do not work out (negative references), we simply use the following formula:

$$\frac{(x - y)}{y} \quad or \quad 100 - 16.15/16.15 = 5.2$$

In the case of the above five references, the critic will have to find 5.2 negative references for each reference that we found, in order to disprove this theomatic design. This means that for all five references, the total number needed to nullify them would be 5.2 × 5, or 26 references, *none of which* contain any features that fall within the cluster of ±2 of the multiples of 153.

And here is something very important. In seeking to compile a list of references that do not work out, a person must always bear in mind that the ones he is using must in general be just as outstanding, clearcut, and significant as the ones that we have found. He should not use an odd collection of phrases or extra-long phrases, which do not attain the same degree of quality as the features that we have found.

A perfect illustration of what we mean by this can be found in Matthew 15:36. Here the text states: "He [Jesus] took the seven loaves and the fishes . . ." (ελαβεν τους επτα αρτους και τους ιχθυας). Interestingly enough, the theomatic value of this phrase is 153 × 31, and the word *loaves* by itself is 153 × 7. But even though these words work out to 153, they could not be fairly used as negative theomatic features, in trying to disprove this design. The five features we found referred directly to fishes, fishing, the net, and so on, and not to the subject of loaves. Therefore, to use this phrase and the word *loaves* would be out of the question.

Another example would be found in Luke 5:5: "And answering Simon said, 'Master, we have toiled all the night, and have taken nothing: but at Thy word I will let down the nets.' And when they had done this, they enclosed a great multitude of fishes." Now the theomatic value of this phrase, after the opening clause "And answering Simon said" is 153 × 97. (επιστατα δι ολης νυκτος κοπιασαντες ουδεν ελαβομεν επι δε τω ρηματι σου χαλασω τα δικτυα και τουτο ποιησαντες συνεκλεισαν πληθος ιχθυων πολυ) However, this complete phrase could not be used for a negative theomatic feature either. Why? Because a long phrase of this nature is quite obviously not as distinct or significant as just the word *fishes* by itself, or the words *multitude of fishes*. The reasons for this should be obvious to any honest observer. Any quotation used for a negative theomatic feature must be of the same general quality as the features that do work out to multiples of 153.

As we mentioned earlier, in order for a person to disprove the theomatic design of the 153 fishes, he would have to find 26 direct references to this topic, none of which contain features that fall within ± 2 of the multiples of 153. In seeking to compile his list of features, the critic is going to run into a little problem. What if during the process of trying to compile a list of features that do not work out, he happens to find another one that does? What then? If this should happen, it would mean that he would then have to find an additional number of references, besides the 26 that he already needs.

A perfect example of another feature that works out is found in Matthew 4:18: "And Jesus walking by the sea of Galilee saw two brethren, Simon called Peter and Andrew his brother, casting a net into the sea: for they were fishermen." The words "casting a net into the sea" have already been shown to have a theomatic value of 153 × 20. But the words that immediately follow, "for they were fishermen" (ησαν γαρ αλεεις), have a theomatic value of 153 × 4. Because we have found another feature that works out (which makes a total of six), we must now recalculate our average percentage, in order to see how many more references are needed, to nullify the six that we have found.

The words "for they were fishermen" have a total of three possible combinations:

For they were fishermen (ησαν γαρ αλεεις)
They were fishermen (ησαν αλεεις)
Fishermen (αλεεις)

And these three combinations give us a statistical probability of 9.49 percent. $1 - (148/153)^3 = 0.09487022$, *i.e.*, 9.487022%. What we must now do is add this number (9.49) to our previous total of 80.74 percent for the first five references. This then gives us a grand total of

90.23, which is then divided by 6, the result being 15.04. To arrive at our final answer, we use the same formula as was shown earlier:

$$\frac{100 - 15.04}{15.04} = 5.65$$

Because the additional reference ("for they were fishermen") has only three combinations, this brings the average up to 5.65 instead of the previous calculation of 5.2. And in order to nullify the six references that we have now found, a person would have to find $5.65 \times 6 = 33.9$, or 34 new references none of which contain any features that fall within the cluster of ± 2 of the multiples of 153.

In the chapter on the 153 fishes, we also showed where the word *draught* was a multiple within ± 2 of 153. This is an outstanding reference to fishes and fishing. Here again, if the critic is going to be looking for references that do not work out, then he will have to count this reference as a hit when he makes his calculations.

In going through the New Testament we found only one or two other references to fishes and fishing that we thought could be classified as outstanding as the ones that we found that did not work out to 153. However, there were many more general references that were multiples of 153. A perfect example of one of these is found in John 21:9. When the disciples disembarked onto the land, "they saw a fire of coals there, and a fish laid thereon, and bread." The words "and a fish laid thereon" (και οψαριον επικειμενον) have a theomatic value of 153×9. We do not think that this is an outstanding reference to fishes and fishing, but if the critic trying to compile a list of features that do not work out thinks that it is, he would have to count it as a hit.

Another example is the word for *fish* in the singular. In the story of the 153 fishes, the text says that they caught *fishes*, plural. For this reason, we limited our calculations to the plural form of the word, but interestingly enough, the word *fish* in the singular (ιχθυν) has a theomatic value of 153×7. If we had taken this fact into consideration, then it would have improved our previous calculations substantially. Both the words *fish* and *fishes* have theomatic values that are divisible by 153.

METHOD 2 AND THE DESIGN ON THE BIRTH OF CHRIST

We will now present a more detailed study of how Method 2 can overwhelmingly prove the existence of theomatics. To illustrate, we will use the same design shown earlier, related to the birth and coming of Christ and the child Jesus. This design contained 32 references, all of which had features that fell within the cluster of ± 2 of the multiples of 111.

The reference from this design with the lowest probability had only four combinations (Reference 29), and the reference with the highest probability (Reference 7) had seventy-two combinations. As was illustrated earlier, we must first of all find out the average probability. In order to do this, we simply add up all of the percentages, and then divide the result by the number of references:

36.93 + 42.48 + 90.47 + 33.95 + 52.17 + 47.55 + 96.38
+ 42.48 + 60.22 + 47.55 + 66.92 + 30.84 + 72.49 + 66.92
+ 20.58 + 80.97 + 36.93 + 42.48 + 42.48 + 39.77 + 30.84
+ 24.16 + 24.16 + 52.17 + 36.93 + 52.17 + 30.84 + 86.84
+ 16.84 + 42.48 + 33.95 + 77.12 = 1559.06

Next, we divide 1559.06 by the number of references, which is 32.

$$1559.06/32 = 48.72$$

Therefore, the average probability for each of the thirty-two references is 48.72 percent probability.

After obtaining the average probability, we then use the standard formula for finding out how many negative references are needed to disprove this design:

$$\frac{100-48.72}{48.72} = 1.05$$

To obtain the final result, we simply multiply 1.05 $\times$ 32, the answer being 33.66, or 34. Notice that in figuring these calculations, we used the percentages from Column 1. This was the chance that at least one of the combinations from each reference would produce a multiple within ± 2 of 111. If we had wished, we could have used the actual probability percentages from Column 2. These would have given us eighty-one references needed, instead of thirty-four, but in order to be conservative, we will use the less impressive figure of thirty-four.

What we are going to do now is demonstrate and prove that it is impossible for any person to find thirty-four completely new references, related to this topic, which do not work out to multiples within ± 2 of 111.

During the process of researching the many references to the birth and coming of Christ and the child Jesus, we carefully took into consideration every single reference found in the New Testament. On only four occasions did we find a reference to this topic that did not contain any features within ± 2 of the multiples of 111. Here are those four references.

The latter portion of Matthew 1:18 states the following: "When His [Jesus'] mother Mary was espoused to Joseph, before they came together, she was found to be pregnant of the Holy Spirit."

Before they came together, she was found to be pregnant of the Holy Spirit (6 combinations—no hits.)

Luke 2:11: "And the angel said unto them, fear not: for, behold I bring you good tidings of great joy, which shall be to all people. For unto you is born this day in the city of David, a savior which is Christ the Lord."

For unto you is born this day in the city of David, a savior which is Christ the Lord (8 combinations—no hits.)

Matthew 2:2: "Now when Jesus was born in Bethlehem of Judea in the days of Herod the king, behold, there came wise men from the east to Jerusalem, saying, 'Where is the one born king of the Jews?'"

Where is the one born king of the Jews (8 combinations—no hits.)

Luke 1:32: "And, behold, you will conceive in your womb, and bear a son, and you shall call the name of Him Jesus. He shall be great, and shall be called the son of the highest."

He shall be great, and shall be called the son of the highest (4 combinations—no hits.)

These four passages of Scripture were the only ones we could find that did not contain any design of 111. However, during the process of compiling these four, we found four additional ones that did work out. Here they are, with all of their combinations.

Reference 33. "Now the birth of Jesus Christ took place in this way:
Mt 1:18   When His mother Mary was espoused to Joseph. . . ."
(10 combinations—1 hit.)

Now the birth of Jesus Christ took place in this way

33–1	του δε Ιησου Χριστου η γενεσις ουτως ην		
33–2	– –	–	
33–3	του –	–	$111 \times 49 \pm 0$
33–4	– –	η	
33–5	του –	η	
33–6	του δε	–	

The birth of Jesus Christ

33–7	του Ιησου Χριστου η γενεσις
33–8	– –
33–9	του
33–10	– η

Reference 34. "And coming into the house they saw the child with
Mt 2:11   Mary the mother of Him, and falling they worshiped
Him." (51 combinations—2 hits.)

And coming into the house they saw the child with Mary the mother of Him, and falling they worshiped Him
και ελθοντες εις την οικιαν ειδον το παιδιον μετα Μαριας της μητρος αυτου και πεσοντες προσεκυνησαν αυτω

(ALL COMBINATIONS PRESENT IN THIS PASSAGE.)

34–1	και	την	το	της
34–2	και	—	—	—
34–3	και	την	—	—
34–4	και	—	το	—
34–5	και	—	—	της
34–6	και	την	το	—
34–7	και	—	το	της
34–8	και	την	—	της	$111 \times 68 \pm 0$
34–9	—	την	το	της
34–10	—	—	—	—
34–11	—	την	—	—
34–12	—	—	το	—
34–13	—	—	—	της

34–14	—	την	το	—
34–15	—	—	το	της
34–16	—	την	—	της

And coming into the house they saw the child with Mary the mother of Him

34–17 και ελθοντες εις την οικιαν ειδον το παιδιον μετα Μαριας της μητρος αυτου

34–18	και	-	-	-
34–19	και	την	-	-
34–20	και	-	το	-
34–21	και	-	-	της
34–22	και	την	το	-
34–23	και	-	το	της
34–24	και	την	-	της
34–25	-	την	το	της
34–26	-	-	-	-

$$111 \times 36 \pm 0$$

34–27	-	την	-	-
34–28	-	-	το	-
34–29	-	-	-	της
34–30	-	την	το	-
34–31	-	-	το	της
34–32	-	την	-	της

They saw the child with Mary the mother of Him

34–33 ειδον το παιδιον μετα Μαριας της μητρος αυτου

34–34	-		-
34–35	το		-
34–36	-		της

The child with Mary the mother of Him

34–37 το παιδιον μετα Μαριας της μητρος αυτου

34–38	-		-
34–39	το		-
34–40	-		της

The child with Mary

34–41 το παιδιον μετα Μαριας

34–42 -

The child

34-43 το παιδιον

34-44 -

And falling they worshiped Him

34-45 και πεσοντες προσεκυνησαν αυτω

34-46 -

They worshiped Him

34-47 προσεκυνησαν αυτω

They saw the child with Mary the mother of Him, and falling they worshiped Him

34-48 ειδον το παιδιον μετα Μαριας της μητρος αυτου και πεσοντες
       προσεκυνησαν αυτω

34-49 -   -

34-50 το   -

34-51 -   της

Reference 35. "And Jacob begat Joseph the husband of Mary, of
Mt 1:16   whom was born Jesus, the one called Christ." (21 com-
          binations—1 hit.)

*And Jacob begat Joseph the husband of Mary, of whom was born
Jesus, the one called Christ*

Ιακωβ δε εγεννησεν τον Ιωσηφ τον ανδρα Μαριας εξ ης εγεννηθη Ιησους
ο λεγομενος Χριστος

(ALL COMBINATIONS PRESENT IN THIS PASSAGE.)

35-1	δε	του	του	ο
35-2	—	—	—	—
35-3	δε	—	—	—
35-4	—	του	—	—
35-5	—	—	—	ο
35-6	δε	του	—	—
35-7	δε	του	του	—
35-8	δε	του	—	ο
35-9	δε	—	—	ο
35-10	—	του	του	—
35-11	—	του	του	ο
35-12	—	του	—	ο

111 × 66 ±1

And Jacob begat Joseph the husband of Mary, of whom was born Jesus

35–13	Ιακωβ δε εγεννησεν τον Ιωσηφ τον ανδρα Μαριας εξ ης εγεννηθη Ιησους
35–14	‒	–	–
35–15	δε	–	–
35–16	–	τον	–
35–17	–	τον	τον
35–18	δε	τον	–

Was born Jesus, the one called Christ

35–19	εγεννηθη Ιησους ο λεγομενος Χριστος
35–20	‒

Was born Jesus

35–21	εγεννηθη Ιησους

Reference 36. "And again, when He brings the firstborn into the
Heb 1:6   world, He says, 'Let all of God's angels worship Him.' "
(30 combinations—1 hit.)

*And again, when He brings the firstborn into the world, He says,
'Let all of God's angels worship him'*

οταν δε παλιν εισαγαγη τον πρωτοτοκον εις την οικουμενην λεγει και

προσκυνησατωσαν αυτω παντες αγγελοι Θεου

(ALL COMBINATIONS PRESENT IN THIS PASSAGE.)

36–1	δε	τον	την
36–2	—	—	—
36–3	δε	—	—
36–4	—	τον	—
36–5	—	—	την
36–6	δε	τον	—
36–7	—	τον	την
36–8	δε	—	την

And again, when He brings the firstborn into the world

36–9	οταν δε παλιν εισαγαγη τον πρωτοτοκον εις την οικουμενην
36–10	‒	–	–
36–11	δε		–
36–12	–	τον	–
36–13	–		την

36–14	δε	τον	–
36–15	–	τον	την
36–16	δε	–	την

Brings the firstborn into the world

36–17 εισαγαγη τον πρωτοτοκον εις την οικουμενην

36–18	–	–
36–19	τον	–
36–20	–	την

The firstborn into the world

35–21 τον πρωτοτοκον εις την οικουμενην

36–22	–	–
36–23	τον	–
35–24	–	την

$$111 \times 29 \pm 1$$

The firstborn

36–25 τον πρωτοτοκον

36–26 –

And let all of God's angels worship Him

36–27 και προσκυνησατωσαν αυτω παντες αγγελοι Θεου

36–28 –

Worship Him

36–29 και προσκυνησατωσαν αυτω

36–30 –

Out of a total of forty references to the birth of Christ and the child Jesus, thirty-six were found to have features that clustered around the multiples of 111. In compiling all of these features, we cut the length of the phrases off at those points where we thought the complete spiritual thought of that particular passage had been enunciated. This, of course, was a matter of judgment on our part. We believe that anyone who carefully examines these features will agree with the length of the phrases, as we took them from the text. If the reader thinks that the length of some of these quotations could be expanded, then he is perfectly welcome to lengthen them as he sees fit. In doing so, however, the overall statistical results would not be changed to any significant degree.

For the original thirty-two references that we previously examined, it was shown that thirty-four negative references were needed to disprove this design. But because four additional references were discovered that contained theomatic design, this means that Method 2 must now be recalculated.

The total probability for the thirty-two references was 1,559.06. The probabilities for References 33, 34, 35, and 36 were 36.93, 90.47, 62.01, and 74.91, respectively. By adding these figures to 1,559.06, we obtain a revised total of 1,823.38. To find the average, this number is divided by 36; the answer is 50.65.

$$\frac{100-50.65}{50.65} = 0.97$$

To obtain the final result, we simply multiply 0.97×36; the answer is 35.07, or 35. Therefore, the number of negative references needed to disprove this design on the birth of Christ is 35.

It has already been shown that four references did not contain any feature that was within ± 2 of the multiples of 111. By subtracting 4 from 35, this still leaves 31 references that must be found, to disprove this theomatic design. But guess what? There are no more references in the New Testament related to this topic. If the would-be critic thinks that there might be some others, he will have to find thirty-one new references, *none of which* contain any features that cluster around the multiples of 111. Where is he going to get them from? We will leave that problem up to him.

We might also add that when the reader gets done compiling his list, his overall results must be just as outstanding as the thirty-six references we have shown. However, we will leave the evaluation of this up to him.

Statistician's note: In order to statistically nullify the thirty-six references that we have found, the negative references should contain approximately the same number of combinations. The average probability for our thirty-six references (using the percentages in Column 1) was 50.65 percent probability. Therefore, the average probability of the negative references should be in the vicinity of 50 percent. It should be noted that this would be necessary to effectively nullify our thirty-six references.

METHOD 3—THE ACID TEST

The methodology you are about to see demonstrated is the most powerful means possible for proving the existence of the theomatic design in the Word of God. Toward the end of Chapter 4 on the 153 fishes, we briefly explained how Method 3 worked. We also explained that it was the acid test for proving theomatics, because on it rests our entire case. Theomatics either stands or falls based on Method 3.

Earlier in this chapter (p. 151), we made mention of a scientific law which states the following: Numbers must occur at random, unless there is a design. If there is no theomatic design present in the Bible, then all of the number values for the words would simply be one great big conglomeration of random numbers.

This statement has profound implications, because on it rests the entire case for the existence of theomatics. For this reason, we shall now make a daring declaration from which there is absolutely no escape: If the theomatic designs we have presented in this book are untrue, then this means that all of these so-called designs were simply created from random numbers. Therefore, any other number values randomly assigned to the letters of the alphabet should produce the same results.

Here is the statistician's report, reproduced in facsimile, describing the objective test that Method 3 offers.

July 17, 1976

Mr. Del Washburn
Theomatics Research Association
13707 Doty #11
Hawthorne, California 90266

Dear Mr. Washburn,

I have considered the material which you sent me concerning your approach to the proof of "theomatic" design in the Bible. In considering your material, I addressed myself in particular to your proposal of the construction of "random interlinears".[3] I am in complete agreement with you in the idea that if there is nothing inherently "special" or "non-random" about the interlinear resulting from the assignment

[3] A "random interlinear" is a Greek-English New Testament with random numbers written over the words instead of the numbers that we use based on the papyrus and Webster's dictionary.

of number values to Greek letters as given in Webster's dictionary, then one should be able to substantially duplicate your findings with any random assignment of number-letter equivalencies. More precisely, if one examines an interlinear resulting from a random assignment of equivalencies in the same manner as you examined the interlinear resulting from the assignment appearing in Webster's, and if there are no special characteristics of the latter assignment, then one should expect to be able to produce results, i.e. theomatic features with the same general probability (or improbability) as those you have been able to produce. In comparing the results of both efforts one should then expect:

As *many* features from the one as from the other.

The features produced from the one would have the same clear significance as those of the other. By this I mean, one would be able to find groups of phrases with the same theological theme, i.e. Jesus, Satan, the flesh, etc., rather than phrases consisting of odd collections of words with no clear theological significance and chosen only for the similarity of the numerical equivalents.

The features would exhibit the same general "clustering" characteristics. In particular, the clustering from the random interlinear should be around multiples of numbers of the same general magnitude as those of Webster's, not smaller numbers. It should be noted that numbers of the same general magnitude would be necessary to produce comparable probabilities of occurrence.

Pursuant to the idea discussed above, I have constructed from a table of random numbers (*Rand Corporation, A Million Random Digits with 100,000 Normal Deviates*, The Free Press, Glencoe, Ill., 1955, p. 993) two random assignments of number-letter equivalencies which may be used to construct random interlinears:

GREEK LETTER	WEBSTER'S ASSIGNMENT	RANDOM ASSIGNMENT A	RANDOM ASSIGNMENT B
alpha	1	300	700
beta	2	10	40
gamma	3	70	800
delta	4	1	5
epsilon	5	400	1
vau	6	9	8
zeta	7	2	70

eta	8	40	50
theta	9	200	200
iota	10	100	600
koppa	20	60	60
lambda	30	4	30
mu	40	80	100
nu	50	600	7
xi	60	7	10
omicron	70	30	3
pi	80	90	4
kappa	90	6	9
rho	100	20	400
sigma	200	8	80
tau	300	3	90
upsilon	400	50	300
phi	500	5	6
chi	600	500	500
psi	700	700	2
omega	800	800	20

In closing I would like to wish you good luck with the forthcoming publication of your book. Please keep me informed.

Sincerely,
La Verne W. Stanton, Ph. d.
Associate Professor and Chair
Department of Quantitative Methods
California State University, Fullerton

In this report, Dr. Stanton is setting forth the basic principles by which a person would have to disprove theomatics. Let's briefly summarize the three points he made concerning the comparison of random numbers with the numbers we used from Webster's dictionary and the papyrus.

"As many features from the one as from the other" means precisely what it says. If we found a total of twenty-five references to a particular topic that contained theomatic features, this means that a person would have to find twenty-five references that contained features from the random assignment, in order to disprove these twenty-five references. Furthermore, let's say that our twenty-five references contained a total of fifty features. This means that this person would also have to pull fifty features from his twenty-five references from the random assignment, in order to disprove the fifty features that we found. The ultimate test is who ends up with the most features.

"The features produced from the one would have the same clear significance as those of the other" means very simply that the overall quality of the features from the random assignment would be equal to ours. This, of course, is a matter of judgment on the part of the observer. If there is any large degree of difference in quality between the two efforts, it will be obvious to any honest observer. Here are several examples of comparison. The two words *Jesus* and *Christ* are more significant than complete phrases such as "Jesus of Nazareth is passing by," or "this is the son of David." Likewise, the name *Satan* by itself would be more significant than the phrase "then cometh the Devil and taketh the word out of their hearts."

"The features would exhibit the same general clustering characteristics. In particular the features from the random interlinear should be around multiples of numbers of the same general magnitude, not smaller numbers." This means that in order for a person to disprove a particular theomatic design, he would have to use a number of the same magnitude as we have used. This does not mean that it has to be the same number. *It could be any number* in the same general range of magnitude.

In the design for the topic of light, we showed how practically every related feature worked out to multiples of 100. In order to disprove this design, the critic would have to use a number as large as 100, but not necessarily the same number.

Since a person can use any number he chooses, what if he chooses a number smaller or larger than one hundred? Let's say that he decides to go with the number fifty. If we found a total of twenty-five references that contained fifty features using the number one hundred, he would then have to find twice as many, or fifty references, containing one hundred features. Why? Because fifty is half of one hundred. But let's say that this person decided to try a larger number, like 150. This means that for every three references we found, he would have to find only two to match ours. However, to make the results as meaningful as possible, a person should stick to a number in the same general vicinity as what we have used.

Method 3 and the Design on the Birth of Christ

Earlier in this chapter, we examined thirty-six references to the birth and coming of Christ and the child Jesus. At that time it was shown that the probability of the first thirty-two of these references occurring was only 1 chance in 177,804,008,500. This was Method 1. Then in Method 2, we explained that in order for a person to disprove these thirty-six references, he would have to find thirty-five more just like them, none of which contained any features that fell within the cluster of ± 2 of the multiples of 111. To do this would be a total impossibility.

Now we come to the crucial issue at hand. All of these calculations of one chance in so many and having to find x number of features that don't work out mean nothing if someone can take any other random assignment of number-letter equivalencies and produce the same results that we have been able to produce. If this should happen, then everything that has been presented in this book would be totally discredited.

We shall now take all forty of the references to the birth of Christ (including the four that did not work out to 111), and see what happens when a person tries to build a like design using random numbers.

The first thing that a person would have to do is find the number that he is going to use in order to disprove this design. Obviously, for any design on *Jesus* to be meaningful, it would have to be a number that is divisible into the name *Jesus*. In the Greek language, the name *Jesus* is spelled three different ways. Each of these spellings has an article to match. This gives us a total of six combinations.

	RANDOM ASSIGNMENT A	RANDOM ASSIGNMENT B
ο Ιησους	266	1,116
Ιησους	236	1,113
του Ιησου	311	1,426
Ιησου	228	1,033
τον Ιησουν	1,461	1,140
Ιησουν	828	1,040

On the table to the right of these combinations, there are two columns of numbers. By taking the two random assignments that Dr.

Stanton provided, we would add up the letters in each spelling of *Jesus*, in order to find out what the number value was. The first column contains the number-letter equivalencies from *Random Assignment A* and the second column from *Random Assignment B*.

For the second phase of our research, we had to have special materials prepared. We took all of the numbers from 1 to 10,000 and then proceeded to find every single factor that was divisible into each of the numbers from 1 to 10,000. For example, take the number 10. It is divisible by 1, 2, 5, and 10. Or take the number 48. It is divisible by 1, 2, 3, 4, 6, 8, 12, 16, 24, and 48; these numbers are all of the numbers—and the only numbers—that can be divided into 48.

Now what a person must first of all do is find all of the numbers that fall within ± 2 of every spelling of *Jesus*. To show how this is done, let's take a sample from one of the pages of this work. The number we will be looking at is 311, the third number in *Random Assignment A*.

```
308   2 4 7 11 14 22 28 44 77 154
309   3 103
310   2 5 10 31 62 155
311   311
312   2 3 4 6 8 12 13 24 26 39 52 78 104 156
313   313
314   2 157
```

The numbers 309, 310, 311, 312, and 313 form the cluster around the number 311. Every number that divides into these five numbers would fall within this cluster. This process would then be applied to the six spellings of *Jesus*, and then all of the numbers placed in a list. Here now are the numbers from both sets of random assignments. For practical reasons, we will list the numbers from 60 on up.

Random Assignment A: 62, 66, 67, 69, 73, 76, 77, 78, 79, 83, 86, 88, 89, 92, 103, 104, 113, 114, 115, 117, 118, 119, 132, 133, 134, 138, 146, 155, 156, 166, 207, 209, 227, 228, 229, 236, 266, 276, 292, 311, 313, 365, 413, 414, 415, 487, 730, 731, 827, 828, 829, 1,459, 1,461

Random Assignment B: 60, 62, 65, 67, 68, 69, 75, 76, 80, 84, 86, 89, 93, 94, 95, 101, 102, 104, 114, 115, 119, 124, 129, 130, 139, 153, 159, 172, 173, 178, 186, 190, 204, 207, 208, 223, 228, 238, 258, 260, 278, 279, 285, 344, 345, 346, 347, 356, 357, 371, 372, 380, 475, 476, 516, 517, 519, 520, 521, 556, 557, 558, 559, 569, 570, 571, 712, 713, 714, 1,031, 1,033, 1,039, 1,040, 1,113, 1,116, 1,117, 1,140, 1,426, 1,427

From these lists, a person could take any number he wished, and try to use it to disprove the theomatic design on the birth of Christ. For demonstration purposes in this chapter, we wanted to use a number as close to 111 as possible. Neither of the random assignments contained a multiple of 111 that was divisible into the name *Jesus*, so in order to be conservative, we decided to try the first number smaller than 111. Interestingly enough, the number 104 was the next smaller number, and it was common to both random assignments.

In performing our calculations, the first thing we did was to go through every combination (beginning back at p. *155*) on the birth of Christ and add up the number values for each word, as given in the random assignments made by Dr. Stanton. We then went through all forty references to see how many features of 104 we could find.

Here are the results of our calculations. If the symbol in each of the random columns looks like this: — – – – –, this means that *no combination* in that particular reference contained a feature that fell within ± 2 of the multiples of 104. For all of the other references, however, there will be numbers following them like these: 11–2; 11–20. If you will turn back to the pages where we listed all of the combinations for the design on the birth of Christ, you will remember these numbers. The number 11–2, for example, shows that the second combination from Reference 11 worked out to a multiple of 104. Also, the twentieth combination from Reference 11 worked out to a multiple of 104.

	Our Observed Results	Random Assignment A	Random Assignment B
Reference 1	10 comb.—2 hits	——	——
Reference 2	12 comb.—1 hit	2-2 2-5	——
Reference 3	51 comb.—3 hits	3-4	3-13
Reference 4	9 comb.—1 hit	4-5	——
Reference 5	16 comb.—1 hit	——	5-7
Reference 6	14 comb.—1 hit	——	——
Reference 7	72 comb.—6 hits	7-16 7-60	7-65 7-69
Reference 8	12 comb.—1 hit	——	8-1
Reference 9	20 comb.—2 hits	9-17	9-13
Reference 10	14 comb.—1 hit	10-9	——
Reference 11	24 comb.—1 hit	11-2 11-20	11-8
Reference 12	8 comb.—2 hits	——	——
Reference 13	28 comb.—7 hits	12-23	——

Reference 14	24 comb.—2 hits	13-5	13-19 13-20
Reference 15	5 comb.—2 hits	——	——
Reference 16	36 comb.—2 hits	16-11 16-20	16-15 16-17
Reference 17	10 comb.—1 hit	——	15-9
Reference 18	12 comb.—1 hit	——	——
Reference 19	12 comb.—1 hit	——	17-5
Reference 20	11 comb.—1 hit	——	18-2
Reference 21	8 comb.—1 hit	——	——
Reference 22	6 comb.—2 hits	——	——
Reference 23	6 comb.—1 hit	——	——
Reference 24	16 comb.—1 hit	24-10	24-7
Reference 25	10 comb.—1 hit	——	——
Reference 26	16 comb.—1 hit	26-7 26-16	——
Reference 27	8 comb.—1 hit	——	27-3 27-6
Reference 28	44 comb.—4 hits	28-16 28-28 28-29	——
Reference 29	4 comb.—1 hit	——	29-4
Reference 30	12 comb.—1 hit	——	——
Reference 31	9 comb.—3 hits	——	——
Reference 32	32 comb.—3 hits	32-26	——
Reference 33	10 comb.—1 hit	33-2	33-8
Reference 34	51 comb.—2 hits	34-14	34-12 34-35
Reference 35	21 comb.—1 hit	35-3	——
Reference 36	30 comb.—1 hit	36-12 36-26	——
Matthew 1:18	6 comb.—0 hits	——	——
Luke 2:11	8 comb.—0 hits	——	——
Matthew 2:2	8 comb.—0 hits	1 feature	——
Luke 1:32	4 comb.—0 hits	——	——

Out of the forty references possible, we discovered that by using the number values given in Webster's dictionary and the papyrus thirty-six of these references contained multiples of 111. The results from the random assignment produced the following: *Random Assignment A* did a little better than *B*. It contained features in nineteen out of the possible forty references. Twenty-one references contained *no* multiples of 104. This was over half. In *Random Assignment B*, sixteen references contained features, while twenty-four did not contain any.

From these forty references, we pulled a total of sixty-five features. And here is where the random assignments totally collapsed. *Random Assignment A* did best, and it contained twenty-seven features altogether, while *Random Assignment B* only contained twenty-one. This is less than a third of what we obtained.

Furthermore, if one were to compare the quality of the features from the random assignments with the quality of our features, he would discover a world of difference. For example, the four most important features in this design would be the following:

Lk 2:17 This child   111 × 26
Lk 2:27 The child Jesus   111 × 12
Rev 12:4 The child of her   111 × 16
Rev 12:5 The man child   111 × 8

In *Random Assignment A,* "the child Jesus" worked out to 104. The other three features missed. But in *Random Assignment B,* none of the features worked out to 104.

In the overall results, *Random Assignment A* performed a little better than *B.* But here is where the random numbers completely fell apart. Without question, the four most important features from Chapter 3 on Jesus were the names *Jesus, Christ, God,* and *Lord.* When we began this experiment, we made sure that the number 104 was divisible into *Jesus.* But when we went back and checked the other three names, the design of 104 completely missed the words *Christ* and *God.* It should be noted that any design on *Jesus* in which these two words did not work out would be meaningless. Furthermore, if a person went through all the other references to Jesus in Chapter 3, the design with random numbers would totally disintegrate.

These results are staggering! This design so collapses when random numbers are used that there is no way anyone could ever disprove theomatics in this manner. In fact, no one can even come close. A person could sit down for a million years, and he would never be able to make thirty-six of these references contain a design with a number as large as 111 and then pull out sixty-five features. By laws of probability this would be next to impossible to do.

In performing this experiment, we first of all had the statistician select the random assignments. This was done so that a person could not say that we had played around with a lot of alphabetical arrangements, and then selected the one that worked the best for us. Furthermore, in order to be conservative, we used a smaller number than 111. By laws of probability, the number 104 should produce more features. And then to be absolutely sure, we performed the experiment twice with two random assignments. The first time we ever tried the experiment was when we used the number 104. Never once did we try other numbers to see which ones worked better in our favor. To do this would be silly, because any other number would not produce any significantly better results.

Method 3 and the Design on Satan

Of all the designs presented in this book, perhaps no other was as powerful as the one mentioned in Chapter 6 on the satanic kingdom. This chapter was the most important chapter for one particular reason —the size of the number 276!

The design on the birth of Christ consisted of the number 111. We have just demonstrated that no one can even come close to building a like design with a number this size, using random numbers. But what about a number 2½ times as large as 111? Let's find out.

Like the name *Jesus,* the name *Satan* has three different forms in Greek. These three spellings have three different articles to match, which gives us a total of six combinations. Here are those combinations.

		RANDOM ASSIGNMENT A	RANDOM ASSIGNMENT B
Mk 3:26	ο Σατανας	1,549	2,360
	Σατανας	1,519	2,357
Mk 1:13	του Σατανα	1,594	2,670
	Σατανα	1,511	2,277
Mt 12:26	τον Σαταναν	2,744	2,384
	Σαταναν	2,111	2,284

Now the first thing we must do is find every number that falls within ± 2 of every single spelling of Satan.

In performing our calculations, we went clear down to the number 138, which is half of 276. The list will contain every number that is divisible into every spelling of Satan, from 138 on up. Following each number there are some letters. These stand for references on Satan, which follow this table. The code for these letters is found on p. 186.

The next thing we did was to take seven references from the New Testament which we thought were the seven most outstanding titles

RANDOM ASSIGNMENT A			RANDOM ASSIGNMENT B		
138 R K	264 A L	532 —	149 E D K	457 R	1,143 —
141 E K L	266 —	549 —	157 K	471 —	1,178 —
145 R K	302 D	686 —	159 R D K	472 E	1,179 —
151 D K	304 R	703 A	163 R L	477 —	1,180 —
152 P R L	305 R K	704 E	167 P A R	534 —	1,181 —
155 A	310 —	755 K	175 —	569 —	1,191 D
168 L	319 K L	756 —	178 R	571 R	1,192 D
169 P	343 —	759 —	207 R D L	589 —	1,193 D
172 E P	352 E	760 L	236 E A	590 K	1,334 —
176 E P L	378 A D	774 —	253 P L	596 E D	1,335 —
177 R D K	380 P L	775 —	254 R K	667 —	1,336 —
183 R K	387 —	796 R	262 R	668 —	2,357 —
189 E A D	392 R	797 —	265 K	759 P L	2,383 —
190 P L	398 R	798 —	267 —	761 —	2,671 —
192 R	399 —	914 —	295 D K	762 K	
196 R	422 L	915 R	298 E D	785 —	
199 P R	457 —	1,055 —	325 P	786 —	
211 L	503 K	1,056 —	326 —	787 —.	
216 R	504 —	1,371 —	334 P A R	794 K	
217 —	506 P R	1,372 —	337 R K	795 —	
221 —	507 P	1,373 —	381 K	890 R	
228 R K	516 P	1,511 —	393 D	1,138 —	
252 —	517 K	1,549 —	397 D K	1,139 —	
253 P A R	528 L	2,111 —	445 R	1,141 —	
258 P K	531 R K	2,113 —	455 P A	1,142 R	

relating to Satan. Here are those references with all of their combinations:

Reference 1. "The evil one." (8 combinations.)

Mt 13:19 ο πονηρος
  πονηρος
Mt 13:38 του πονηρου
  πονηρου
1 Jn 2:13 τον πονηρου
  πονηρου
1 Jn 5:19 τω πονηρω
  πονηρω

Reference 2. "The prince of the power of the air." (8 combinations.)
Eph 2:2

τον αρχοντα της εξουσιας του αερος
αρχοντα εξουσιας αερος
τον αρχοντα εξουσιας αερος
αρχοντα της εξουσιας αερος
αρχοντα εξουσιας του αερος
τον αρχοντα της εξουσιας αερος
αρχοντα της εξουσιας του αερος
τον αρχοντα εξουσιας του αερος

Reference 3. "The accuser of the brethren of us." (8 combinations.)
Rev 12:10

The accuser of the brethren of us

ο κατηγωρ των αδελφων ημων
κατηγωρ αδελφων ημων
ο κατηγωρ αδελφων ημων
κατηγωρ των αδελφων ημων

The accuser of the brethren

ο κατηγωρ των αδελφων
κατηγωρ αδελφων
ο κατηγωρ αδελφων
κατηγωρ των αδελφων

Reference 4. "Beelzebub, the ruler of the demons." (11 combina-
Lk 11:15   tions.)

Beelzebub, the ruler of the demons

Βεεζεβουλ τω αρχοντι των δαιμονιων
Βεεζεβουλ αρχοντι δαιμονιων
Βεεζεβουλ τω αρχοντι δαιμονιων
Βεεζεβουλ αρχοντι των δαιμονιων

Beelzebub, the ruler

Βεεζεβουλ τω αρχοντι
Βεεζεβουλ αρχοντι

Beelzebub

Βεεζεβουλ

The ruler of the demons

τω αρχοντι των δαιμονιων
αρχοντι   δαιμονιων
τω αρχοντι   δαιμονιων
αρχοντι των δαιμονιων

Reference 5. "The dragon." (8 combinations.)

Rev 12:4 ο δρακων
       δρακων

Rev 12:7 του δρακοντος
       δρακοντος

Rev 13:4 τω δρακοντι
       δρακοντι

Rev 20:2 τον δρακοντα
       δρακοντα

Reference 6.
Rev 9:11 "A king, the angel of the bottomless pit, whose name in Hebrew is Abaddon, and in Greek he has the name Apollyon." (21 combinations.)

A king, the angel of the bottomless pit, whose name in Hebrew is Abaddon, and in Greek he has the name Apollyon

βασιλεα τον αγγελον της αβνξσσου ονομα αυτω Εβραιστι Αβαδδων και εν τη Ελληνικη ονομα εχει Απολλυων

(ALL COMBINATIONS PRESENT IN THIS PASSAGE.)

τον	της	τη
τον	—	—
—	της	—
—	—	τη
τον	της	—
—	της	τη
τον	—	τη

A king, the angel of the bottomless pit

βασιλεα τον αγγελον της αβυσσου
βασιλεα   αγγελον   αβυσσου
βασιλεα τον αγγελον   αβυσσου
βασιλεα   αγγελον της αβυσσου

The angel of the bottomless pit

τον αγγελον της αβυσσου

   αγγελον   αβυσσου

τον αγγελον   αβυσσου

   αγγελον της αβυσσου

Whose name in Hebrew is Abaddon, and in Greek he has the name Apollyon

ονομα αυτω Εβραιστι Αβαδδων και εν τη Ελληνικη ονομα εχει Απολλυων

ονομα αυτω Εβραιστι Αβαδδων και εν   Ελληνικη ονομα εχει Απολλυων

Abaddon

Αβαδδων

Apollyon

Απολλυων

Reference 7. "He's a liar and the father of lies." (4 combinations.) Jn 8:44

οτι ψευστης εστιν και ο πατηρ αυτου

   ψευστης εστιν και   πατηρ αυτου

οτι ψευστης εστιν και   πατηρ αυτου

   ψευστης εστιν και ο πατηρ αυτου

Now our purpose in presenting these seven outstanding references is to draw from them a number that we will use in trying to disprove this particular theomatic design. In performing our calculations, the first thing we did was to take every single number divisible into every spelling of Satan and then try to divide it into every combination contained in these seven references. These numbers listed on p. 184 are followed by letters. Each letter represents one of the seven references, as follows:

E–The evil one
P–Prince of the power of the air
A–Accuser of our brethren
R–Beelzebub, the ruler of the demons

D–The dragon
K–A king, the angel of the bottomless pit
L–He's a liar and the father of lies

Take, for example, the first number from the list, which is 138. It is followed by the letters R and K. This means that 138 was found to be divisible into "Beelzebub, the ruler of the demons" (R) and "a king, the angel of the bottomless pit" (K). Five of the remaining seven references contained no combination divisible by 138.

The purpose in performing this experiment is to narrow down all of these numbers in order to find out which is the best number. In *Random Assignment A*, six numbers were found to contain three out of the possible seven references (141, 152, 176, 177, 189, and 253). In *Random Assignment B*, only five numbers contained three references (149, 159, 167, 207, and 334). These numbers were the ones that produced the best overall results, but the most important part was that *no number* produced more than three references. This means that every single number missed on at least four of the seven references.

What we are going to do now is show the reader that there is absolutely no design present when random numbers are used. We have taken every one of these numbers that produced three or more combinations (141, 152, 176, 177, 189, and 253 from *Random Assignment A* and 149, 159, 167, 207, and 334 from *Random Assignment B*), and tried to divide them into all the references we showed in Chapter 6 on the subject of Satan and hell.

This statistical study is quite large, and because of the limits of space, it would be impossible for us to show all of it. Earlier in this chapter we listed all of the combinations from every reference on the topic of the birth of Christ and the child Jesus. To do so again on the design related to Satan would take a tremendous number of pages, so we have decided to give a summary of our results.

The first thing we are going to do is take from each random assignment one number that produced the best overall results. This number would be the number that produced the most references out of the possible seven. Also, it would be the number with the lowest probability, the least likely to occur.

In *Random Assignment A*, six numbers produced three references. The largest of these numbers was 253. In *Random Assignment B* there were five numbers that produced three references, the largest of which was 334. Both of these numbers (253 and 334) are closest in magnitude to 276, and for this reason they will give us a fairly accurate statistical analysis. We shall see how well these numbers perform when we try to build a similar design using a random assignment of numbers to the references of Satan and hell.

Interestingly enough, both of these numbers (253 and 334) worked out on the same three references ("prince of the power of the air," "accuser of the brethren," and "Beelzebub, the ruler of the demons"). This means that both of these numbers missed completely on "the evil one," "the dragon," "a king, the angel of the bottomless pit . . . ," and "he's a liar and the father of lies." These four references are now completely out of the picture. This means that in order to catch up, both of these numbers (253 and 334) must now produce better results than we produced with 276 on the remaining features. Let's see how well they perform.

We shall now list all of the references shown in Chapter 6 on the subject of Satan and hell, excluding the seven already shown. We will quote the complete verse or portion surrounding the reference, and the phrase we used for the reference will be italicized. The Greek words from that particular reference will be given with the articles and conjunctions underlined. The number of combinations derived from that particular phrase is given, as before, but not shown in detail. The number of "hits" is also given, with indications of whether 253 or 334 was divisible into at least one of these combinations.

Reference 8.   *"And if I cast out demons by Beelzebub,* by whom do
Mt 12:27   your sons cast them out." (10 combinations—no hits.)
    και ει εγω εν Βεεζεβουλ εκβαλλω τα δαιμονια

Reference 9.   "But some of them said, 'He casts out demons by Beel-
Lk 11:15   *zebub, the ruler of the demons.'* " (8 combinations—no
    hits.) The words "Beelzebub, the ruler of the demons"
    have been excluded from this reference, because they
    were already examined in *Reference 4.*
    εν Βεεζεβουλ τω αρχοντι των δαιμονιων εκβαλλει τα δαιμονια

Reference 10.   "I will no longer talk much with you, *for the ruler of this*
Jn 14:30   *world is coming,* and hath nothing in me." (8 combina-
    tions—no hits.)
    ερχεται γαρ ο του κοσμου αρχων

Reference 11. "Concerning righteousness, because I go to the Father,
Jn 16:11   and you will see Me no more; *concerning judgment,*
because the ruler of this world has been judged." (16
combinations—no hits.)

περι δε κρισεως οτι ο αρχων του κοσμου τουτου κεκριται

Reference 12. "Now is the judgment of this world, *now is the ruler of*
Jn 12:31   *this world cast out."* (4 combinations—no hits.)

νυν ο αρχων του κοσμου τουτου εκβληθησεται εξω

Reference 13. *"Ruler of this world."* (8 combinations—no hits.)
Jn 12:31   ο αρχων του κοσμου τουτου
Jn 16:11
Jn 14:30

Reference 14. "Be sober, be watchful. *Your adversary, the devil, goes*
1 Pet 5:8   *about as a roaring lion, seeking whom he may devour."*
(10 combinations—no hits.)

ο αντιδικος υμων διαβολος ως λεων ωρυομενος περιπατει ζητων

τινα καταπιειν

Reference 15. "And He said to them, *'I beheld Satan fall from heaven*
Lk 10:18   *as lightning.'"* (8 combinations—no hits.)

εθεωρουν τον Σαταναν ως αστραπην εκ του ουρανου πεσοντα

Reference 16. *"And if Satan also is divided against himself, how shall*
Lk 11:18   *his kingdom stand."* (16 combinations—253–334.)

ει δε και ο Σατανας εφ εαυτον διεμερισθη πως σταθησεται η

βασιλεαι αυτου

Reference 17. *"Behold I have given you authority to tread on serpents*
Lk 10:19   *and scorpions and all the power of the enemy; and noth-*
ing shall hurt you." (47 combinations—no hits.)

ιδου δεδωκα υμιν την εξουσιαν του πατειν επανω οφεων και

σκορπιων και επι πασαν την δυναμιν του εχθρου

Reference 18. *"Get thee behind Me Satan, for thou mindest not the*
Mk 8:33   *things of God, but the things of men."* (13 combinations
—253.)

υπαγε οπισω μου Σατανα οτι ου φρονεις τα του Θεου αλλα τα των

ανθρωπων

Reference 19. "Then the lawless one will be revealed whom the Lord
2 Thess 2:9 Jesus will slay with the breath of His mouth and bring
to nothing by the outshining of His presence *of whom
is the coming according to the operation of Satan with
all power and signs and lying wonders.*" (24 combinations—no hits.)

ου εστιν η παρουσια κατ ενεργειαν του Σατανα εν παση δυναμει

και σημειοις και τερασιν ψευδους

Reference 20. "So I would have younger widows marry, bear children,
1 Tim 5:15 rule their households, and give the enemy no opportunity [also 276] to revile us. *For some have already turned
aside to follow Satan.*" (8 combinations—no hits.)

ηδη γαρ τινες εξετραπησαν οπισω του Σατανα

Reference 21. "And no wonder, *for even Satan transforms himself into
2 Cor 2:11 an angel of light.*" (5 combinations—no hits.)

ουτος γαρ ο Σατανας μετασχηματιζεται εις αγγελον φωτος

Reference 22. "*And He was in the wilderness forty days being tempted
Mk 1:13 by Satan.*" (10 combinations—no hits.)

και ην εν τη ερημω τεσσερακοντα ημερας πειραζομενος υπο του

Σατανα

Reference 23. "*Then Jesus was led up by the spirit into the wilderness
Mt 4:1 to be tempted by the devil.*" (26 combinations—no
hits.)

τοτε ο Ιησους ανηχθη εις την ερημον υπο του πνευματος

πειρασθηναι υπο του διαβολου

Reference 24. "*Put ye on the whole armor of God that ye may be able
Eph 6:11 to stand against the craftiness of the devil.*" (44 combinations—253–334.)

ενδυσασθε την πανοπλιαν του Θεου προς το δυνασθαι υμας στη-

ναι προς τας μεθοδειας του διαβολου

Reference 25. "Above all taking the shield of faith *by which ye will be
Eph 6:16 able to quench all the fiery darts of the evil one.*" (24
combinations—no hits.)

εν ω δυνησεσθε παντα τα βελη του πονηρου τα πεπυρωμενα

σβεσαι

Reference 26. "But He Who was born of God keeps him, *and the evil*
1 Jn 5:18   *one does not touch Him."* (4 combinations—no hits.)

και ο πονηρος ουχ απτεται αυτου

Reference 27. "Be angry but do not sin; do not let the sun go down
Eph 4:27   on your anger, *and give no opportunity to the devil."* (2
combinations—no hits.)

μηδε διδοτε τοπον τω διαβολω

Reference 28. *"Be subject therefore to God and resist the devil and he*
Jas 4:7   *will flee from you."* (10 combinations—no hits.)

υποταγητε ουν τω Θεω αντιστητε δε τω διαβολω και φευξεται αφ
υμων

Reference 29. *"And the devil who had deceived them was thrown into*
Rev 20:10   *the lake of fire and sulfur* where the beast and false
prophet are." (27 combinations—253.)

και ο διαβολος ο πλανων αυτους εβληθη εις την λιμνην του πυρος
και Θειου

Reference 30. "The ones by the way are the ones hearing; *then cometh*
Lk 8:12   *the devil, and taketh away the word out of their hearts."*
(12 combinations—no hits.)

ειτα ερχεται ο διαβολος και αιρει τον λογον απο της καρδιας
αυτων

Reference 31. *"The one doing sin is of the devil, for the devil has*
1 Jn 3:8   *sinned from the beginning."* (28 combinations—253.)

ο ποιων την αμαρτιαν εκ του διαβολου εστιν οτι απ αρχης ο
διαβολος αμαρτανει

Reference 32. "And even if our gospel is hid, it is hid only to those who
2 Cor 4:4   are perishing, in whose case *the god of this age has
blinded the minds of the ones not believing,* to keep
them from seeing the light of the gospel." (32 combinations—334.)

ο Θεος του αιωνος τουτου ετυφλωσεν τα νοηματα των απιστων

Reference 33. "And the good seed, these are the sons of the kingdom,
Mt 13:38   *and the tares are the sons of the evil one."* (14 combinations—no hits.)

τα δε ζιζανια εισιν οι υιοι του πονηρου

Reference 34. "And the tares are the sons of the evil one, *and the*
Mt 13:39   *enemy who sowed them is the devil.*" (10 combinations
—no hits.)

ο δε εχθρος ο σπειρας αυτα εστιν ο διαβολος

Reference 35. "And he said to them, *'An enemy has done this.'* " (3
Mt 13:28   combinations—no hits.)

εχθρος ανθρωπος τουτο εποιησεν

Reference 36. "And there was war in heaven, *Michael and his angels*
Rev 12:7   *made war with the dragon.*" (17 combinations—253.)

ο Μιχαηλ και οι αγγελοι αυτου του πολεμησαι μετα του δρακοντος

Reference 37. "*And the dragon was cast down, the great serpent of old,*
Rev 12:9   *who is called the devil and Satan.*" (79 combinations—
253–334.)

και εβληθη ο δρακων ο μεγας ο οφις ο αρχαιος ο καλουμενος
διαβολος και ο Σατανας

Reference 38. "*Then the dragon was enraged with the woman,* and
Rev 12:17   went off to make war with the rest of her seed." (12
combinations—334.)

και ωργισθη ο δρακων επι τη γυναικι

Reference 39. "*And he laid hold of the dragon, the serpent of old, who*
Rev 20:2   *is called the devil and Satan.*" (52 combinations—253.)

και εκρατησεν τον δρακοντα ο οφις ο αρχαιος ος εστιν διαβολος
και ο Σατανας

Reference 40. "And when the thousand years are ended, *Satan will be*
Rev 20:7   *loosed out of his prison.*" (6 combinations—no hits.)

λυθησεται ο Σατανας εκ της φυλακης αυτου

FINAL ANALYSIS

We have just examined all of the features shown in Chapter 6
related to the topic of Satan. Here now is a chart showing a summary
of the results:

Reference 1	—	—	*Reference 21*	—	—
Reference 2	253	334	*Reference 22*	—	—
Reference 3	253	334	*Reference 23*	253	334

Reference 4	253	334	Reference 24	—	—
Reference 5	—	—	Reference 25	—	—
Reference 6	—	—	Reference 26	—	—
Reference 7	—	—	Reference 27	—	—
Reference 8	—	—	Reference 28	—	—
Reference 9	—	—	Reference 29	253	—
Reference 10	—	—	Reference 30	—	—
Reference 11	—	—	Reference 31	253	—
Reference 12	—	—	Reference 32	—	334
Reference 13	—	—	Reference 33	—	—
Reference 14	—	—	Reference 34	—	—
Reference 15	—	—	Reference 35	—	—
Reference 16	253	334	Reference 36	253	—
Reference 17	—	—	Reference 37	253	334
Reference 18	253	—	Reference 38	—	334
Reference 19	—	—	Reference 39	253	—
Reference 20	—	—	Reference 40	—	—

When we began this experiment, we started with all the numbers divisible into the name *Satan*. We then narrowed down all of these numbers by dividing them into seven of the most outstanding references. This was done to find out which was the best number from each random assignment. Next, we tried to divide 253 and 334 into the remaining references shown in Chapter 6.

There are other ways this experiment could be conducted. One could take a set of features different from the seven we used, in order to try to find the best number. However, no different process from the one we tried would produce any significantly better results overall. The reason for this is the scientific law of randomness. For example, if a person were to flip a coin enough times, it would be feasible that out of ten flips, he could obtain nine heads and only one tail. But the law of randomness states that a coin has a 50–50 chance of landing on either heads or tails. If this person were to flip the coin one hundred times, it would be next to impossible for him to obtain ninety heads and only ten tails. A thousand flips would be even harder. The more times a coin is flipped, the closer the results will come to being 50-50.

For this reason, out of forty references to Satan, no single number is going to produce overall results substantially better than any other number. In the foregoing experiment we used a number smaller and a number larger than 276. The number 253 produced eleven out of the possible forty references, and 334 produced only eight references. This is just about what one would expect from sheer randomness.

Take the number 253 as an example. This number is now twenty-nine references behind what we were able to produce (40 − 11 = 29). This means that for one to disprove this theomatic design, he would have to find other references from the New Testament, which did not work out to 276, but which he can show work out to 253. When that happens, he would have produced results equal to what we have been able to produce. Since the number 253 is smaller than 276, this means that he would actually have to find more references than what we found; if he tried the number 334, he would have to find fewer references, because 334 is larger than 276.

In going through the New Testament, we discovered that more than 75 percent of the times the words *Satan* and *devil*[4] were mentioned features of 276 could be found. Many of these references were quite general and in no way outstanding.

As it has been stated, a person would have to find twenty-nine new references to Satan that contain multiples of 253, or thirty-two new references that contain multiples of 334, in order to catch up with the results obtained from the forty references we just examined. In order to obtain these needed references, a person would have to obtain them from references we did not consider in the forty just examined.

Here is the problem our critic will encounter. What if during the process of looking for these features of 253 and 334, he happens to find others that come out to 276? What then? If this should happen, then it means that in order to not lose any ground, he has to make those references contain a design of 253 or 334. If he fails to do this, he will fall further behind, which means that he will need more references than the twenty-nine or thirty-two originally needed.

Now in order to illustrate the problems that will be encountered in trying to do this, we will list seventeen more direct references to Satan, all of which work out to multiples of 276.

In Matthew 4:5 we find the following words:

The devil took Him to the holy city and set Him on the 276 × 21
pinnacle of the temple

[4]In checking all the spellings of the word *devil* in the singular, we discovered that neither 253 or 334 were divisible into it. The word *devil* in the plural (οι διαβολοι) has a theomatic value of 276. In Greek, the word *devil* (διαβολος) means "slanderous, accusing falsely."

Mt 4:5 *παραλαμβανει αυτον ο διαβολος εις την αγιαν πολιν και εστησεν αυτον
επι πτερυγιον ιερου*

Later on, in the same passage, the following words are found:

Again, the devil took Him to a great high mountain,   276 × 28
and showed all the kingdoms of the world and their glory
Mt 4:8 *παλιν παραλαμβανει αυτον διαβολος εις ορος υψηλον λιαν και δεικνυσιν
αυτω πασας τας βασιλειας του κοσμου και δοξαν αυτων*

Paul had the following words to say in 1 Timothy, chapter 3: "For if a man does not know how to rule his own household, how can he care for the church of God? He must not be a recent convert, lest being conceited he fall into the judgment of the devil."

Lest being conceited he falls into the judgment   276 × 16
of the devil
1 Tim 3:6 *τνα μη τυφωθεις εις κριμα εμπεση του διαβολου"*

In his second epistle to Timothy, Paul stated the following: "God may perhaps grant that they will repent and come to know the truth, and escape from the snare of the devil, having been held captive by him to do his will."

Escape from the snare of the devil, having been   276 × 18
held captive by him to do his will
2 Tim 2:26 *εκ διαβολου παγιδος εζωγρημενοι υπ αυτου εις το εκεινου θελημα'*

Existing in the following words, there is another design of 276: "He himself likewise partook of the same nature, that through death he might destroy the one having the power of death, that is, the devil."

The one having the power of death is the devil   276 × 15
Heb 2:14 *το κρατος εχοντα θανατου εστιν τον διαβολον*

An outstanding reference is found in 1 Jn 3:10: "By this the children of God and the children of the devil are manifest."

The children of the devil are manifest   276 × 9
1 Jn 3:10 *φανερα εστιν τα τεκνα διαβολου"*

In Revelation 12:12 we find these words: "Woe to the earth and the sea, for the devil has come down to you having great wrath, knowing that he hath but a short time."

For the devil has come down   276 × 4
Rev 12:12 οτι κατεβη διαβολος΄

Now we shall turn and focus our attention on some specific references to Satan. In Matthew 12:26 the following words are found: "And if Satan casts out Satan, he is divided against himself; how then shall his kingdom stand?"

Satan casts out Satan, he is divided against himself;   276 × 28
how then shall his kingdom stand?
Mt 12:26 ο Σατανας τον Σαταναν εκβαλλει εφ εαυτον εμερισθη πως ουν
σταθησεται η βασιλεια αυτου΄

Satan casts out Satan he is divided against himself   276 × 13
Mt 12:26 Σατανας τον Σαταναν εκβαλλει εφ εαυτον εμερισθη΄

Here are the words from Mark 4:15: "And these are the ones by the way, where the word is sown. And when they hear, immediately comes Satan and takes away the word having been sown in them."

Immediately comes Satan and takes away the word   276 × 13
Mk 4:15 ευθυς ερχεται Σατανας και αιρει τον λογον

Jesus said the following to Simon Peter before going to the cross: "Simon, Simon, Behold, Satan has desired to have you that he may sift you as wheat."

Behold, Satan has desired to have you that he may sift you   276 × 12
Lk 22:31 ιδου Σατανα εξητησατο υμας σινιασαι

Earlier in this book we examined a reference that concerned the power of Satan, which had a theomatic value of 1,500, the number of power. Here is that complete verse: "To open their eyes and turn them from darkness to light, and from the power of Satan to God."

And from the power of Satan to God   276 × 11
Acts 26:18 και της εξουσιας του Σατανα επι Θεον΄

Paul said this, in writing to the Corinthian church: "What I have forgiven, if I have forgiven anything, has been on the account of you in the person of Christ, lest we are taken advantage of by Satan."

By Satan   276 × 4
2 Cor 2:11 υπο Σατανα΄

A well-known verse is the one in which Paul speaks of having a thorn in his flesh: "And to keep me from being too exalted by the abundance of revelations, I was given a thorn in the flesh, a messenger of Satan to buffet me, lest I should be exalted above measure."

A thorn in the flesh, a messenger of Satan to buffet me   276 × 11
2 Cor 12:7 σκολοψ σαρκι αγγελος Σατανα ινα με κολαφιζη"

In writing to the church at Thessalonica, Paul said the following: "Wherefore we would have come unto you, even I, Paul, once and again; but Satan hindered us."

Satan hindered   276 × 6
1 Thess 2:18 ενεκοψεν Σατανας"

In Revelation 2:13 Jesus is found speaking to the church at Smyrna: "And you held fast My name and you did not deny My faith even in the days of Antipas, My witness, the faithful of Me, who was killed among you where Satan dwells."

Was killed among you where Satan dwells   276 × 11
Rev 2:13 απεκτανθη παρ υμιν οπου ο Σατανας κατοικει"

Several times Revelation speaks of the synagogue of Satan. Here is an example of that feature:

Those of the synagogue of Satan who say they are Jews   276 × 38
and are not, but lie
Rev 3:9 εκ συναγωγης του Σατανα των λεγοντων εαυτους Ιουδαιους ειναι και
ουκ εισιν αλλα ψευδονται"

Do you remember the four features we showed in Chapter 6, which spoke of "Beelzebub, the ruler of the demons." Here now is another reference on this topic:

He is possessed by Beelzebub, and by the ruler of the   276 × 20
demons he casts out the demons
Mk 3:22 Βεεζεβουλ εχει και οτι εν τω αρχοντι των δαιμονιων εκβαλλει τα δαιμονια

This concludes our statistical study of the references to Satan. These seventeen references just shown were found after we had written Chapter 6. At this time we have not gone through any of these references in order to find out whether or not they contain features of 253 or 334. Quite frankly, this would not be necessary. By laws of probability, a person would only be able to pick up a handful of references using either 253 or 334. After going through these seventeen references with all of their combinations, he would be much further behind than he had been previously. And the element that clinches it is that there are not enough other references left in the New Testament by which he could disprove this design, even if he made all of them work out to 253 or 334.

Furthermore, the features with the numbers 253 and 334 in no way match the quality of those that we found. The references shown in Chapter 6 are by far the most outstanding possible from the entire New Testament. A careful examination will reveal that the quality of the seventeen references just given is much lower than those given in Chapter 6. And the numbers 253 and 334 have already missed on 75 percent of those references from Chapter 6.

We did something else in this experiment that we did not have to do. In the probability study given previously on the birth of Christ, we not only pulled thirty-six references, but we also took into consideration the number of features from those references. In the design on 276 that we just examined, we did not do that. If we had, the final results would have been even more in our favor, because many of the references contained two, three, or four multiples of 276, whereas with the numbers 253 and 334 this was not so.

Method 3 and the Design on Hell

As we have demonstrated, it would be totally impossible for a critic to come close to building a similar design on Satan by using random numbers. A person could try and use any number he wished, and he would never be able to produce as many references as what we have been able to produce with the number 276. But let us say hypothetically that a person was able to eventually build a like design using random numbers. If this should happen, he still would not have disproven the design on 276. Ultimately, he would have to duplicate the other designs related to the other topics presented in Chapter 6.

In his report, Dr. Stanton stated that a person would have to find as many references as what we have found, just as outstanding, using a number of the same magnitude we used. Here is where Method 3 really shines forth. In Chapter 6, we showed a complete design on hell with the number 276, the same number used in the satanic design. This means that in order to now disprove the design on 276, the critic would have to build a like design on hell using the same number that he used in trying to disprove the design on Satan.

In other words, the critic cannot change his number when he comes to the topic of hell. In Chapter 6, we did not change our number, so why should he be allowed to change his? Earlier, we narrowed down all of the numbers to find out which was the best number for Satan. The result was the two numbers, 253 and 334. This means that now either of these two numbers would have to be used in trying to disprove the design on hell. (Of course, he could use any other number that he had started out with on the design of Satan.)

What we have done next is to take from Chapter 6 what we thought to be the nineteen most outstanding references to the topic of hell. Let us now see how well they perform when we run the numbers 253 and 334 through these references.

Reference 1. In this reference we will look at the Greek word *gehenna*, which means hell. Also, we will examine the references which speak of *in gehenna*. (8 combinations —334.)

Mt 5:22 την γεενναν

γεενναν

Mt 10:28 γεεννη

Mt 5:33 της γεεννης

γεεννης

Mt 5:22 εις την γεενναν

εις   γεενναν

Reference 2. Likewise we will examine the Greek word *hades* which also means hell. (8 combinations—no hits.)

Lk 10:15 του αδου

αδου

Lk 16:23 τω αδη

αδη

Rev 6:8 ο αδης

αδης

Acts 2:27 εις αδην

αδην

Reference 3.   "You serpents, you brood of vipers, *how shall you escape*
Mt 23:33   *the judgment of hell?*" (8 combinations—no hits.)

πως φυγητε απο της κρισεως της γεεννης

Reference 4.   "And calling he said, 'Father Abraham, have mercy on
Lk 16:24   me, and send Lazarus that he may dip the tip of his
finger in water and cool my tongue; *for I am suffering
in this flame.*" (8 combinations—no hits.)

οτι οδυνωμαι εν τη φλογι ταυτη

Reference 5.   "For I have five brothers, so that he may warn them,
Lk 16:28   *lest they also come to this place of torment.*" (20 combinations—no hits.)

ινα μη και αυτοι ελθωσιν εις τον τοπον τουτον της βασανου

Reference 6.   "And in the time of the harvest I will say to the reapers,
Mt 13:30   *'Collect ye first the tares and bind them in bundles to
burn them.'*" (12 combinations—no hits.)

συλλεξατε πρωτον τα ζιζανια και δησατε αυτα εις δεσμας προς
το κατακαυσαι αυτα

Reference 7.   "And they will collect out of His kingdom all causes of
Mt 13:42   sin and all evildoers, *and cast them into the furnace of
fire.*" (16 combinations—no hits.)

και βαλουσιν αυτους εις την καμινον του πυρος

Reference 8.   *"There shall be weeping and gnashing of teeth."* (6
Mt 13:42   combinations—no hits.)

εκει εσται ο κλανθμος και ο βρυγμος των οδοντων

Reference 9.   *"Hell fire."* (8 combinations—no hits.)
Mk 9:43   την γεενναν το πυρ
Mt 5:22   την γεενναν του πυρος

Reference 10.   *"Unquenchable."* (3 combinations—334.)
Mt 3:12   ασβεστω
Mk 9:42   το ασβεστον
            ασβεστον

Reference 11.   *"Where their worm dieth not and the fire is not
Mk 9:48   quenched."* (4 combinations—no hits.)

οπου ο σκωληξ αυτων ου τελευτα και το πυρ ου σβεννυται

Reference 12. "If thy right eye offend thee, pluck it out, and cast it
Mt 5:29   from thee; *for it is better that thee lose one of thy mem-*
bers than that thy whole body be cast into hell." (17
combinations—253.)

συμφερει γαρ σοι ινα αποληται εν των μελων σου και μη ολον
το σωμα σου βληθη εις γεενναν

Reference 13. "But I will warn you whom to fear: *Fear him who after*
Lk 12:5   *he has killed has power to cast into hell."* (10 combinations—334.)

φοβηθητε τον μετα το αποκτειναι εχοντα εξουσιαν εμβαλειν εις
την γεενναν

Reference 14. "And then I will declare to them, *'I never knew you;*
Mt 7:23   *depart from Me, ye that work iniquity.'* " (14 combinations—no hits.)

οτι ουδεποτε εγνων υμας αποχωρειτε απ εμου οι εργαζομενοι την
ανομιαν

Reference 15. "Then He will also say to those on his left, *'Depart from*
Mt 25:41 *Me, ye cursed, into everlasting fire prepared for the devil*
and his angels.' " (48 combinations—no hits.)

πορευεσθε απ εμου κατηραμενοι εις το πυρ το αιωνιον το ητοιμασμενον τω διαβολω και τοις αγγελοις αυτου

Reference 16. "And these will go away into everlasting punishment."
Mt 25:46 (4 combinations—no hits.)

και απελευσονται ουτοι εις κολασιν αιωνιον

Reference 17. "Whoever says, Thou fool! shall be in danger of hell
Mt 5:22   fire." (8 combinations—no hits.)

ος δ αν αεπη μωρε ενοχος εσται εις την γεενναν του πυρος

Note: This feature was within ± 3 of 276. Because it is
such an outstanding reference, we should consider it in
this random experiment.

Reference 18. "For wide is the gate, and broad is the way leading to
Mt 7:13   destruction." (36 combinations—253.)

οτι πλατεια η πυλη και ευρυχωρος η οδος η απαγουσα εις την
απωλειαν

Reference 19. "*And for it has been appointed unto man once to die,*
Heb 9:27   *and then the judgment.*" (7 combinations—no hits.)
και καθ οσον αποκειται τοις ανθρωποις απαξ αποθανειν μετα δε
τουτο κρισις

Here is a summary of the results:

Reference 1	—	334	*Reference 11*	—	—
Reference 2	—	—	*Reference 12*	253	—
Reference 3	—	—	*Reference 13*	—	334
Reference 4	—	—	*Reference 14*	—	—
Reference 5	—	—	*Reference 15*	—	—
Reference 6	—	—	*Reference 16*	—	—
Reference 7	—	—	*Reference 17*	—	—
Reference 8	—	—	*Reference 18*	253	—
Reference 9	—	—	*Reference 19*	—	—
Reference 10	—	334			

Out of a total of nineteen references, we found that only
two were divisible by 253, and three of the references contained
multiples of 334.

Summary and Conclusion

The methodology presented in this chapter can be applied to any
theomatic design in the Bible. In Method 1, we saw that each design
has only one chance in so many of occurring. Method 2 proved that
a person would have to find x amount of features that do not work out
in order to disprove those that do. And last, Method 3 was the acid
test for either proving or disproving theomatics. Here it was demonstrated that no other number-letter equivalencies can produce these
designs except those that God placed in the papyrus.

Everything that was presented in this book had rationality behind
it. First of all, we did not choose the number equivalencies for the
letters ourselves. Instead, we had only one choice. We had to go with
what was standardized and found in Webster's dictionary and the
papyrus. This limited us to one set of equivalencies. Second, the numbers used for the designs are found right in the text. The number 8 was
in the text, as were the numbers 153, 10,000, 276, 666, 144, and so

on. What meaning would it have if we showed that all of the references related to fishing came out to multiples of 147? The text specifically states that 153 fishes were caught! Or what meaning would it have if the references to the mark of the beast came out to 654? *We had to use the numbers that God placed in the text!*

Never once did we use the ridiculous process shown in this chapter in trying to build our designs. However, we have allowed the critic to use any random assignment he wishes, and to use any numbers for multiples he wishes. We ourselves did not have this luxury. We were limited to the numbers in the papyrus and the numbers that God placed in the text.

In conclusion, we can only state that no argument will ever explain away the fact that only those values found in the papyrus can produce these designs. No amount of subjectivism will ever explain away the objective truth of theomatics.

When someone can take any other random assignment and produce complete designs equal to those presented in this book, then we will admit publicly that even though we were sincere, we were sadly mistaken. We can assure the reader that that day will never come. *God may allow man to condemn, criticize, and even abuse this truth, but He will never ever allow anyone to duplicate these designs with any random assignment of numbers to the letters of the Greek alphabet other than those that He Himself placed in the papyrus. In fact, no one will even come close.*

APPENDIX:
Special Information for Greek Scholars

In this book, we have had one primary goal: to make known to all concerned that there exists in the Bible a mathematical design called "theomatics." This book has been written with the general public in mind, and its purpose is to make these findings known to the Christian as well as the non-Christian world.

For this reason, we have tried to steer away from making this book a scholarly treatise only, for the minority of those so inclined. In the future, our approach to theomatics will be more critical, and we will aim our research and writing toward the academic community. At the same time we will continue to write material for the nonacademic community as well. The factor of utmost importance is that the masses receive the benefit of this truth as well as the scholars. Nevertheless, the scholarly approach is essential, if the former is to keep its credibility.

In these concluding pages, we would like to discuss in fairly general terms two areas of importance related to the Greek of the New Testament. First of all, we will look at some information concerning textual criticism. Second, we will make a more detailed analysis of the grammatical structure of Greek in its usage of the definite article.

Which Text?

In Chapter 9, we discussed some of the basic problems surrounding textual criticism, as it relates to theomatics. We also mentioned that in this book we used the Nestle text exclusively. The Nestle text we used, however, was not the one that gives all the varying readings at the bottom of each page. Instead, it is the *straight* Nestle text that appears in interlinear form.[1] The only time we made an exception to this text was in the book of Revelation. Here we compared the Nestle text with the Chester Beatty papyrus (P[47]). The reason for this is that we have come to the conclusion in our years of Bible research that Revelation is probably the worst established text in the New Testament. There are very few early manuscripts of Revelation. Furthermore, there are remarkable variances among some of these manuscripts.

In approximately a dozen instances, we chose the papyrus reading over the Nestle reading if there was a difference between the two. However, there were some instances where the Nestle text was correct. If the scholar discovers that any feature in this book differs from the straight Nestle text, then that reading was taken from the Chester Beatty papyrus.

An important note: In making our statistical calculations, we have made it a rule that we would only use a feature if it works out in the Nestle text. Here is why. If we were to choose among the different textual readings, then in figuring our statistical calculations, we would have to take into consideration every possible reading from all the texts, no matter how poor. This would open us up to criticism, and at the same time reduce our statistical credibility.

What we decided to do was limit ourselves to the straight Nestle text. If we found that a feature worked in the papyrus and not in Nestle's, we counted it as a miss. For statistical purposes, it only counted if it worked in the Nestle text. This also means that any person trying to discredit theomatics would also be limited to the straight Nestle text, in using Method 3.

In the future, we will compare all of the various texts. This will no doubt throw light on which readings are true and which are false. Here is one quick example of how theomatics can throw light on textual criticism. Revelation 14:3 states the following: "And no one could learn the song except the 144 thousands, the ones purchased from the earth." There are two differences for this passage between the papyrus and Nestle's. First of all, the number 144 is given with the letters of the alphabet in the papyrus, whereas in Nestle's it is written out with words. Second, the word *thousands* is spelled differently. In the papyrus it is χειλιαδες, but in Nestle's, the ε is dropped (χιλιαδες).

[1]Marshall, Rev. Alfred, *The Interlinear Greek-English New Testament* (Grand Rapids: Zondervan, 1958).

In going through the Nestle text we found no design of 144 present, but in the papyrus the following presented itself:

And no one could learn the song except the 144   144 × 32
thousands, the ones purchased from the earth
Rev 14:3 και ουδεις εδυνατο μαθειν ωδην ει μη αι ρμδ χειλιαδες οι
  ηγορασμενοι απο γης΄

The 144 thousands, the ones purchased from the earth   144 × 17
Rev 14:3 αι ρμδ χειλιαδες ηγορασμενοι απο της γης΄

The 144 thousands   144 × 7
Rev 14:3 ρμδ χειλιαδες΄

These results would definitely indicate that the correct reading was found in the papyrus. This is only one example of several that we have found, where theomatics can throw definite light on which readings are true and which are false.

In conclusion, we would like to offer a personal comment on textual criticism. The work that has been done in the area of textual research down through the centuries has been outstanding. Eberhard Nestle and others have brought us very close to the original text. The outstanding work that these men have done should be appreciated by all those who love to study the Bible in its original languages.

Theomatics has added a whole new dimension to textual criticism. For this reason, we have concluded that in using theomatics, the best form of textual criticism will be to take the best texts of our day (such as Nestle's), and compare these with the earliest papyrus fragments. In this way, small spelling variations and other corrupt readings that slipped through can be weeded out, as in the above feature on the 144 thousands.

A Further Discussion of Greek Grammar

There was a time when the scholars who dealt with the original text of the New Testament regarded its Greek as a special Holy Ghost language, prepared under divine direction for the scripture writers. When the fallacy of this conception began to grow evident, two opposing schools developed. . . .[2]

[2]H. E. Dana and Julius R. Mantey. *A Manual Grammar of the Greek New Testament* (Toronto: Macmillan, 1955), p. 9.

The above quotation was taken from one of the finest textbooks on New Testament Greek grammar currently being used in our seminaries. Sadly, such is the prevailing attitude of many present-day scholars toward the Greek of the New Testament. The modern trend has been to discount or limit the divine inspiration of the Scriptures by putting the study of Greek syntax on a historical basis alone. The entire scope of New Testament research in recent times has been, strictly speaking, historical.

Quite obviously, this is the only way in which it is presently possible to pursue an adequate study of New Testament Greek grammar. The great strides forward in this direction, particularly at the turn of the century, have helped scholars to understand the original languages better. The work of A. T. Robertson has become a milestone for the linguist. The volumes of research, which he compiled, are phenomenal.

In spite of all its benefits, the historical approach has given scholars an excuse to push aside the fact that New Testament Greek, or *koine*, is a specially prepared Holy Ghost language. Instead, they have regarded it as nothing more than a transitional phase in the development of the Greek. Needless to say, the authors of this book strongly dispute any historical approach that discredits New Testament Greek as a divinely prepared language and places it solely in a historical category.

We believe—and theomatics proves—that God simply used the historical development of the Greek to design a language whereby he could place the mathematics in His Word. Each Greek word had to be formed so that the letters, when added together, came out to the right number value that God had predetermined. When the proper time came, God in His sovereignty moved upon the writers of the Bible by the Holy Spirit, and they, without knowing it, placed the right word here and the right word there. Each word was in the spelling, or syntactical case, that God intended it to be, and when God wanted the article placed in the text, the writer would add that, too.

This is why in our analysis of the Greek of the New Testament, the cart must be placed after the horse. The historical development of the grammar is not the end in itself. It is only the means to the end. Theendistheomatics—the Bible formed and written by God mathematically. One of the factors that enables the theomatic structure to flow together is the Greek definite article.

THE GREEK DEFINITE ARTICLE

Earlier in this book we pointed out that the key to the theomatic design is understanding the use of the Greek article. We also pointed out that the article could be removed, and that the theomatic designs flowed between the articles. This statement needs further comment.

Probably the one area of criticism that theomatics will receive at the hands of Greek scholars is our inclusion or deletion of the definite article from the theomatic features. The immediate reaction of some critics will be to attack us on this basis. The reason for this is that many of those individuals trained in seminaries are taught that the definite article in Greek contains certain exegetical or theological significance in interpretation. As a result, scholarship has tried to attach a mystical significance to the presence or absence of the article in the text.

A careful study will reveal, however, that this approach is totally arbitrary and subjective. There is not a Greek scholar or theologian alive that can prove that the definite Greek article has any meaning (interpretive significance) whatsoever.[3]

In Chapter 2, on the definition of the theomatic structure, we quoted from Dana and Mantey that "there are no 'rules' for the use of the article in Greek." Here is the complete paragraph surrounding that statement:

> In harmony with its basal significance there are certain constructions in which the article is normally used. We employ the term "regular" here in the sense of ordinary, and not as implying use in keeping with any fixed rules. There are no "rules" for the use of the article in Greek, but there is a fundamental principle underlying its significance—as we have seen in the foregoing section—and this gives rise to normal usage. *Deviation from this normal usage may occur at the will of the writer.*[4]

Koine, or the Greek language of the New Testament, was rarely written. It was primarily a spoken language. When an orator wished to make a strong point of emphasis, he would add the article to his speech. This is why the New Testament writers wrote as if they were

[3]This excludes instances where the article deviates from its basal significance and becomes a demonstrative pronoun. Other examples are when o is translated as *which* and η is translated as *or.* In these places, we did not remove the article. We only removed it in instances where its basic purpose was to simply add emphasis. Furthermore, in our statistical calculations we took into consideration every combination possible, with and without the articles. Cf. p. 153.

[4]Dana and Mantey, *Manual Grammar,* p. 141.

speaking the words; and this is also why the articles were included in the text. As Dana and Mantey stated, deviation from the normal usage of the article "may occur at the will of the writer," but they also state that "in rare cases it is possible that the writer employed the article at random."[5]

This very admission destroys any set rules for the usage of the article in Greek, and demonstrates that the original function of the article was for added emphasis. The article could occur simply at the will of the writer.

Here is the crux of the matter. Who is the writer of the Bible? If it is God, do you not think that He has a purpose behind the placement of the article in the text. Is God simply employing the article at random? Scholarship cannot answer all the questions of the article, but theomatics can.

ARTICLE INCONSISTENCY

A perfect example of a scholar trying to attach a mystical significance to the article is found in the Greek word for God (Θεος). Let us now examine a statement made by Webster back in 1864:

> Θεος occurs without the article (1) where the Deity is contrasted with what is human, or with the universe as distinct from its Creator, or with the nature and acts of evil spirits, (2) when the essential attributes of deity are spoken of, (3) when operations proceeding from God are appropriated to one of the three Divine Persons, (4) when the Deity is spoken of as heathens would speak, or a Jew who denied the existence of the Son and of the Holy Spirit. But the article *seems to be used* (1) when the Deity is spoken of in the Christian point of view, (2) when the first person of the blessed trinity is specially designated, unless its insertion is unnecessary by the addition of πατηρ, or some distinctive epithet.[6]

Dana and Mantey comment on this by saying that "this analysis is doubtless more exact and detailed than the facts will support, but it certainly shows admirable discrimination."[7] Webster was hard-pressed to establish a rule and fails to do so. Robertson states it best when he

[5]*Ibid.*, p. 143.
[6]*Ibid.*, p. 140.
[7]*Ibid.*, p. 140.

says, Θεος, as to the article, "is treated like a proper name and may have it or not have it."[8]

If the text may have it or not have it, and there are no rules for its usage with Θεος, then the scholar is making something out of nothing. In order to prove that the article with Θεος has any meaning, the critic will have to show a definite reason in every instance why the article is present or not present.

One of many examples of how the article baffles all of the intellectuals is found in its usage with proper names. We will now quote at length Dana and Mantey.

> It is instructive in dealing with this problem to observe the use of the article with Ιησους [Jesus]. The word occurs nine hundred and nine times in the New Testament (according to Moulton and Geden). It is used three hundred and fifty-nine times without the article. In one hundred and seventy-five of these instances the emphasis is on the Messianic significance of the name, which means "a deliverer"; forty-one times the emphasis is upon the name as a designation rather than upon the identification of the person—approximating the force of our expression "a man named"; ten times it is used in the vocative without the article. In several instances these anarthrous uses are in salutations, where the absence of the article is doubtless due to the general custom in the New Testament and the papyri of not using the article in salutations. *But there are one hundred and thirty-three times that* Ιησους *occurs without the article, for which we can find no evident reason.* Though this is but fifteen percent of the occurrences of the word and thirty-four percent of the anarthrous constructions, yet it is sufficient to prove that we are as yet unable to lay down any rigid principle according to which we can explain the use of the article with proper names.[9]

Robertson's conclusion, too, is that "no satisfactory principle can be laid down for the use or non use of the article with proper names."[10]

---

[8]Robertson, *A Grammar of the Greek New Testament* (Broadman: Nashville, 1934), p. 761.
[9]Dana and Mantey, *Manual Grammar*, p. 143.
[10]Robertson, *Grammar*, p. 761.

THE ONE FACTOR THAT CLINCHES IT

Here now is another quote from Dana and Mantey:

It is important to bear in mind that we cannot determine the English translation by the presence or absence of the article in Greek. Sometimes we should use the article in the English translation when it is not used in the Greek, and sometimes the idiomatic force of the Greek article may best be rendered by an anarthrous noun in English. The best guide in this matter is well informed common sense. . . .[11]

There are thousands of examples from the New Testament where the article does not determine translation. See a typical example in "the Son of God" on p. 16 of this book. Robertson further confirms this by saying that the Greek article "is not a matter of translation."[12] Robertson further says, "Whenever the article occurs the object is certainly definite. When it is not used the object may or may not be."[13]

Here is the clincher. If the object may be definite with or without the article, then why the article at all? As you can see, this means that if every single definite article were eliminated from the New Testament, the entire English translation could remain exactly the same. Robertson confirms this by stating that the article "is not essential to language."[14] If it is not essential, then why is it there? Or why would eliminating it change the meaning? Let's find out.

WHY GOD PUT THE ARTICLE IN THE TEXT

Existing in the Bible, there are thousands upon thousands of theomatic designs, all flowing together through each and every passage, to form the complete mathematical structure of the Bible. Throughout this book we have declined to show many of these designs, because our purpose at this time is to establish an overall consistency with the larger and more persistent key numbers.

Now we are faced with a problem. Because the theomatic designs in the Bible are so vast, and because there are so many of them, how

[11]Dana and Mantey, *Manual Grammar*, pp. 150–151.
[12]Robertson, *Grammar*, p. 756.
[13]*Ibid.*, p. 756.
[14]*Ibid.*, p. 756.

is it possible for all of them to fit and flow together? The answer is the Greek article. Here is a perfect illustration.

In John 8:12 Jesus is referred to as the "light of the world." Since Jesus is the light of the world, it is not surprising to find that these words with the articles work out to the number 3,440, which is in the cluster of multiples of 111, the number of Jesus.

Light of the world   111 × 31
Jn 8:12 το φως του κοσμου'

Let's say for argument's sake that in theomatics we never removed any of the articles. This would then mean that "light of the world" would only have one value, which would be 3,440, or 111 × 31. Now let's pretend that now we are going through the text looking for features that work out to 100, which is the number of *light.* After examining a few references we come to the term "light of the world," which is probably the most famous reference in the entire Bible to the topic of light. *Here is where the complete theomatic design would bog down if the articles were not removed.* How can a multiple of 111 become a multiple of 100? The term "light of the world" not only bespeaks Jesus, but also the subject of light!

Here then is the beautiful part of the theomatic design. When the two articles το and του are removed, the term "light of the world" has a theomatic value of 2,300, or 100 × 23, the number of light. *Now the complete design fits together perfectly:* Jesus, the light of the world (111), and the subject of light (100). When the articles are removed these words carry the exact same meaning—light of the world—but the theomatic value changes.

Light of the world   100 × 23
Jn 8:12 φως κοσμου

Here is another example. 2 Thessalonians 2:3 refers to "the man of sin, the son of perdition." This phrase contains four articles. If we remove the first three, the following will result:

The man of sin, the son of perdition   666 × 6
2 Thess 2:3 ανθρωπος ανομιας υιος της απωλειας'

In the first portion of this phrase, we find the words "the man of sin." When these words appear with their two articles (which were removed in the feature of 666), we then have a theomatic value of

2,260. Interestingly enough, the words "image of the beast" from Revelation 13:15 also have a value of 2,260. Obviously, there is some connection.

The man of sin   2,260
2 Thess 2:13 ο ανθρωπος της ανομιας

Image of the beast   2,260
Rev 13:15 η εικων του θηριου

If you then take the words "the son of perdition" with their two articles, you have a theomatic value of 2,385. Interestingly enough, Revelation 13:12 states that "the ones dwelling on the earth shall worship the first beast."

The son of perdition   2,385
2 Thess 2:13 ο υιος της απωλειας

The first beast   2,385
Rev 13:12 το θηριον το πρωτον"

At this time, we do not understand the complete significance behind these numbers, but that is not the important thing yet. In this pioneering effort, it is only necessary for us to show that the articles must taken out in order for all of these designs to flow together. For "the man of sin, the son of perdition" to come out to 666, three of the articles must be removed; in order for the other designs to flow together, the articles must be left in.

Furthermore, if you take the complete phrase with all of the articles, you get the following:

And is revealed the man of sin, the son of perdition   276 × 21
2 Thess 2:3 και αποκαλυφθη ο ανθρωπος της ανομιας ο υιος της απωλειας'

All of the combinations throughout the passages—with or without the articles—are what makes it possible for all of the designs to flow together. Without the option of article removal, the whole theomatic structure would be so rigid that God would not have the flexibility He needed to make all of these designs fit together.

Not only do the articles make this possible, but the conjunctions as well. Many times throughout the book we eliminated the conjunctions δε, γαρ, and ουν. Here is an example: In Matthew 15:14 we find the words, "But if the blind lead the blind, they shall both fall into the ditch" (τυφλος δε τυφλον εαν οδηγη). As opposed to the English, the little Greek conjunction δε (but) appears in the middle of these Greek words instead of at the beginning. This phrase would then read "blind leading the blind" instead of "but if the blind lead the blind."

Here is another example. In Galatians 3:19 we find the following words: "Why therefore the law? Because of transgressions it was added" (τι ουν ο νομος; των παραβασεων χαριν προσετεθη). By removing the word ουν (therefore), this phrase would then be: "Why the law? Because of transgressions it was added." Here again, the conjunction fulfills the same basic purpose as the article, in enabling the theomatic design to flow together.

Comment. As a rule, the conjunctions δε, γαρ, and ουν always appear preceded by an article or another word. Never once in this book did we show a phrase preceded by a straight conjunction. Here is an example: Matthew 13:39 states: "And the enemy sowing them is the devil" (ο δε εχθρος ο σπειρας αυτα εστιν ο διαβολος). The δε here is preceded by the article ο. As a rule, we could remove δε, but never ο without δε. In other words, the phrase would never be shown as: "δε εχθρος ο σπειρας αυτα εστιν ο διαβολος."

Another rule we followed was to never remove a conjunction from the center of a complete phrase. We only eliminated the conjunction when it appeared at the beginning of a phrase.

Sometimes a phrase containing a design will appear with the conjunction. Many times this will make for an awkward translation. A feature found in Revelation 21:22 bears this out: "For the Lord God almighty and the lamb are the temple of it" (ο γαρ κυριος ο Θεος ο παντοκρατωρ ναος αυτης εστιν και το αρνιον). The first words in this phrase "for the Lord God almighty" have a theomatic value of 111 × 29, the number of Jesus. Obviously, it does not sound very good to say "for the Lord God almighty," even though the design is present when the conjunction γαρ is in the phrase.

Another example is found in Revelation 7:15: "And the one sitting on the throne will spread His tabernacle over them." The Greek words "and the one sitting on the throne" (και καθημενος επι του θρονου) have a theomatic value of 111 × 18. In English this phrase does not sound very good with the conjunction *and* (και); however, in Greek, the design and the meaning are present with the word και.

Another word having great significance in the theomatic design is the conjunction οτι. This little Greek word carries the meaning of "that," "because," and other conjunctions, but many times it is not even translated. Sometimes it is used as the equivalent of quotation marks, in which case it is not translated. In our research we have come to the basic conclusion that the primary function of this word closely resembles that of the article, in that it adds emphasis and carries over the meaning from something previously said. Its purpose is thus theomatic. However, in this book we almost never removed it from the center of a phrase as we did with the articles.

In conclusion, the purpose of all the articles and conjunctions is to allow God the complete flexibility He needs is constructing the theomatic design of the Bible, and in allowing it to all fit and flow together. The whole idea behind the Greek case system and all the various combinations of articles, conjunctions, and so on is expressly to enable God to place the theomatic design in His Word. Every single word was designed mathematically by God so that He could bring forth the mathematics. Theomatics will not change to any great extent the basic rules of grammar now applicable to the Greek language, but it can throw light on why certain things are the way they are. This, in turn, will give us a much better understanding of the grammar and its purpose.